WebObjects®

web application
construction kit

SAMS
201 West 103rd Street, Indianapolis, Indiana 46290

WebObjects Web Application Construction Kit

International Standard Book Number: 0-672-32074-6

Library of Congress Catalog Card Number: 00-109551

Printed in the United States of America

First Printing: May 2001

04   03   02   01   4   3   2   1

Trademarks

Warning and Disclaimer

Executive Editor
Jeff Schultz

Development Editor
Scott Meyers

Managing Editor
Charlotte Clapp

Project Editor
Elizabeth Finney

Copy Editor
Rhonda Tinch-Mize

Indexer
Chris Barrick

Proofreader
Danny Ponder

Technical Editors
Ron Davis
Tor Manders

Team Coordinator
Amy Patton

Interior Designer
Gary Adair

Cover Designers
Alan Clements
Dan Armstrong

Contents at a Glance

Table of Contents

About the Author

George Ruzek is an independent consultant and teacher specializing in server-side software development. George first started programming graphics and sound at age 13 on an Atari 800, and later on a Commodore Amiga. He then attended Virginia Commonwealth University, majoring in Electronic Music. After graduating with a B.S. in Math specializing in Computer Science, George went to work at Fannie Mae. He spent his time there writing software in C, C++, and Visual C++ on Windows and Unix, and Objective-C on NeXTSTEP. He then went to work at BLaCKSMITH (http://www.blacksmith.com) in McLean, Virginia, where he learned WebObjects from the great software engineers there. As a Director at BLaCKSMITH, George became familiar with a number of server-side technologies and frameworks. Because of his early adoption of Java at BLaCKSMITH, he was given the nickname "Java George." When not in front of a computer, George spends his time with his kids or playing the piano. He's also a true video game junkie. George can be reached by e-mail at java_george@pobox.com.

Dedication

This book is dedicated to the memory of my father, Don H. Ruzek.

Acknowledgments

Thanks to the many talented software engineers at BLaCKSMITH who have helped me learn this and other technologies over the years, and whose enthusiasm for this technology has really fueled this book. Thanks especially to Randy Tidd, who helped with all my EOF questions and to Mike Hovan, who taught me the foundations of these frameworks.

I would also like to thank my Editor at Sams, Jeff Schultz. Jeff was the catalyst for this book, and his contagious energy and excitement have really kept me going.

But most of all, I'd like to thank my wonderful family: Lisa, Seattle, and Rex. Thanks for supporting me and giving me the time to complete this endeavor. Your smiling faces and warm hugs make me feel lucky every day.

Tell Us What You Think!

As the reader of this book, *you* are our most important critic and commentator. We value your opinion and want to know what we're doing right, what we could do better, what areas you'd like to see us publish in, and any other words of wisdom you're willing to pass our way.

As an Executive Editor for Sams, I welcome your comments. You can e-mail or write me directly to let me know what you did or didn't like about this book—as well as what we can do to make our books stronger.

Please note that I cannot help you with technical problems related to the topic of this book, and that due to the high volume of mail I receive, I might not be able to reply to every message.

When you write, please be sure to include this book's title and author as well as your name and phone or fax number. I will carefully review your comments and share them with the author and editors who worked on the book.

E-mail: feedback@samspublishing.com
Mail: Jeff Schultz
           Executive Editor
           Sams Publishing
           201 West 103rd Street
           Indianapolis, IN 46290 USA

INTRODUCTION

The year is 1995, and the platform is OPENSTEP. Developers are working at a major telecommunications firm building client/server applications using Objective-C and an object/relational mapping system called Enterprise Objects Framework. The decision to use the EOF/Objective-C combination rather than some of the other alternatives such as Visual C++ is considered questionable by management. Objective-C developers are hard to find and high-priced, the learning curve for the technology is perceived to be steep, and the OPENSTEP software from NeXT computers is expensive. The extra money spent in consultants, training, and licenses will be saved in reduced development time, so the story goes. At the height of the project, versions with major new pieces of functionality were released biweekly, and the testers could not keep the pace of the development staff. The stability of the code was due in large part to the OPENSTEP development environment, and the ability to easily add major pieces of functionality is attributed to the flexibility and strength of the Enterprise Objects Framework, version 2.0.

Developing for OPENSTEP had its drawbacks, which have led to its demise. The OPENSTEP operating system lacked applications and was unfamiliar for most users. It was also expensive to license at $1,500 a copy. NeXT computers ported the OPENSTEP frameworks to Windows NT, which allowed the users to use NT and run the familiar applications, but NeXT never worked out a reasonable runtime license. Also around this time, the trend was to begin deploying thin application clients using Web servers and browsers. This was the environment that formed the precursor to the WebObjects framework.

The original goal of WebObjects was to allow OPENSTEP developers to build Web applications rather than the traditional client/server applications, and still use the same development techniques. WebObjects is considered an application server because the application resides on the server and is served to the clients as requested. WebObjects uses EOF to access databases, so most of the database code written in the client/server applications could be ported to WebObjects with little or no changes. The WebObjects frameworks were rough in the beginning, but stable and usable by the 3.0 release in 1997. The 3.0 release also contained something very important to the future of WebObjects: the ability to access the entire EOF and WebObjects framework from Java. The price for WebObjects is still an issue at this stage, and for many a barrier to using it.

An Apple product since 1997 when Apple bought NeXT, the current version of WebObjects contains a Java API to the Objective-C frameworks. In an attempt to increase market share, the price for WebObjects was reduced dramatically by Apple in 2000. The 100% Java libraries and the dramatic price reduction are indications that Apple has decided to open its arms to developers in the application server market.

WebObjects has many advantages over its competitors. The first advantage is reliability. It has been around for a long time and has been optimized for performance. It's also designed really well: easy for the experienced developer to customize parts of the framework and easy to get some spiffy sites up and running quickly. It's object-oriented, really. These days a number of APIs claim to be object-oriented, but through poor design they fail to gain full advantage of object-oriented programming. It's also based on components. WebObjects was around long before Java Beans or Enterprise Java Beans, and the basic building block of WebObjects is the component. It is economical. WebObjects sells for a fraction of the competitors' price, and contains more features than most. Finally, it's just cool. Most WebObjects developers think it's the coolest thing since Luke blew up the Death Star. It was voted JavaWorld's "1999 Application Server of the Year" mostly due to feverish voting by the developers who use it.

WebObjects and EOF are powerful frameworks that can be customized in a number of ways by the experienced developer. They can also be daunting and unapproachable to the beginner. Armed with *WebObjects Web Application Construction Kit*, you will be able to unlock the power of these frameworks. The goal is to empower you with the knowledge of how to complete the most common tasks that you will be asked to accomplish as a WebObjects developer.

Is This Book for You?

This book is the definitive tutorial on WebObjects and is designed for the beginning to intermediate developer. If you are a Perl programmer who is looking for another way to write your Web applications, this book is for you. If you are a college student or professor who has taken advantage of the WebObjects discount, this book is for you. If you are a Mac programmer who wants to use WebObjects to write killer Web apps, this book is also for you. This book, coupled with hard work, will give you what it takes to be a professional WebObjects developer.

This book is not for everyone, however. If you are interested in learning programming, WebObjects is not the place to start. WebObjects is based on a number of technologies, each complex on its own. So, if you want to use WebObjects, there are some things you have to know.

What You Need to Know

This book is designed for the experienced developer who is interested in learning how to become productive using the WebObjects frameworks. This book assumes that you understand the following:

- Java

- Relational databases

- HTML

The server-side programming in WebObjects can be done in either Java or Objective-C. Apple has advertised that WebObjects version 5.0 will be 100% Java, so all the examples and discussions in the book will focus on using Java with WebObjects. Because of this, knowing the language is crucial for understanding this book. You don't have to understand all of Java, just the syntax for creating classes, methods, instances, and inheritance. This also assumes that you understand object-oriented programming concepts. If you fully understand the basics of the Java Language, you should be fine.

The WebObjects database frameworks do a good job of sheltering the developer from having to write SQL, but a solid knowledge of how relational databases work is essential for understanding the discussions of database access throughout this book. You don't have to know how to write SQL, but you should know what relational database tables, columns, and primary and foreign keys are and how they're used.

You should also understand concepts such as compound primary keys and how to create many-to-many relationships.

Similar to the database frameworks, the WebObjects frameworks shelter the developer from writing HTML. Once again, you don't have to write HTML, but you need to understand the structured format of HTML and be familiar with how to create a HTML table at a minimum.

What You Need

You will need a copy of WebObjects 4.5 and a Windows NT/2000 or Mac OS X machine. To run WebObjects, you need about 800MB of free hard drive space, 96-128MB of RAM (more is better), and about a 300MHz processor, either Pentium III or G3. WebObjects will take up about 600MB of hard drive space, and you need some room to build your applications. 96MB should be considered the bare minimum, and 128MB will be adequate. To be comfortable in Windows, 256MB should be used. The processor speed is not as critical as memory, slower processors will just run, well, slower.

How is This Book Organized?

The book was designed to get you up and running with a database-driven WebObjects application as quickly as possible. The database access frameworks are the most complicated of the frameworks supplied with WebObjects, so the majority of the book is focused on this framework. This book is really divided into three sections:

- WebObjects Fundamentals
- Enterprise Objects Framework
- Advanced topics

The first section discusses all the basic knowledge required to start writing a WebObjects application.

- Chapter 1, "Introducing and Installing WebObjects," leads you through the installation process.
- In Chapter 2, "Creating a Model," you will learn about the fundamentals of setting up the database model.

- Chapter 3, "WebObjects Components," is a discussion of the component architecture vital to creating a WebObjects user interface. In this chapter, you will create dynamic Web pages.

- Chapter 4, "Adding Navigation," discusses navigation between components in WebObjects.

The second section is an in-depth discussion of Enterprise Objects Framework, which is used to access the database.

- Display groups are used in Chapter 5, "Using Display Groups," to easily display database data in a WebObjects application.

- Chapter 6, "Retrieving Objects," provides an in-depth discussion of different ways to retrieve data out of a database.

- In Chapter 7, "Writing Enterprise Object Classes," you will learn how to write classes that encapsulate business logic.

- Chapter 8, "Using Inheritance with EOF," is a guide to using inheritance for persistent database classes.

- Validating the data entered by the user is the topic for Chapter 9, "Validating Data."

The last part contains advanced topics that are used by experienced WebObjects developers.

- Chapter 10, "Advanced UI," discusses advanced user interface options available in the WebObjects framework.

- Reusable components and frameworks will be discussed in Chapter 11, "Creating Reusable Components."

- Improving application efficiency by using Direct Actions is discussed in Chapter 12, "Using Stateless Transactions."

- Chapter 13, "Optimizing Database Access," delves into various ways to improve database performance.

- And Chapter 14, "Deploying Your Application," is a discussion of deploying WebObjects applications.

Companion Web Site

The companion Web site to this book, www.wowack.com, contains supplemental exercises that can be performed along with solutions and the code examples from the book. In addition, I provide answers to frequent questions asked by other readers. And, considering how dynamic the Web is, more information might be there by the time you read this.

Let's Get Started

It is intended that this book will be read from beginning to end. By the end of the book, you should be a solid WebObjects developer. You will have a good understanding of numerous WebObjects classes and be able to build an application in no time. You will be able to access and maintain data in a relational database and incorporate business rules in your completed application. So let's get started!

PART I

WEBOBJECTS FUNDAMENTALS

CHAPTER 1

INTRODUCING AND INSTALLING WEBOBJECTS

In this chapter, you will install WebObjects and verify that the installation has been completed successfully. You will also install the sample database and build an example project to make sure that everything is working so that you can begin using the tools to develop WebObjects applications.

This book is intended to be read while interacting with your computer. Basically, when you see some steps for completing an activity, try them. The book has also been written to be read consecutively from beginning to end: A lot of information in any given chapter is dependant on the information from previous chapters.

So, what you will need for this chapter is: A WebObjects 4.5 CD-ROM and a computer suitable for the WebObjects development environment, either an Intel machine running Windows NT/2000 or a G3/G4 running Mac OS X Server. From now on the term *Windows* will refer to Windows NT or 2000 and *Mac* will refer to Mac OS X Server. Even though you can probably get by with the minimum requirements as defined by Apple, you will be a lot better off if you have at least 128MB of RAM (256MB for Windows) and 1GB of free hard drive space. Separate instructions are included throughout the book for both Windows and Mac, although most instructions are the same for both platforms unless otherwise noted.

What Is WebObjects?

A lot of different ways can be used to describe what WebObjects is and what it can do for you. One way is to look at the different features and describe exactly what they do. These features are as follows:

- Application server
- Object-Relational mapping system
- Component-based HTML generation
- Development environment

Application Server

When you purchase a copy of WebObjects, you get a reliable, scalable application server. Similar to the way a *file server* is a repository for files and a *mail server* stores e-mail, an *application server* acts as the repository for your application. The application itself is *served* to application clients. Any changes to the application are also automatically served. Using WebObjects, applications can be served using HTML, a Java applet, or a Java application as the user interface. This is illustrated in Figure 1.1.

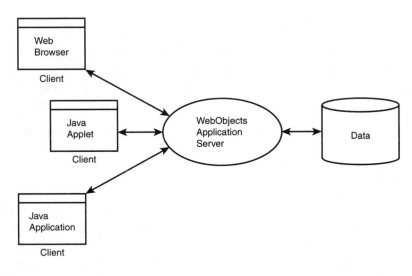

Figure 1.1
WebObjects serves the application to many clients.

WebObjects applications are deployed as application *instances*, and can be deployed on one or several machines. Also, several application instances can be deployed on the same machine (including several instances of the same application). Detailed deployment information is available in Chapter 14, "Deploying Your Application."

Object-Relational Mapping System

WebObjects is also installed with an advanced object to relational mapping system called *Enterprise Objects Framework*, or EOF. This is arguably the one of the best reasons to use WebObjects instead of other products. EOF is a mature framework for converting rows of data in a relational database to objects. EOF is a sophisticated framework that does a large amount of the mundane development work for you, but also allows programmatic customization at any level. It allows you to place all the business logic for your domain in the classes that also store your data. This allows you to reuse that data and that business logic across applications. Once you are familiar with EOF, creating new complex applications becomes trivial, as does making changes or additions to an existing application. Also, EOF handles the generation of SQL for you (for the most part), so it makes it easier to migrate your completed application from one database system to another.

Component-Based HTML Generation

Another impressive part of WebObjects that is sometimes overlooked is the WebObjects framework, which maps objects to HTML. The power of this framework lies in its design, which is component-based rather than object-based. This component-based architecture allows the mixing of scripted, Java, and Objective-C components. This architecture also allows you to create reusable components, saving in development time. Also supplied are a number of pre-built dynamic elements that fit seamlessly into the architecture, giving you a head start on your software development.

Development Environment

Included with the installation is a development environment consisting of the following development tools:

- **Project Builder**—The tool used for managing your entire project and editing your source files. You can build and run your project directly from Project Builder.

- **WebObjects Builder**—An HTML editor with the ability to add/modify WebObjects-specific tags, along with some code generation and component bindings.

- **EOModeler**—The tool used to create models for EOF. An EOModel contains the definition of how objects map to relational database data.

- **WOInfoCenter**—This is where all the documentation on WebObjects is stored, including API reference, tutorials, and online books. It is actually a WebObjects application and will launch your browser when started.

- **File Merge**—This useful utility is used to graphically display the differences between two files, and it allows the user to choose what text to save and what to delete when merging the files.

- **Java Browser**—This small utility uses the Java reflection API to display information about Java packages, classes, methods, and instance variables. It is extremely useful in determining undocumented API.

The really great thing about these tools is that they were written using the same APIs across platforms, which means that they look and "feel" the same in Windows and Mac OS X Server. There are only a few differences in the two platforms; the most prominent is in the placement of the menu.

Some other tools installed on Windows are Unix command-line applications such as ls, grep, and make (see Figure 1.2). This is provided to give the experienced Unix developer some familiar and useful command-line tools, and so that all the tcsh scripts created on Mac OS X can execute on Windows, making the software more compatible. For example, the same makefile is used to build the application on Windows NT/2000, Mac OS X, and Solaris.

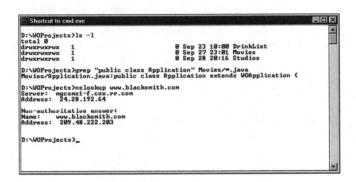

Figure 1.2
Installing WebObjects on Windows makes a number of command-line Unix commands available to Windows developers.

Installation

Both the Mac and Windows installation are included on the same CD-ROM. Go ahead and put in the CD and let's get started with the installation.

Windows NT/2000

If you haven't done so, you should install a Web server. Microsoft's IIS comes with Windows 2000, and that's the one used in the examples throughout the book. To add IIS to your Windows 2000 installation, double-click Add/Remove Programs in the control panel (Start, Settings, Control Panel). In this dialog box, choose Add/Remove

Windows Component. This opens the Windows Component Wizard, shown in Figure 1.3. The second option is for Internet Information Services. If it is checked, your Web server is installed. If not, go ahead and check it, click Next, and follow the directions to install the server. You will need the Windows 2000 CD for this.

Note

A Web Server isn't absolutely necessary for development, as the standard mode of development uses the *Direct Connect* adaptor, which allows clients to directly connect to the application. However, if you want to learn how to deploy the application, you will need to install a Web server, and it's done the easiest before you install WebObjects.

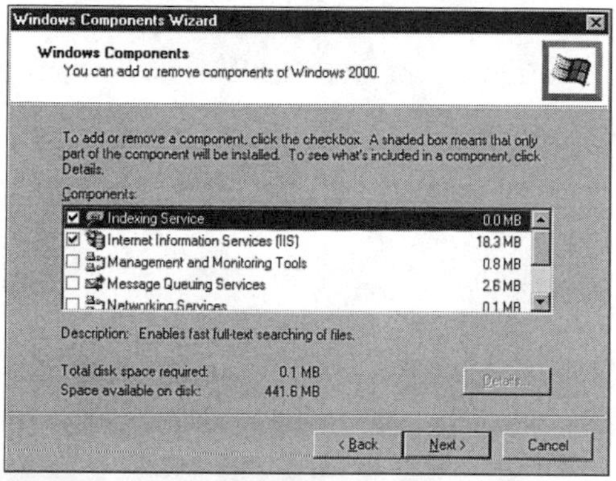

Figure 1.3
The Windows Component Wizard.

Double-click the WebObjects CD and navigate to the Windows folder. Double-click the Setup.exe application.

1. The first step is to enter the serial number, your name, and your company name (see Figure 1.4). The serial number is on the WebObjects CD case. If you're using WebObjects for personal use, you still need to enter something for the company name to enable the Next button. I always like to make up a company name in those situations. Click the Next button.

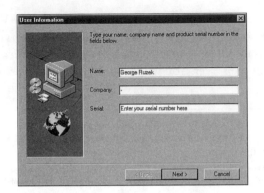

Figure 1.4
The first step is to enter your name, company, and the serial number.

2. Accept the license agreement and click Yes (see Figure 1.5).

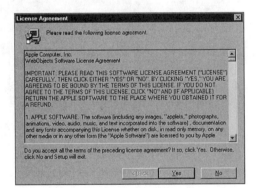

Figure 1.5
The License Agreement dialog box.

3. Next choose a destination directory. It should be the \Apple directory on one of your hard drives. About 400MB are required for the standard installation, but you should have double that amount to be safe. Click the Next button (see Figure 1.6).

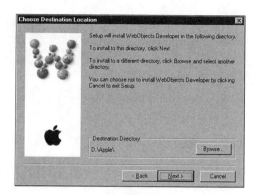

Figure 1.6
The Destination Location dialog box.

4. Now choose the infamous installation type. For this installation, you should just choose a Typical installation. That installs everything except the GNU source code. So if you want that, select Custom. Click Next (see Figure 1.7).

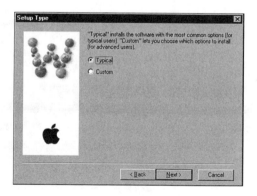

Figure 1.7
The Setup Type dialog box.

5. The seemingly innocent dialog in Figure 1.8 is a little dangerous. If you enter a folder name that exists in the system path before the WebObjects folders, none of your WebObjects applications will run. This is because of the order in which the Apple DLLs are found. If you have installed the Web server, enter the scripts directory of the Web server. Otherwise create a directory in your file system that is not in the path and enter that directory. DO NOT enter c:\, d:\, c:\WINNT, or d:\WINNT. Enter the scripts directory of the Web server.

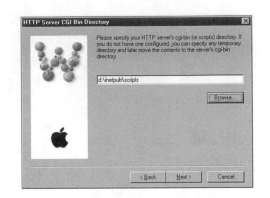

Figure 1.8
\inetPub\scripts *is the default scripts directory for IIS.*

6. Now enter the document root directory for your web server. If you have not installed a Web server, you should create a directory as you did in step 5. Click the Next button (see Figure 1.9).

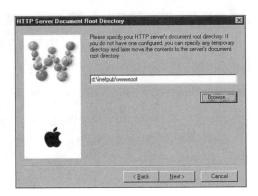

Figure 1.9
\inetPub\wwwroot *is the default document root directory for IIS.*

7. Leave the program group as WebObjects because it's referenced that way throughout the book (see Figure 1.10).

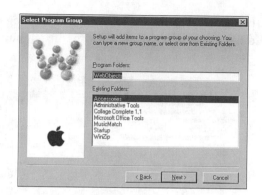

Figure 1.10
The Select Program Group dialog box.

Installation might take quite a while, so you can either skip forward and read about the difference between the Mac and Windows versions or install WebObjects on your Mac.

Mac OS X Server

Installation on the Mac is a bit easier than the Windows installation. OS X Server comes installed with Apache, and you are not given a lot of options, which means that there are not as many options as the Windows installation.

1. Insert the WebObjects Developer CD-ROM and double-click the icon that appears on your desktop to start browsing the CD contents in the file viewer. Navigate to the Mac_OS_X_Server folder and double-click the WebObjectsDeveloper.mpkg file. This will launch the Installer application (see Figure 1.11).

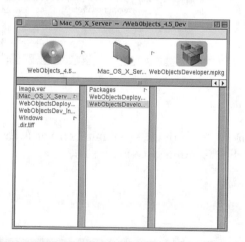

Figure 1.11
The WebObjects installation package is found on the CD in the Mac_OS_X_Server folder.

2. You are then presented with the Package Selection dialog box (see Figure 1.12). Simply leave the defaults selected and click the Install button.

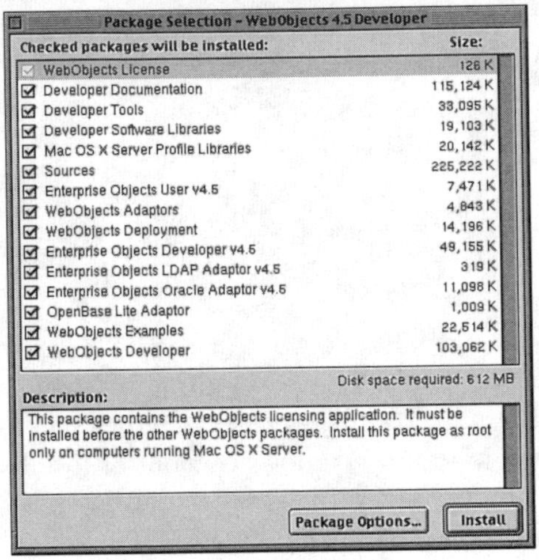

Figure 1.12
The Package Selection dialog box.

3. Now enter the serial number that appears on the CD case that came with WebObjects and click the OK button (see Figure 1.13).

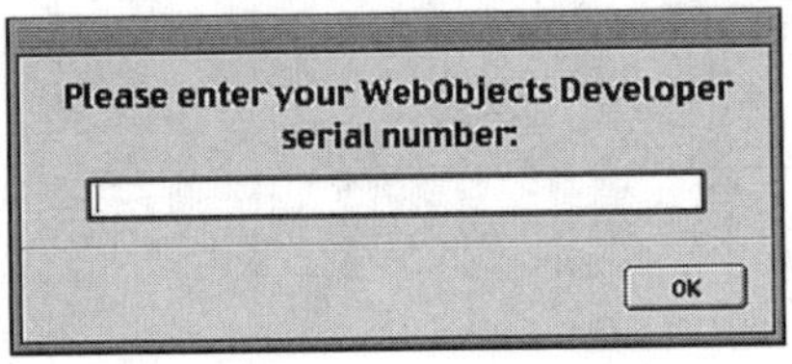

Figure 1.13
The serial number dialog box.

4. You will be presented with the serial number. Verify that this is the correct number and click Continue (see Figure 1.14).

Figure 1.14
Serial number verification dialog box.

At this point, the WebObjects frameworks and all the tools will be installed on your computer (see Figure 1.15). This will take a while.

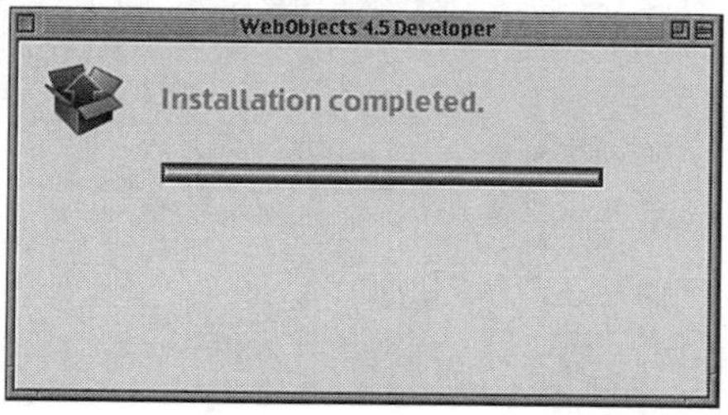

Figure 1.15
If everything goes well, you should see this dialog box.

Installing the Update

For WebObjects 4.5, at the time of this writing, three updates have been released. It is only necessary to install the third update as it includes the changes made in the first update. Another update might be available by the time you read this. These updates can be found at `http://til.info.apple.com/`. Do a search on "WebObjects and update," and you should find an article with instructions on installing the latest update.

Other Post-Installation Instructions

Some post-installation instructions are in the documentation contained in the WOInfoCenter. Go ahead and run the WOInfoCenter. In Windows it can be started by selecting Start, WebObjects, WOInfoCenter. On the Mac, select Apple, WebObjects, WOInfoCenter. The WOInfoCenter contains reference documentation, release notes, and developer guides.

For the release notes, select Release Notes, WebObjects, WebObjects Post Installation Instructions (see Figure 1.16). Most importantly, steps to verify the installation should definitely follow these steps before continuing. This document also contains instructions for installing Oracle, Sybase, or Informix client libraries. If you are planning to use one of these databases with WebObjects, you should follow these instructions at this time as well.

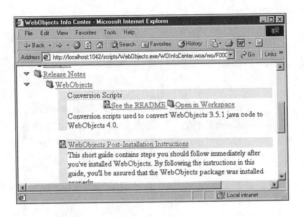

Figure 1.16
The WebObjects Info Center has a lot of good documentation, and the post installation instructions contain useful information.

Differences Between Windows and Mac

Not many differences exist between the Mac and Windows versions of these products. All the software was developed using the Yellow Box libraries, which consist of compiled Objective-C code and Java wrapper classes that access the compiled code. For the most part, the Yellow Box frameworks have all been ported to Windows, so porting of the tools is a simple recompile (depending on what your idea of simple is), unless you use platform-specific libraries. In order to preserve the visual integrity between platforms, the OS X Server display model, *Display Postscript*, was also ported to Windows, and is installed with WebObjects. Also, as noted previously, all the necessary Unix commands were ported to Windows so that the scripts and make files could be easily ported. The result is fantastic: The tools look and behave the same between platforms.

> **Note**
> The display model for OS X Server has been changed from Display Postscript to Display PDF with the release of OS X, and the new display layer is called Quartz. Currently Apple has announced no plans to port this new display layer to Windows, which will mean that the future tools might look and behave considerably different between Macs and Windows.

The primary difference between the two platforms is how you get to the developer tools and the location of the menus. On Windows, the tools are located in Start, Programs, WebObjects. On the Mac, the tools are located in Apple, WebObjects. The menus are located just under the title bar of the main window in Windows and at the top of the screen on the Mac.

Some development differences exist on the two platforms, mainly in the file paths and in the installation. The installation differences have been noted previously in this chapter. The files are located in a similar directory structure on the Mac and Windows, but the difference is the location of the root folder. On Windows, the root folder is the \Apple folder on the drive that WebObjects was installed. On OS X, the root folder is the /System folder. From this root folder, there is a set of other folders that contain executables, documentation, headers, and other resources used by WebObjects (see Table 5.1).

Table 5.1

The WebObjects Folders

Folder	Contents
(root)/Demos	Demo applications, mostly non-WebObjects related.
(root)/Developer	All the developer applications. An Applications folder is in here that contains all the developer tools. Also, there is an Examples folder that contains sample applications and tools for creating the sample database.
(root)/Documentation	This is an entire subtree of various types of documentation, including developer guides, release notes, and a Getting Started guide. You probably will not need to access this through the file system. It can all be accessed through the WOInfoCenter.
(root)/Library	The Library folder contains most of the software that is required by WebObjects to operate. For example, on Windows there's a subfolder called System, which contains the essential files for emulating the OS X environment in Windows. Also found in the Library folder is the Frameworks folder, which contains all the necessary frameworks such as WebObjects, Foundation, and the EO frameworks. Also on Windows, check out the Executables folder to determine the Unix commands that are now available to you. (They're the .exe files).

These folders are not identical in content between Windows and Mac, just similar. It's probably a good idea at this point to take a minute to become familiar with this directory tree.

Installing the Sample Database

The examples throughout the book use the sample databases that come with WebObjects. There are two sample databases, Movies and Rentals. The Movies database is a set of movie titles, actors, directors, and plot summaries. Using the Movies database alone, you could create an application similar to www.imdb.com, the Internet Movie Database. The Rentals database stores information about renting movies, and allows you to create an application that tracks movie rentals. This is a great example for a number of reasons: The domain is interesting and everyone can relate to it; there are two databases, allowing you to create them in two different physical locations; and there is enough complexity to try out almost all aspects of WebObjects.

To install the sample databases, run the Enterprise Objects examples Setup Wizard. Step 1 will be different for each platform because the path is different. The rest of the steps will be the same for Windows or Mac OS X.

1. **Windows**—Using the file viewer, navigate to the directory where you installed WebObjects, probably C:\Apple. From there, navigate to the Developer\ Examples\EnterpriseObjects\SetupWizard.app directory. Double-click SetupWizard.exe.

   Mac OS X—Using the file viewer, navigate to /System/Developer/Examples/ EnterpriseObjects. Double-click SetupWizard.app.

2. The Welcome screen is then shown. Click Next to continue (see Figure 1.17).

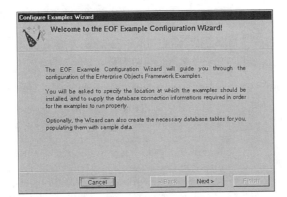

Figure 1.17
The Movies and Rentals database setup wizard.

3. You will then be asked the location to install the EOF examples. Choose your home directory for OS X, or a suitable location for Windows. Do not choose a location within the WebObjects install directory (C:\Apple or similar). Click Next to continue (see Figure 1.18).

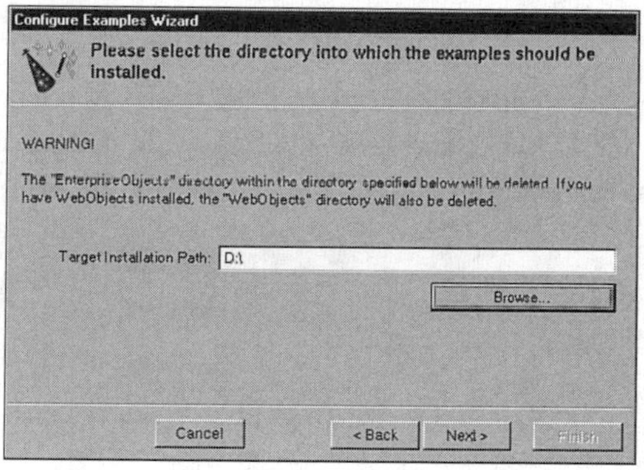

Figure 1.18
Choose the location to install the examples.

4. Choose an adaptor for the Movies database. An *adaptor* is a set of software that EOF uses to access a specific database. As new databases are developed or as new versions are released, only the adaptors need changing. If you have access to Oracle or Sybase databases and have the permissions to create tables, choose one of these databases (see Figure 1.19). Also, if you have an ODBC data source such as Microsoft Access, you can choose that as well. Otherwise, choose OpenBaseLite. OpenBaseLite is a single-user relational database from a company named OpenBase that ships with WebObjects. Click Next to continue.

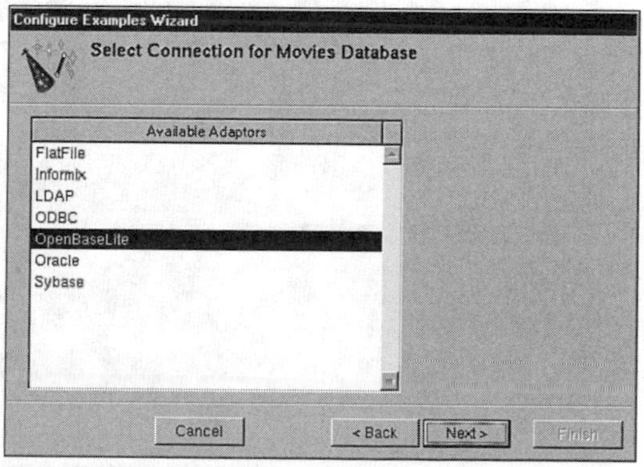

Figure 1.19
You can choose from a number of database adaptors.

5. You will then be prompted to enter adaptor connection information. If you have chosen Oracle or Sybase, you will be prompted for a username, password, and server. OpenBaseLite stores all the data for a particular database in files (see Figure 1.20). The database itself is a directory with the .db extension. Creating a new database is as simple as specifying the name of the directory to be created. Click the Create button and select a directory name. In OS X, place the database in your home directory. In Windows, place it in a suitable location. Either way, it's probably a good idea to create a folder where you will place all your databases, such as WODatabases. Name the file **Movies.db**. Click OK on the Adaptor dialog to continue.

Figure 1.20
OpenBaseLite stores all information in files on the file system.

6. What about adaptor information for the Rentals database? Remember that there are two databases installed. You have the option of choosing a different adaptor for each one (see Figure 1.21). By doing this, you can see how EOF seamlessly integrates data from different sources. However, it is easier for the beginner to combine all the data into one database. For this reason, choose the same adaptor that you chose in step 5 and click Next.

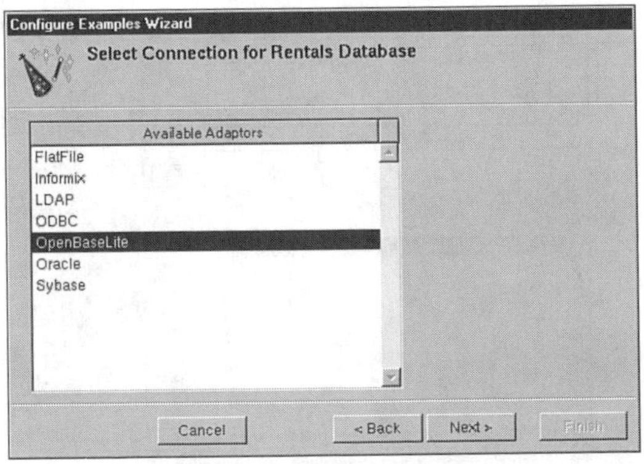

Figure 1.21
You can choose a separate adaptor for the Rentals database.

7. You are then prompted to enter the connection information for the Rentals database (see Figure 1.22). Because you are choosing the same database, this will look familiar. If you chose OpenBaseLite for your adaptor, do not click the Create button for the Rentals database. This would create a new database for Rentals, and we simply want to put all the rental information in the movies database that we created before. So you can either type in the path to the movies database file or click Browse and navigate to it using the file viewer. Click OK when done.

Figure 1.22
The adaptor connection dialog for the Rentals database.

8. You must then specify how the database is to be populated. Because you're creating these databases from scratch, choose the Create Tables and Populate Them with Sample Data option (see Figure 1.23). At this point, click the Finish button and you're done. The Wizard will take some time to copy the example applications, create the databases, and populate them with data. Click Next.

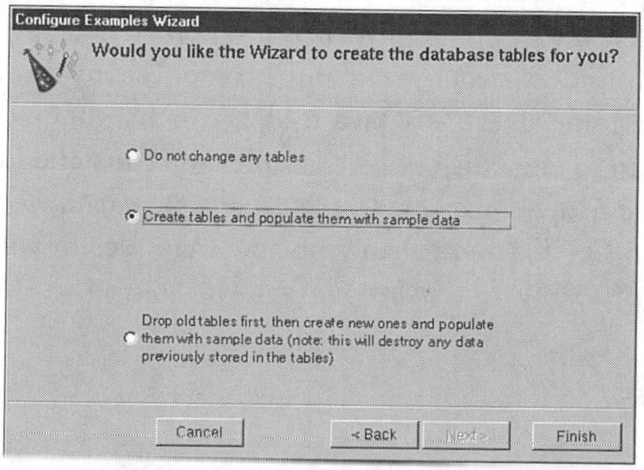

Figure 1.23
The first time you run the examples setup, choose the second option.

> **Note**
> If you really mess up the data while developing and testing your application, you can always re-run the wizard and select the third option, which is to re-create the database by dropping all tables, creating them again, and populating them with data.

> **Note**
> Choosing the third option will trigger a number of database error dialogs because there will be no tables to drop.

It will take a while for the process to complete (see Figure 1.24). It will copy all the examples to the directory you specified, create the database tables, and populate them with data.

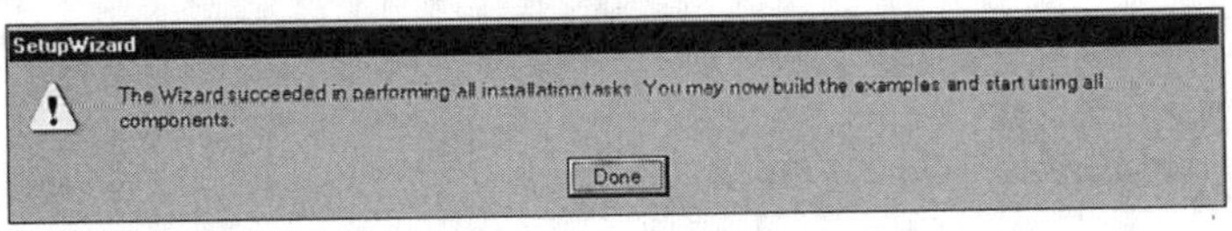

Figure 1.24
You should see this window at the end of the setup.

Testing the Database Setup

To test the database setup, you can build and run one of the examples using the Project Builder application. The Project Builder window is shown in Figure 1.25. Remember where you told the SetupWizard to copy the examples? You will need that location now. Two folders, WebObjects and EnterpriseObject, are within that folder. In the WebObjects folder there is a Java folder, which contains a Movies folder. This is the project you will open. This book's examples were installed in D:\WOExamples, so the full path to the Movies project is D:\WOExamples\WebObjects\Java\Movies. If you're working on OS X, you probably put the examples in your home directory, so your path would probably be ~/WebObjects/Java/Movies.

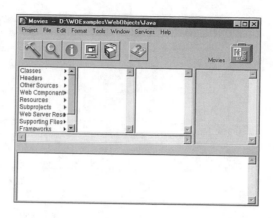

Figure 1.25
The Movies project is a good one to run to test your WebObjects installation.

There are two ways to open a project in Project Builder. One way is to navigate to the project folder in your file viewer and double-click the PB.project file. Every project has a PB.project file that specifies the files in the project, the type of project, the project name, and so on. When you install the developer tools, a file association is made between .project files and Project Builder.

Another way to open the project is to open it directly in Project Builder. In Windows it's in the Start menu under Programs, WebObjects. On the Mac, it's in the Apple menu under WebObjects. After Project Builder is loaded, select the Project, Open menu item. Navigate to the project folder and click the Open button.

To test your application, you first need to build it. Bring up the build panel by clicking the Hammer button. Then build the program by clicking the Hammer button on the build window. This is known as the double-hammer. All the build information is displayed in the build panel (see Figure 1.26).

Note
If you don't click the Hammer button on the build panel, your application will not build. This has caused a bit of frustration for some developers who, anticipating a lengthy build process, click the initial Hammer button on the Project Builder main window, get up to get some coffee, and return to their desks only to realize that the **second** Hammer button was not clicked. It kind of makes one feel like a yellow-skinned cartoon character created by Matt Groening.

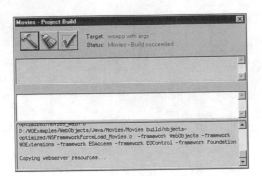

Figure 1.26
The build panel.

 If the build succeeded (and it should), you will then need to run your
application. This is done through the Launch panel. This panel is brought up
using the Launch button. You will then need to click the Launch button on this panel
to run the project (see Figure 1.27). The Launch button will then become a stop sign.
To stop the application, click this button again.

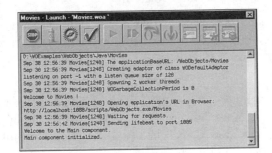

Figure 1.27
The launch panel.

After you've clicked the second Launch button, the project will start, and—assuming
that your file associations are working properly—your browser will be launched with
the application running (see Figure 1.28).

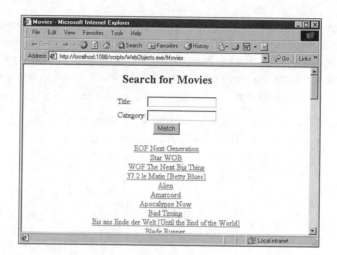

Figure 1.28
The Movies sample application. The one you build will look a lot nicer.

Tip
On the Mac, OmniWeb is the standard browser. Everything should work fine, except sometimes OmniWeb does not register for HTML files appropriately. If this is the case, your application will start, but the browser will not automatically launch. You can launch the browser yourself. It's located in /Local/Applications/Internet/OmniWeb and enter the URL located in the launch panel. The easiest fix to the problem is to reboot your machine.

Summary

In this chapter you installed WebObjects and the sample database. You also started using Project Builder to build and run a WebObjects application. This is a crucial first step, which will allow you to continue with the confidence and knowledge that WebObjects is installed correctly. If you had problems however, help is available. Take a look at the "Troubleshooting" section in the WOInfoCenter. This section is located in the Release Notes, WebObjects, Post Installation Instructions section. If you can't find the answer there, go to Apple's technical info library at http://til.info.apple.com. A lot of good information is located there. Another place to look is the

OmniGroup mail list archive, which can be found at http://www.omnigroup.com. The mailing lists are found if you follow the Community, Developer Resources, Mailing Lists hyperlinks. Finally, don't forget to check out http://www.wowack.com. If a number of readers are encountering the same problem, chances are good that a solution has been posted here.

In Chapter 2, "Creating a Model," you will start with the first stages of a project, which is to use EOModeler to define your model.

CHAPTER 2

CREATING A MODEL

Since the beginning of time, we have been looking at ways to do things better using tools. Yeah, we can dig a hole with our hands and fingers, or we can use a cave bear's femur, a hollowed-out bamboo stick, or maybe a shovel. If it's a big hole, we could dig for a while using a femur, or rent a Caterpillar 416C center-pivot backhoe loader. What tool to use sometimes depends on the size of the job and the amount of your budget. Enterprise Objects Framework can be considered a tool for your use if you liken call-level SQL to digging a hole.

Sure, you know SQL. You're the fastest SQL hole digger this side of the Mississippi. But SQL is work, and implementing a solid, object-oriented design on top of call-level SQL takes a bit of work and thought power. This effort could have been used to make your application better, and this is where your tool can help you. EOF is the Caterpillar 416C center-pivot backhoe loader for all your call-level SQL hole digging.

As discussed in Chapter 1, "Introducing and Installing WebObjects," the *Enterprise Objects Framework (EOF)* is a set of classes that map relational database data to objects. A number of great features are built into EOF, and it is a thoroughly tested, mature framework that has been used in production systems for years. The goal of this framework is to provide a stable base of classes that allow the developer to focus on the business problem at hand rather than the database implementation.

One of the problems when creating a framework that "takes care of the dirty work" is allowing the developer to customize the way certain parts of the framework behave and extend classes to provide additional features. This is where EOF, along with the other Apple frameworks, really comes up big. There is a lot of abstraction in EOF, allowing custom classes to be substituted for existing framework classes. Because of the abstraction and the amount of features provided by EOF, examining the framework can be daunting at first. It makes the initial learning curve substantially higher than other frameworks, but the benefits down the road are well worth the effort.

This book follows a plan to introduce EOF with some of the easier-to-use classes followed by digging in deeper to the class hierarchy and examining the "guts," performing customizations and more difficult tasks. This chapter introduces you to EOF, and the following topics will be covered:

- Basic EOF principles

- Creating an EOModel from an existing database

- Modifying the database structure

- Modifying an EOModel

Introduction to EOF

EOF consists of a number of different classes, separated into *layers*. For WebObjects applications, there are two layers to be concerned with: the *access* layer, or EOAccess, and the *control* layer, or EOControl. The Java classes in these layers are contained in the com.apple.yellow.eoaccess and the com.apple.yellow.eocontrol packages.

Note
Documentation about the classes in these layers can be accessed from the WOInfoCenter under Reference, Enterprise Objects Framework (see Figure 2.1). A third layer to EOF is called EOInterface, which is not used with WebObjects; and a fourth layer is called EODistribution, which is used with the Java client portion of WebObjects. However, this book does not discuss Java client.

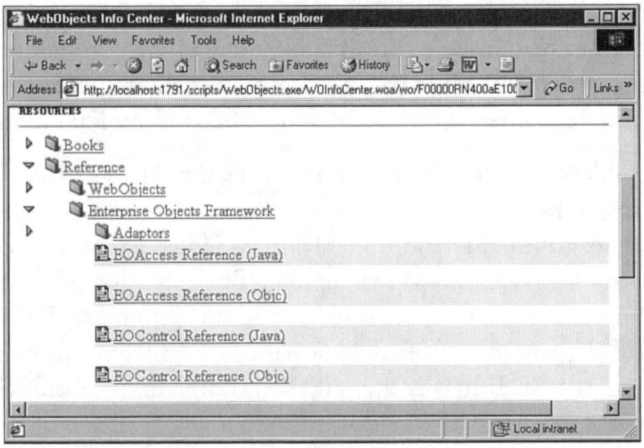

Figure 2.1
WOInfoCenter—Enterprise Objects Framework Reference.

Layers

The layers in EOF are a bit like the layers in a big corporation. Consider a busy executive who wants to ship a document. She gives it to her assistant, who fills out the appropriate paperwork and passes it to the mail room, who picks a vendor and ships it. If the mail room chooses a different vendor, the process works the same, and neither the executive or the assistant know the difference.

Consider that you are the executive interfacing with your assistant (the control layer), who accesses the database through the mail room (the access layer). You don't really know what it takes to get the letter out there, you just know it needs to go. The assistant (control layer) knows the steps to follow to send the letter, but which vendor will be used is unknown and to a certain extent it doesn't matter. The mail room (access layer) directly accesses the delivery vendor (database) and ships the letter.

The advantage of this process is that you don't really need to know the details, so you don't need to specify the details either. There are problems with this, however. Let's say that the mail room decides to use a new vendor that doesn't deliver on Saturday, when the old one did. The package that would have been delivered on Saturday is delayed by a couple of days. You suddenly have to change the way you do things to adapt to the new mail vendor.

EOAccess

This layer provides all the low-level access to the database. The purpose of this layer is to provide an abstraction of the database-specific code so that the higher layers can interface directly with objects. This layer alone satisfies the requirement of EOF being an object-to-relational-mapping system. There are two principle sets of classes in this layer, the database classes and the adaptor classes.

The *adaptor* classes (`EOAdaptor`, `EOAdaptorChannel`, `EOAdaptorContext`) are all abstract. These classes are intended to be overridden by a concrete adaptor, such as the Oracle adaptor. The purpose of these classes is to generate SQL, provide correct data type conversion, and properly access the database. The source code for some of the adaptors is provided, and it's possible to write an adaptor for other databases, including non-relational ones. Unsupported adaptors are also available, such as JDBC and DB2 adaptors. See `http://til.info.apple.com` for more information about these adaptors.

The database classes (`EODatabase`, `EODatabaseChannel`, and `EODatabaseContext`) act as the conduit between the adaptor and control layers. These classes are responsible for converting the raw data from the adaptor classes into *Enterprise Objects*, or *EOs*, along with managing database connections and transactions at a higher level. The database classes also verify data integrity for updates. This will be discussed in Chapter 12, "Using Stateless Transactions." The database classes use an EOModel to determine how to convert raw SQL data into EOs. Later in this chapter, you will create an EOModel.

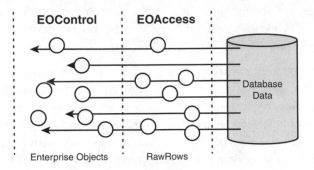

Figure 2.2
The classes in the EOAccess layer.

Note
Objects are directly retrieved from the database as *raw rows*, using the EOAccess layer's classes. These objects are promoted to Enterprise Objects and passed to the EOControl layer. Most of your code will interact with the classes in this layer.

EOControl

After the EOs are fetched from the database, they're passed to the control layer. The EOControl layer keeps an eye on what happens to the objects, tracking any updates, inserts, and deletes. There are also methods in the control layer for specifying which objects to retrieve and in what order. The class that brings everything together in the control layer is the EOEditingContext class. Editing context objects track of all the EOs in the system. When you tell an editing context to save its changes, it makes the appropriate changes in the database. The end result is that there's a lot less work for you to do.

Java to Objective-C
The EOF classes provided by Apple are written in Objective-C. Java developers have access to these classes using the "Java wrapper" classes provided by Apple. The Java wrapper classes allow your Java code to access Objective-C code. These classes use the Java to Objective-C bridge to access the compiled Objective-C objects. The bridge is more than just native interfaces, it contains methods to morph certain Objective-C objects into Java objects. For example, the Objective-C NSString class is morphed to a java.lang.String when objects are passed across the bridge. This means that the Java and Objective-C APIs are quite similar.

Mapping EOs to Databases

Before discussing the mapping between database tables and data to objects, it's probably a good idea to define what an enterprise object is. Basically, an *enterprise object* contains key-value pairs that represent a row in the database. The *key* is basically the column name, and the *value* is what was in that row in the database. Enterprise objects are also assigned an editing context, and the EO notifies the editing context when changes are made. EOEnterpriseObject is a Java interface defined in the EOControl layer, and its documentation can be found in the WOInfoCenter. Table 2.1 contains the most useful methods from this interface.

Table 2.1

Useful EOEnterpriseObject Methods

Method	Description
public Object valueForKey (String key)	Returns the value for the key specified.
public void takeValueForKey (Object value, String key)	Sets the value for the key provided.

These methods are implemented in two concrete classes: EOCustomObject and EOGenericRecord. The implementation makes the maximum use of polymorphism, allowing for a good bit of customization if necessary. This will be discussed in Chapter 13, "Optimizing Database Access."

The EOModel

One of the principles to EOF is the creation of the EOModel, which defines how objects are mapped to the database. This file is created in EOModeler. Mapping is done by specifying three different items: entities, attributes, and relationships. In general, relational database tables map to classes, the rows in the tables map to EOs, and the attributes are keys in the EOs.

- **Entity**—The Entity defines which class the table in the database maps to. The default is EOGenericRecord, which is a general-purpose data storage class.

- **Attribute**—An attribute defines which column a particular key is mapped to.

- **Relationship**—One of the better features of EOF, relationships map how logical database joins are represented. Relationships are specified as either one-to-one or one-to-many.

It is understandable if this much information seems overwhelming, it's a lot of information. As you read through the chapters, the details will be revealed. You should at least have the understanding of how everything fits together at a high level before undertaking the next step, which is to create an EOModel using EOModeler.

Using EOModeler

The purpose of the EOModel is to define how relational database data maps to enterprise objects, or EOs. EOModeler is the tool to use in order to create an EOModel. You can use EOModeler to create an EOModel from an existing database, or you can create a database from an EOModel, or anywhere in between. Because we installed the sample database in Chapter 1, we can go ahead and use that to create a new EOModel.

> **Caution**
> The rest of this chapter assumes that you have installed the sample database from Chapter 1. If you have not done this, now is a good time to go back and install it.

Creating a Model from a Database

In order to access the movies and rentals data from your WebObjects application, you need to create an EOModel. Here are the steps for creating the movies EOModel:

1. Start EOModeler by selecting the Start, Programs, WebObjects, EOModeler menu items in Windows. On the Mac, the menu selections are Apple, WebObjects, EOModeler.

2. In EOModeler, select the Model, New menu items (see Figure 2.3). This dialog should look familiar. Choose the same adaptor you used in the first chapter and click Next.

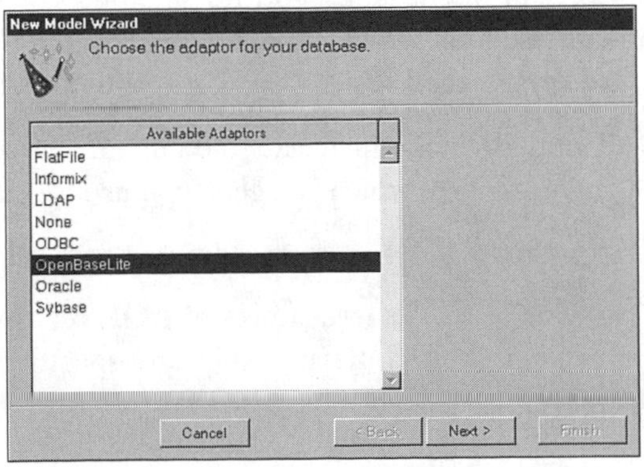

Figure 2.3
The New Model Wizard.

3. Depending on the adaptor you selected, you will receive a different login panel. Figure 2.4 shows the OpenBase Lite login panel. If you're using OpenBase Lite, find the database you created in Chapter 1 using the Browse button and click OK. Otherwise log in using the values you used in Chapter 1 and click OK.

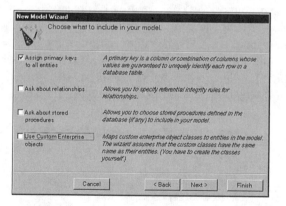

Figure 2.4
The OpenBase Lite Adaptor login panel.

4. Now you're asked what to include in the model (see Figure 2.5). All these values can be changed later. To keep it simple, uncheck everything except Assign Primary Keys to All Entities. The other options are discussed later. Click the Next button.

Figure 2.5
The Choose What to Include in Your Model dialog box.

5. This step is crucial. At this point, EOModeler attempts to determine the database schema. If it is successful, you should see a set of database tables. You can pick and choose which tables you want to use in your model (see Figure 2.6). If you leave a table out, it will be extremely difficult (close to impossible) to

retrieve data from that table in your code. Leave everything selected and click the Next button.

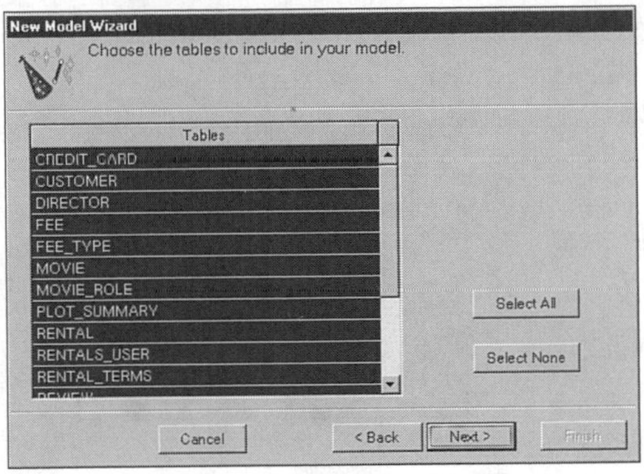

Figure 2.6
The new model wizard will find all the tables in an existing database.

6. EOModeler attempts to determine the primary keys for all the tables and the relationships between the tables. Depending on your database, you might or might not see another dialog before the main EOModeler window. Oracle, for example, stores enough information in the database to be able to determine everything without asking you. OpenBase Lite stores a lot of information, but has trouble with the compound primary keys. You will be prompted to enter the compound primary keys for the tables that have them. The first one is the Director table, and the primary keys are `movieId` and `talentId` (see Figure 2.7). In Windows, hold down the Ctrl key while selecting the two items; on the Mac, hold down the Command key. Then click Next.

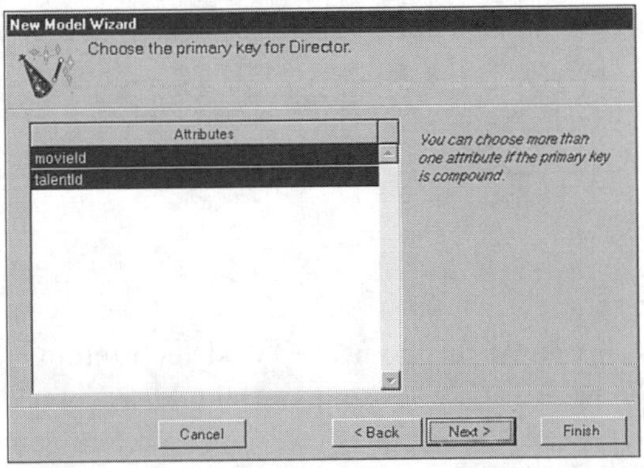

Figure 2.7
The primary keys for the Director entity.

7. Finally, enter the same primary keys for the MovieRole table, `movieId` and `talentId` (see Figure 2.8). Click Finish to continue.

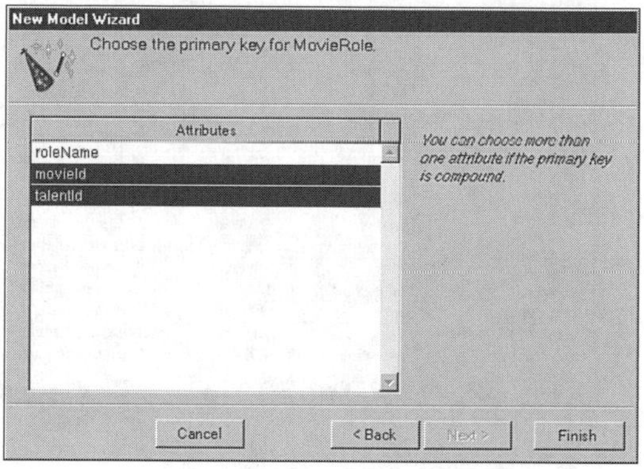

Figure 2.8
The primary keys for the MovieRole entity.

You should now be presented with the EOModeler window once again; this time populated with entities from your database. Go ahead and save your model as **movies.eomodeld** in a directory of your choice, somewhere that you will remember. You have now created a model file. Next you will learn about the different features of EOModeler.

Browsing the Model

One of the first things that you'll want to do is take a look at what's in the model. The main items are the entities, which contain attributes and relationships. Let's start by examining the entities.

Entities

The main objective of the entity is to map the database table to a class. The default is for all entities to be EOGenericRecords. This will work until you want to store some custom business logic in your model. In that case you would make the class name the same as your entity name. This is discussed in Chapter 7, "Writing Enterprise Objects Classes."

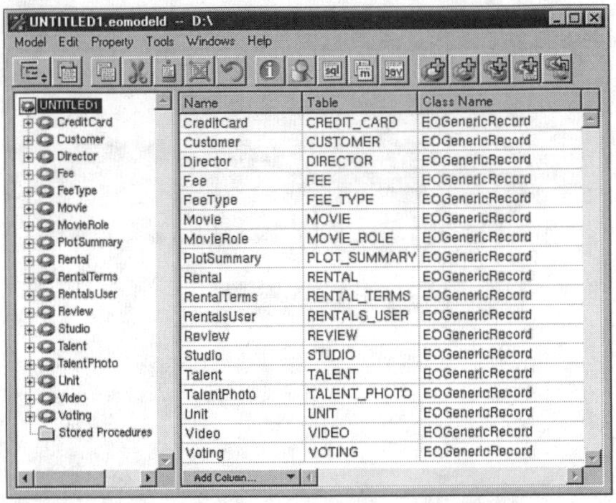

Figure 2.9
The EOModeler main window.

The entities are located down the left side of the window represented as little orange rings around yellow circles. The class and table names for all entities are initially displayed in the main window. To find out more about an entity, select it in the left window. When selected, the right part of the window changes to display the attributes and relationships for the entity (see Figure 2.10).

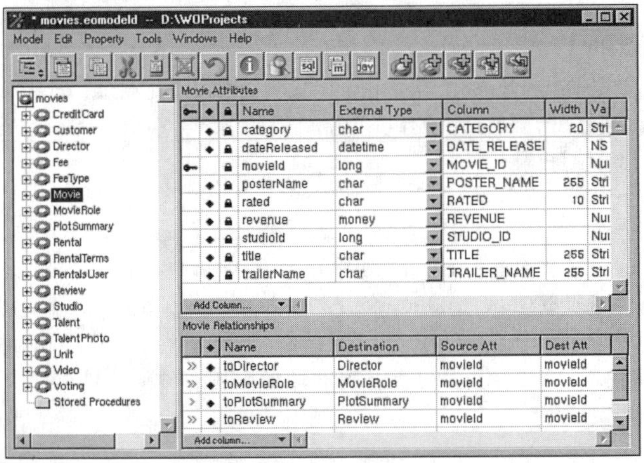

Figure 2.10
The Movie entity is selected.

To find out more about the entity, click the Inspector button while the entity is selected.

This is a user interface paradigm that is followed throughout the Apple tools, clicking the Inspector button displays detailed information about the selected item. There are also potentially different inspectors for the same item. Clicking the buttons at the top of the inspector reveals different types of entity inspectors (see Figure 2.11).

Figure 2.11
The Movie Entity Inspector dialog box.

The different entity inspectors will be discussed in detail later in the book. When finished, simply close the inspector by clicking the Window Close button.

Attributes
When an entity is selected, the attributes are displayed in the upper right part of the window. Attributes specify the table column associated with a given key (see Figure 2.12). Attributes can be marked as editable or read-only, and can allow `null` (see Figure 2.13).

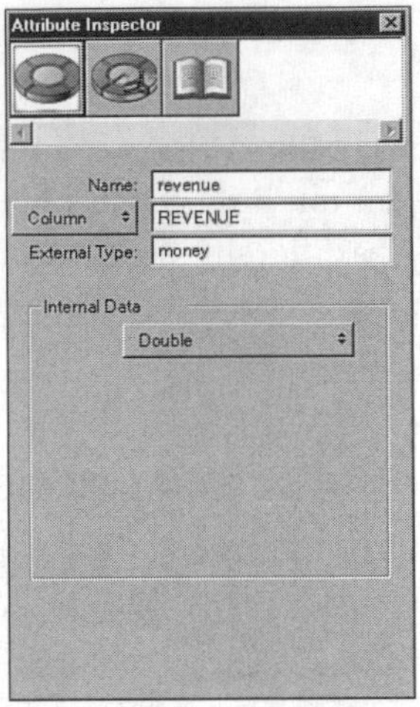

Figure 2.12
The revenue Attribute Inspector dialog box.

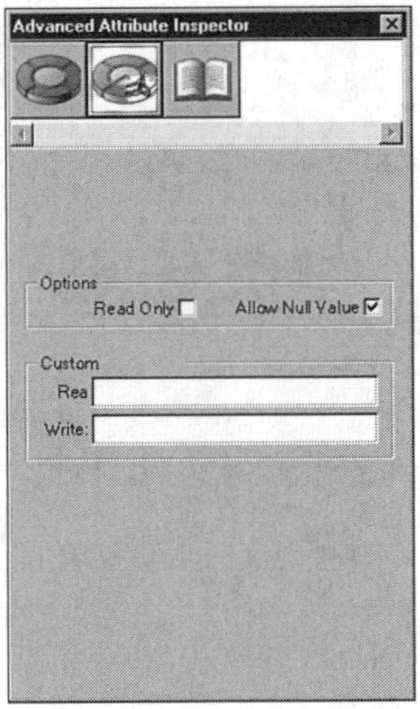

Figure 2.13
The Advanced Attribute Inspector dialog box for the revenue attribute.

The column can be an actual column or one derived from a couple of different columns (see Figure 2.14). For example, assume that you're storing rectangle data with width and height columns. You could also have an area column that is derived from the width and height. The Table Column attribute would be width*height.

The derived columns are dependant on the database to support the operation. Also, derived columns rely on the database to compute the column. For these reasons derived columns are not used much. Listing 2.1 demonstrates the SQL that is generated from the derived column in Figure 2.14.

Figure 2.14

A Derived column. The equation entered must be supported by the underlying database.

Listing 2.1

The SQL Generated from a Derived Column

```
SELECT  t0.length*t0.width, t0.length, t0.rect_id, t0.width
FROM RECTANGLE t0
```

Browsing Data

Just to make sure that everything's working okay, or just to see what's in the database, you can browse the database data using the Browse Data icon. Just select an entity and click the button. If you select an attribute rather than the entire entity, only the attribute is browsed.

Relationships

One of the advantages of using a relational database is the normalization of data; that is, the non-duplication of data. For example, let's say that you want to store employee names and their division names. Let's also say that you have five employees in the Sales and Marketing division. If you store the division name in the employee table, it's considered un-normalized. Table 2.2 shows what this looks like. Notice that if the name of the division needs to be changed to Sales, five records are affected. Also notice the errors. There are a lot of disadvantages to storing un-normalized data; one is the opportunity for data errors to creep into your application.

Table 2.2

The Employee Table

Employee ID	Name	Division
1	Fred	Sales and Marketing
2	Jane	Sales & Marketing
3	Sal	Sales and Marketing
4	Martha	Sales and Mktng
5	Jimbo	Sales and Marketing

To normalize this, the division name is taken out of the Employee table and added to a separate table called Division, as shown in Table 2.3. To indicate that an employee is part of a division, the division's primary key is placed in the employee table. This is considered a *foreign key*.

Table 2.3

The Division Table

Division ID	Name
1	Human Resources
2	Sales and Marketing
3	Administration

In Table 2.4, The division name has been replaced with the primary key for the appropriate division. Now if the division's name needs changing, it's only changed in one place.

Table 2.4

The Normalized Employee Table

Employee ID	Name	Division ID
1	Fred	2
2	Jane	2
3	Sal	2
4	Martha	2
5	Jimbo	2

It can be said from the previous example that a one-to-one relationship exists from the Employee table to the Division table. There is only one division per employee. It can also be said that a one-to-many relationship from the Division table to the Employee table. A division has many employees.

This is a greatly simplified explanation of normalizing relational data. There's a great book on the subject called *Database Design for Mere Mortals: A Hands-On Guide to Relational Data* by Michael J. Hernandez.

That's how relationships work at the database level. Now let's find out how they work in EOF.

EOF Relationships

Modeling these in EOF is quite simple, and there are many options for your relationships. Consider the relationships between the Studio (see Figure 2.15) and Movie entities. A partial set of the data is shown in Figures 2.16 and 2.17.

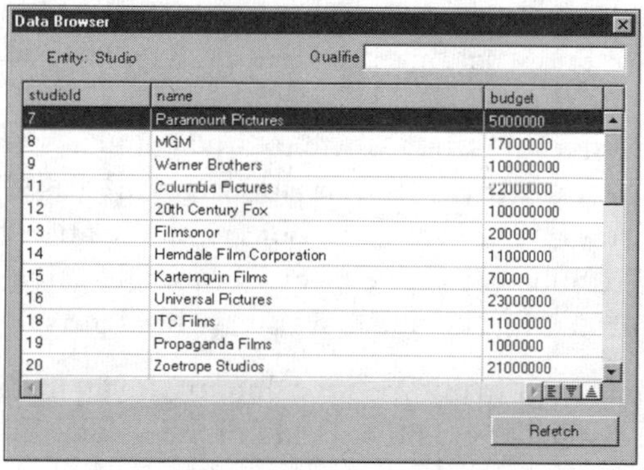

Figure 2.15

The studios.

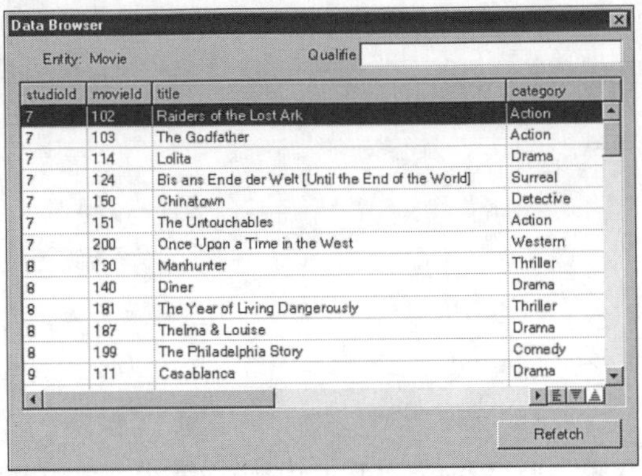

studioId	movieId	title	category
7	102	Raiders of the Lost Ark	Action
7	103	The Godfather	Action
7	114	Lolita	Drama
7	124	Bis ans Ende der Welt [Until the End of the World]	Surreal
7	150	Chinatown	Detective
7	151	The Untouchables	Action
7	200	Once Upon a Time in the West	Western
8	130	Manhunter	Thriller
8	140	Diner	Drama
8	181	The Year of Living Dangerously	Thriller
8	187	Thelma & Louise	Drama
8	199	The Philadelphia Story	Comedy
9	111	Casablanca	Drama

Figure 2.16

The movies for studios 7, 8, and 9.

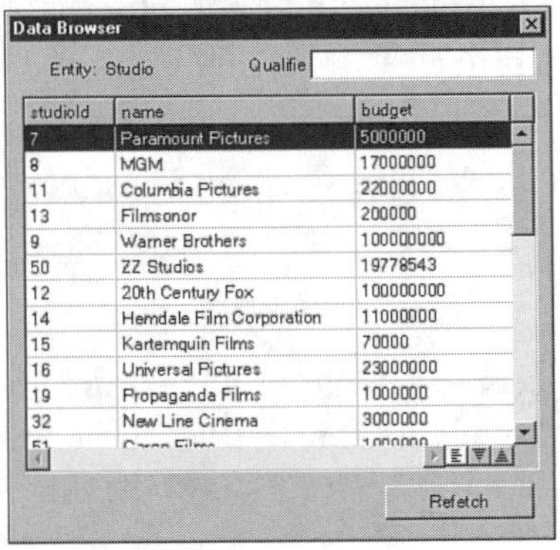

studioId	name	budget
7	Paramount Pictures	5000000
8	MGM	17000000
11	Columbia Pictures	22000000
13	Filmsonor	200000
9	Warner Brothers	100000000
50	ZZ Studios	19778543
12	20th Century Fox	100000000
14	Hemdale Film Corporation	11000000
15	Kartemquin Films	70000
16	Universal Pictures	23000000
19	Propaganda Films	1000000
32	New Line Cinema	3000000

Figure 2.17

The studios. These `studioIds` *should match the* `studioIds` *for the movies in Figure 2.16.*

A "to-one" relationship exists from Movie to Studio and a "to-many" relationship exists from Studio back to Movie. Both relationships are based on the `studioIds` being equal. When these rows are converted to objects, the relationships are converted to keys. The "to-one" relationships are converted to single-value keys and the "to-many" relationships are converted to keys that are arrays of objects.

The Studio entity has a "to-many" relationship to Movie, meaning that every Studio object has a `NSArray` called `movies` that holds all the movies for that studio. Also, the `Movie` entity has a "to-one" relationship to `Studio`, meaning that every movie has a possible reference to a studio. This is shown in Figure 2.18.

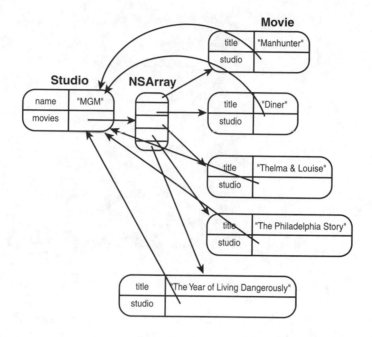

Figure 2.18
The Movie and Studio objects when retrieved from the database.

The names of the relationships are defined in EOModeler. The naming convention is for "to-one" relationships to be the name of the destination entity with a lowercase first letter. For example, the "to-one" relationship from Movie to Studio is called `'studio'`. The naming convention for the "to-many" relationships is also the name of the destination entity starting with a lowercase first letter, with an s appended to the end. The "to-many" relationship from Studio to Movie is called `'movies'`.

Relationships in EOModeler

The good news about relationships is that they're easily created in EOModeler. All you really need to know is the type of relationship, the source and destination entities, and the keys used for the join. The relationships for an entity are located in the bottom right half of the window. To inspect one, select it and click the Inspector button. The inspector for the to Movie relationship is shown in Figure 2.19.

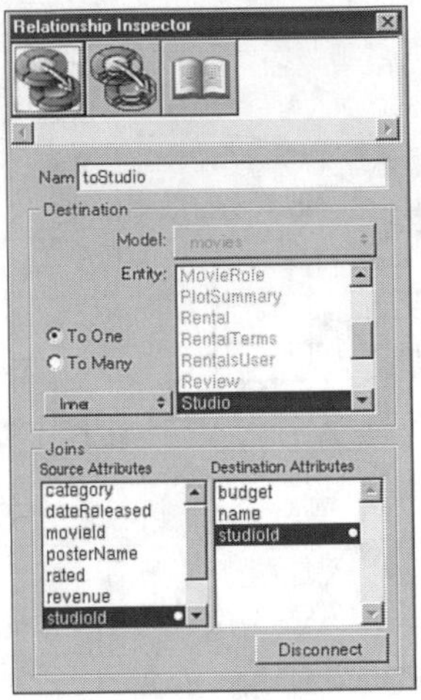

Figure 2.19
The "to-one" relationship from movie to studio.

Notice that if you used the OpenBase Lite database, all the relationships are named to something. This is a really bad way to name relationships. Just think about asking a studio for its toMovie. A better name for that relationship would be movies because you would naturally ask a studio for its movies.

Some advanced options for relationships exist. Take a look at the Advanced Relationship Inspector by clicking the middle button at the top of the inspector. This inspector is shown in Figure 2.20. Here is where you can set some optimizations using batch fetching, the delete rule, and the optionality. Batch Fetching will be discussed in Chapter 13.

Optionality

This specifies whether the relationship is mandatory; that is, whether it is mandatory that an object is on the other side of the relationship. If this is set to Mandatory, EOF will not allow you to set the relationship to null. It's similar to Allow Null Values in the attribute inspector.

Delete Rule

One of the age-old problems with relational databases is what to do when data is removed from the database. More specifically, what do you do with the related data? For example, if you remove a studio from the database and there are movies with that studio ID, what do you do with those movies? EOF allows you to choose what happens depending on the relationship. Table 2.5 describes the delete rule options.

Figure 2.20

The Advanced Relationship Inspector for a "to-one" relationship.

Table 2.5

Delete Rule Options

Delete Rule	Description
Nullify	Any relationships to the object being deleted will be nullified. For example, if a Studio is deleted that contained Movies, all of that Studio's movies will have a `null` relationship back to the Studio table
Cascade	All associated objects are deleted. If the delete rule for the `studio` relationship from Movie to Studio is set to Cascade, the associated Studio is deleted as well as the Movie.
Deny	If objects exist across the relationship, does not let the object be deleted. For example, if a Studio contains movies, it cannot be deleted if the delete rule across the `movies` relationship is Deny.
No Action	Doesn't do anything. This option has the potential to open up the situation in which records have foreign keys for records that do not exist. For example, imagine deleting a Studio that has movies. If the associated movies are not modified, they will all refer to the now deleted studio.

Owns Destination

Setting the Owns Destination flag to a relationship means that if an object is removed from a relationship, it will be removed from the database. In the Movies database, there is a Customer entity with a to-many relationship to the Rental table, which should be called `rentals`. The `Rental` entity stores information about a particular rental that occurred. If a `Rental` is not associated with a `Customer`, it isn't of much use, so the Customer is said to *own* the destination. Now if a `Rental` is removed from the `Customer`'s `rentals` relationship, it's also removed from the database.

Propagate Primary Key

This setting is applicable to relationships in which the source key is the primary key and the destination key is also a primary key (or part of a compound primary key). The source key will be propagated to any newly inserted objects in the relationship. For example, the `Talent` entity has a to-one relationship to the `TalentPhoto` entity, where the primary keys of both entities are the same, `talentId`. In this case, it would be appropriate to say that the primary key is propagated from `Talent` to `TalentPhoto`.

With this knowledge under your belt, it's a good idea to go through the model and set some appropriate names for the relationships as well as set some of the values on the advanced entity inspector for those relationships.

Adding to the Model

EOModeler is useful also when designing or adding to applications. You have the ability to add, modify, and remove entities, attributes, and relationships using the icons in Table 2.6. After you make changes to the model, you can create and execute the SQL to make the appropriate database changes directly in EOModeler. Note that any changes to a particular database table will erase any information in that table. Even though some databases have the ability to add columns to tables, this is not supported in EOModeler. Any table structure changes require that the table is dropped and recreated.

Table 2.6

Model Modification Toolbar Icons

Icon	Description
	New entity
	New attribute
	New relationship
	New fetch specification
	Flatten selected property

Creating Entities

To create an entity, simply select the Create Entity icon or use the Property, Add Entity menu item. You will need to set the entity's name and the table name.

Creating Attributes

To create an attribute in an entity, select the entity and click the Create attribute button or use the Property, Add Attribute menu item. You will need to set the attribute's name, the column name, the database type, and the internal type. Attributes can also be copied and pasted. This is useful if you have multiple attributes of the same type, or if you want to copy the primary key for an entity and paste it into another entity as a foreign key.

Primary Key

The primary key for an entity is set by clicking the key column for the appropriate attribute. If the entity has multiple primary keys, multiple columns can be selected.

Class Attributes

The diamond specifies the class attribute setting for the attribute. If an attribute has a diamond next to it, it is considered to be a class attribute. Otherwise, it's something that EOF tracks, but is not necessarily available from your code. In Figure 2.21, the class attributes for the Studio entity are the Studio's name and budget. The studioId is not a class attribute, meaning that you can't just ask any given studio what its studioId is.

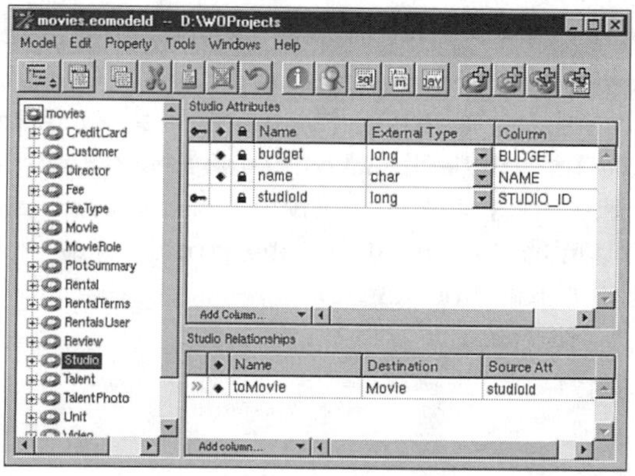

Figure 2.21
The Class Attribute icon is the diamond next to the attribute name.

So you're asking, "Why wouldn't I want to know what the primary key is?" The answer is, "so you won't mess it up." The sole purpose of primary keys is so the relational database can uniquely identify different rows in the database. After the objects get in memory, they can be uniquely identified by their memory address. EOF keeps track of the primary keys, so you don't. When you insert an object, EOF will generate a new unique primary key for you. EOF will also manage your foreign keys through relationships, so these do not need to be class properties either.

In general, everything is a class property except the primary and foreign keys. Now is a good time to unset the class property diamonds for all primary and foreign keys in your model.

Locked Attribute

The Lock icon is used to check for update conflicts, which will be discussed in Chapter 7. In general, columns with very large sets of data like blobs are not locked. For now, you don't need to do anything with this icon, just keep it there for everything.

Creating Relationships

You can create a relationship by selecting the entity and using the Create Relationship button or by using the Property, Add Relationship menu item. If you immediately bring up the inspector and set all the relationship values *except* the name, an appropriate name will be generated for you when you click the Connect button in the relationship inspector.

Altering the Database from EOModeler

If you have added any entities, you can create the underlying database tables using the Generate SQL button. This button brings up the SQL Generation dialog (see Figure 2.22), which displays the SQL that will be executed on the database. SQL for any entity you have selected will be displayed. If you have the entire model selected, the SQL to create all the tables will be displayed. You can either save the SQL or execute it on the server. If you have changed the table structure for an existing entity and executed the SQL for that entity, any existing data in that table will be lost because the table is dropped and re-created.

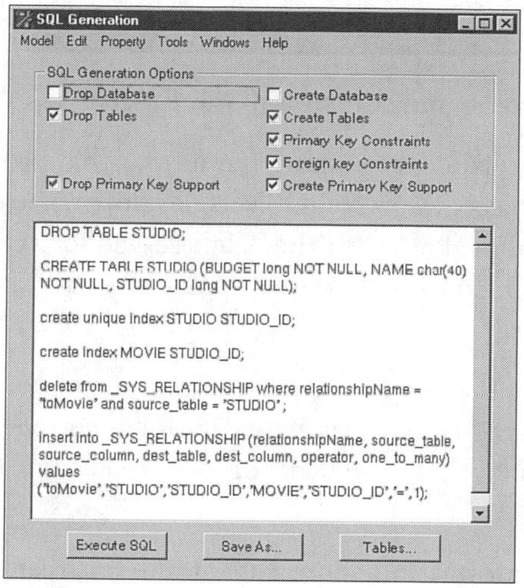

Figure 2.22
The SQL Generation dialog.

Switching the Adaptor

One of the great EOModeler features is that you can switch adaptors at any point. All the data types are converted appropriately. At that point you can click the Generate SQL button to create the table structure in the new database. This is useful if the first part of your development takes place on a single-user database such as OpenBase Lite or Access, and you want to convert your database to a more scalable one such as Oracle or Sybase.

You can switch the adaptor by selecting the Model, Switch Adaptor menu items. Note that the data is not moved between databases, only the table structure.

When switching database adaptors, some of the functionality in your existing application might behave differently depending on the underlying database. One example of this is in the SQL `like` statement. Oracle performs a case sensitive `like` whereas OpenBase Lite performs a not case sensitive `like`. If your application depends on a certain type of `like` operation, it might not behave correctly without modification. The bottom line is that if you know you are going to switch adaptors, you should switch sooner rather than later.

Summary

In this chapter you got an introduction to the Enterprise Objects Framework, or EOF.

EOF is an object-to-relational mapping framework that provides a large amount of power to the WebObjects. As a WebObjects developer, the complexities of database development are hidden along with the database-vendor specific code. EOModeler is used to create the EOModel that is used to map the database tables and columns to classes and attributes.

EOF is divided into a few layers: the most important to you at this point are the EOAccess and EOControl layers. Database data is converted to Enterprise Objects or EOs in the EOAccess layer. The EOControl layer tracks updates, inserts, and deletes of Enterprise Objects.

For more overview information about EOF, there's a great document in the WOInfoCenter under Books, Enterprise Objects, Enterprise Objects Frameworks Developer's Guide. "Part I: Enterprise Objects Frameworks Essentials" would be good to read for a different perspective. Also, check out http://www.wowack.com/. Answers to common reader questions will be posted and grouped by chapter.

Q&A

Q **Considering that EOF is a database layer abstraction, how much of a performance hit is taken by using it?**

A It depends; for most simple queries, there isn't much overhead involved. Some extra copies of the rows are stored in the access layer and a few extra methods called, but nothing that will noticeably impact your response time. For more complex queries and multitable joins, non-optimized EOF can get fairly ugly. The good news is that you have the ability to optimize and customize the way EOF behaves.

CHAPTER 3

WEBOBJECTS COMPONENTS

Component-ware, have you heard of it? It's supposed to replace *OOP (object-oriented programming)* as the software development paradigm of choice. The most popular components these days are JavaBeans, followed closely by Microsoft's COM and Enterprise JavaBeans. Using components speeds your development process, reduces the number of bugs, and in general makes life good, so the story goes. The potential of component-ware is to allow the developer to piece together an application without much (if any) coding using prebuilt components.

Components can be considered a little like LEGOs. You know how all the LEGO pieces magically fit together; it's the same with components. Now, you know the reason the LEGOs fit together so smoothly is that their pegs are just the right size to fit into the under side of the blocks. There's a specification somewhere in LEGOLAND that says what size the pegs and blocks should be. Because there's a specification for how blocks fit together, and because of the incredible price of LEGOs, a number of companies are creating LEGO knock offs that fit into LEGOs. The reason they fit is because they adhere to the same specification.

Components usually come with a specification, like LEGOs, and the also magically fit together like LEGOs. Just because everything fits together doesn't mean that what you're building will work, however. And, components are generally a little more difficult to fit together than LEGOs.

So, how are components different than objects? Well, components are objects that adhere to a certain specification. Components can also contain additional resources, such as text files that describe themselves. Objects are a lot more flexible than components because you really can do anything you want with objects. All components have to be accessible in a certain way, which gives the component developer a little less freedom.

In WebObjects, the components represent dynamic pages of your application. You will be the component developer, and your tools will be WebObjects Builder and Project Builder. Begin by starting your first WebObjects project.

In this chapter, you will

- Create a new WebObjects project using Project Builder

- Learn about WebObjects components

- Create a few WebObjects components

- Use WOHyperlinks to navigate between WOComponents

Creating a New WebObjects Application

This section will be a tutorial on creating your first WebObjects application. The application used here will display a random number when the main page refreshes. Start by creating a new WebObjects application using Project Builder.

Using Project Builder

Project Builder is found in the WebObjects program group under either the Start menu in Windows or the Apple menu on the Mac. When you initially start Project Builder, a project will not be loaded. On Windows, you will see the Loaded Projects window; on Mac, you will simply be presented with the Project Builder menu.

Creating a Project

To create a new project, select the Project, New menu items. You will be presented with the new project dialog box (see Figure 3.1 and Figure 3.2).

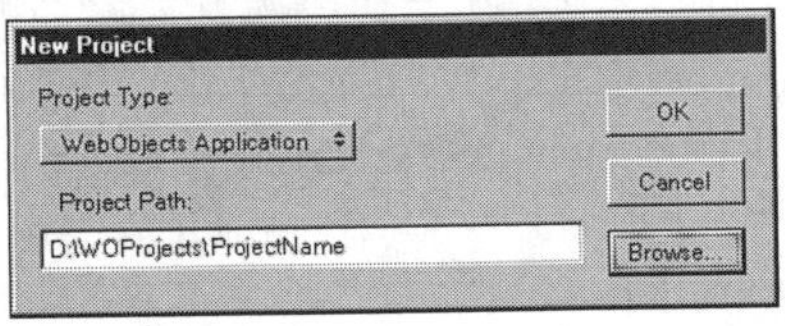

Figure 3.1
The Windows New Project dialog box.

Project Builder manages many different types of projects. The project type that you will use throughout this book is the WebObjects Application type.

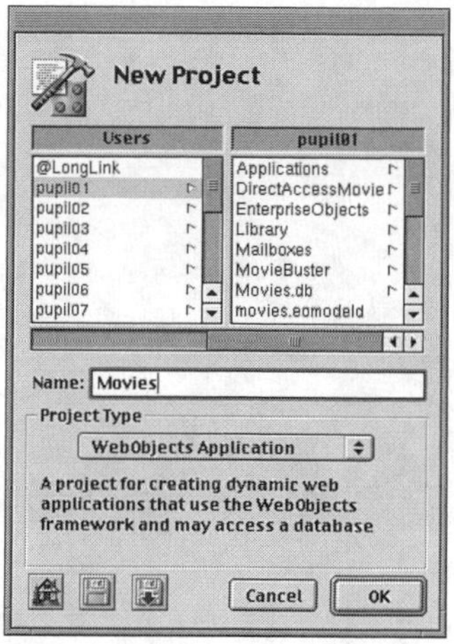

Figure 3.2
Mac OS X New Project dialog box.

> **Caution**
> The WebObjects Application type is different from the Application project type, which is the default. If you choose the Application project type, you will not be able to create a WebObjects application.

In the New Project dialog box, you will need to enter the path for your new project. The name of the project is the last part of the path that you enter. For example, on Windows if you choose `c:\Projects\WebObjects\Movies`, the name of your project is Movies. Also if you choose that path, the `Movies` directory will be created in the `c:\Projects\WebObjects` directory. The other directories need to be there, however.

Go ahead and create a new WebObjects Application project called `Movies`. On the Mac, place it somewhere in your home directory. On Windows, place it in an appropriate directory. You will then be presented with the WebObjects Application Wizard, which is shown in Figure 3.3.

The WebObjects Application Wizard allows you to start your application with some pre-generated code. It also allows you to pick the language used in the application. Set the Available Assistance to None and the Primary Language to Java.

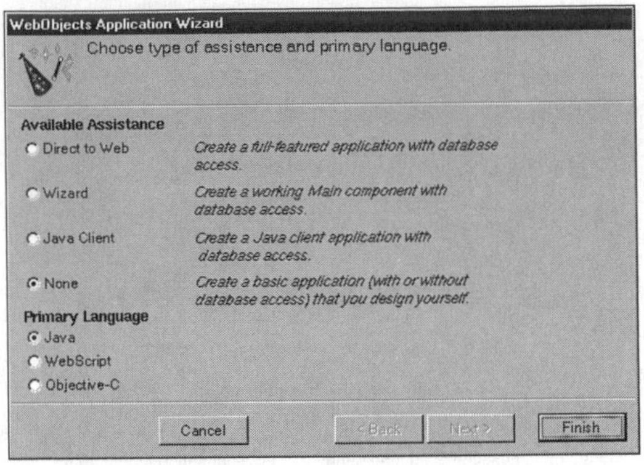

Figure 3.3
The WebObjects Application Wizard.

Examining the Project

After you have created the project, you will be presented with the Project Builder main window, as shown in Figure 3.4. The upper portion of the window allows you to browse your project; the lower portion is a text editor for files that you select.

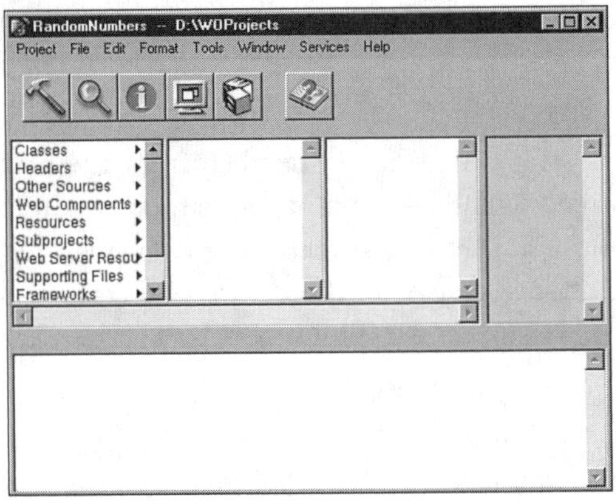

Figure 3.4
The Project Builder main window.

The files in your project are divided into *suitcases*, each holding a different type of file. These suitcases are not necessarily subdirectories within your project directory, rather a logical way to group files. The number and type of suitcases depends on the type of project selected (see Table 3.1).

Table 3.1

Project Builder Suitcases and Their Contents for a WebObjects Application Project

Suitcase	Contents
Classes	Java and Objective-C class files. The initial contents should be `Application.java`, `Session.java`, `DirectAction.java`, and `Main.java`.
Headers	Header files for C, C++, or Objective-C files, not used in Java-only projects.
Other Sources	Anything else that needs to be compiled. This is where you would put C files. The file containing the `main()` function is located here.
Web Components	The components that make up your application are here. Each component is a folder that contains an HTML and WOD file. The class file for the component is in the Classes suitcase.
Resources	Any server-side resources that are not directly available to the client. The EOModel goes here.
Subprojects	You have the ability to break your project into a number of smaller projects, and these would go here. This is useful when working with a team of engineers.
Web Server Resources	Anything that is intended to be available to the client such as images.
Supporting files	Files that are used to create the application, but will not be deployed with the application. Makefiles are here, but it's rare that you would have to modify them. Templates for newly created files are also in this suitcase. These can be modified to add copyright and trademark information.
Frameworks	Frameworks consist of reusable code and resources, and these go here. If you purchase a third-party product framework, it would go here.
Libraries	Compiled libraries to be used with C, C++, or Objective-C code.
Non Project Files	This suitcase contains any files opened that are not part of your project.

Setting Preferences

One thing that you want to do in Project Builder is set the preferences appropriately (see Figure 3.5). The preferences window is displayed by selecting the Edit, Preferences menu items. Set the tab size in the Editing preferences. The Editing preferences are modified by clicking the Editing button in the left portion of the window. For some reason, the default is 8. Most developers prefer 4.

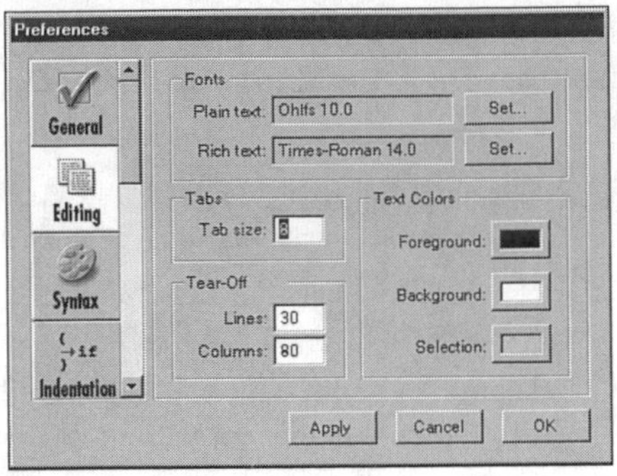

Figure 3.5
One task when using Project Builder is to set the tab size appropriately.

The editor in Project Builder helps the developer with editing the files through things like smart indentations. Depending on your coding style, the default values could either be really helpful or really detrimental. Most developers will find the default values quite irritating. If you fall into that category, do not throw your copy of WebObjects out the window, there are a number of options for customizing the way the Project Builder editor behaves. These options can be found under the Indentation part of the preferences dialog box (see Figure 3.6).

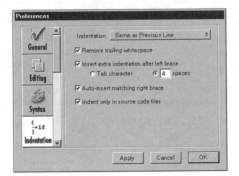

Figure 3.6
The Indentation part of the Preferences dialog box can be used to change the way the Project Builder editor behaves.

Project Settings

You can also set project options using the Inspector. The Build attributes allow you to customize how the application is built, including search orders and destination directories. Project Attributes allow you to change the name of your project (Figure 3.7). You have the option of changing the name of the directory in which the project is located when changing the project name.

Figure 3.7
The name of the project can be changed in the Project Inspector.

Project Find

Project Builder comes with some complex find functionality. You have the ability to search and replace text throughout the entire project. The Project Find is also smart enough to determine the differences between references to a term and the definition of the term (see Figure 3.8).

What results are displayed is dependent on the type of find. The different types and their effect are described in Table 3.2.

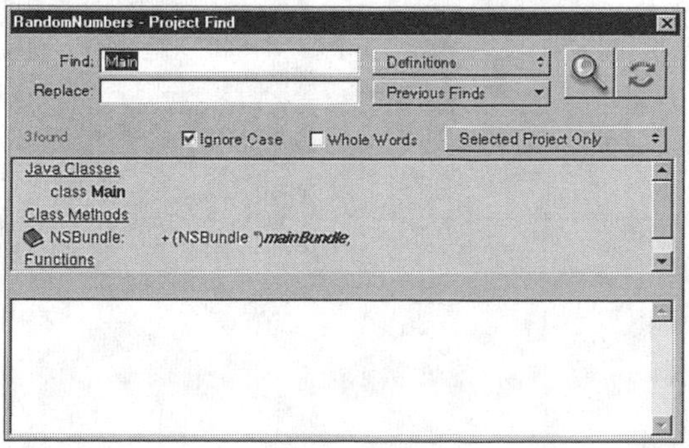

Figure 3.8
The Project Find panel. Clicking on the results displays the location where the item was found.

Table 3.2

Project Builder Find Types

Find Type	What's Displayed
Definitions	Where the text is defined in your code. This is useful when searching for a method definition.
References	This searches your code for where the item is defined and where references are made to the item. This returns a superset of the Definitions search. This is useful if you want to rename a method. You can rename the definition and everywhere it is referenced.
Textually	This is the classic find; the text is searched everywhere. If the text is found anywhere in the code in your project, it's displayed in the results.
Reg Expr'n	Stands for Regular Expression. This will search everything in your project. It is similar to the Textually find, but it extends to non-code files such as your HTML, WOD, and make files.

Class Browser

 Another Project Builder feature is the class browser (see Figure 3.9). This allows you to browse the class hierarchy, viewing the methods for each class. One of the disadvantages of using the class browser for Java developers is that the documentation displayed is for Objective-C. Java developers should use the WOInfoCenter, or learn Objective-C.

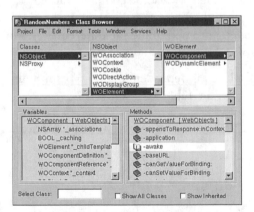

Figure 3.9

The Class Browser dialog box.

Using WebObjects Builder

WebObjects Builder is used to edit your WebObjects components, where each component represents a page of your application. The components are located in the Web Components suitcase. You should have only one at this point, `Main.wo`. Double-click this component to open it in WebObjects Builder (see Figure 3.10).

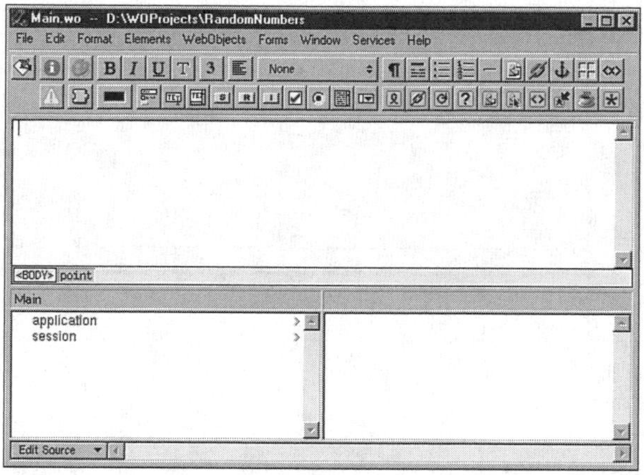

Figure 3.10
WebObjects Builder is used to edit your WOComponents.

WebObjects Builder consists of an HTML editor, a component bindings editor, and a code generator. The top part of the WebObjects Builder window is used to edit the HTML for a component. The bottom part of the window displays the attributes for the component and allows you to browse key-paths for the component's attributes. Component bindings and code generation will be discussed later in this chapter. The HTML editor will be tackled first.

Editing HTML

There are two ways to edit HTML in WebObjects Builder, using the graphical and source editing modes. *Graphical* editing mode is a WYSIWYG editor that renders the HTML as you edit it (see Figure 3.11). Graphical editing mode gives you a good idea on how the final product will look, but it's no substitute for viewing the HTML in your browser. Using the graphical editing mode, you can change font sizes and styles, add HTML tags such as paragraphs, line breaks, and horizontal rules. You can also add and modify HTML tables.

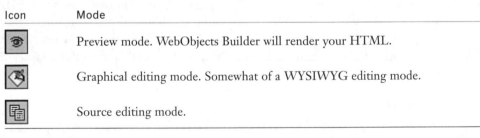

Figure 3.11
The WebObjects Builder Graphical Editing Mode.

Source editing mode allows you to modify the HTML source. You can switch between source and graphical editing modes using the pop-up button on the toolbar all the way to the left. The icons for the different editing modes are described in Table 3.3.

Table 3.3
WebObjects Builder Editing Modes

Icon	Mode
	Preview mode. WebObjects Builder will render your HTML.
	Graphical editing mode. Somewhat of a WYSIWYG editing mode.
	Source editing mode.

In the source editing mode, you can manually edit the HTML (see Figure 3.12). This is useful if you want to add tags that aren't available through the user interface or want to have more control over the editing. More than likely, the raw HTML that you're looking at is fairly ugly. To reformat it to look a bit better, select the Format, Reformat HTML menu item.

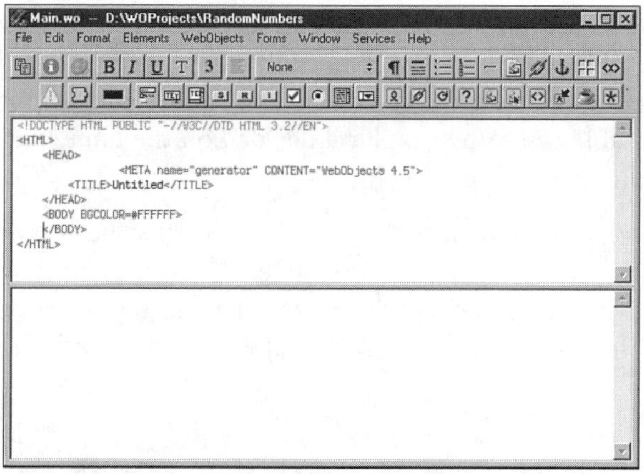

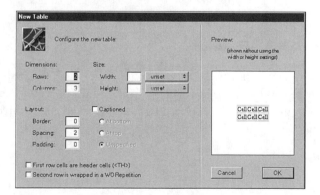

Figure 3.12
WebObjects Builder in source editing mode.

The bottom half of the screen allows you to modify the WebObjects definition file, which will be discussed later in this chapter.

Using HTML Tables

Any self-respecting Web page makes considerable use of HTML tables. Tables allow you to format the HTML in nice, even rows and columns. Tables can also be nested inside of one another for greater control. To easily create a HTML table, you need to be in graphical editing mode (see Figure 3.13). Select the HTML table icon.

Figure 3.13
The New Table dialog box.

The HTML table dialog box allows you to specify the rows, columns, and other table attributes. The table *padding* is the distance, in pixels, between the table rows and columns. The table *spacing* is the distance between the table cell border and the contents of the table cell. After you have decided on the table that you want, simply click OK to create it.

Use the Inspector to edit the table's structure after it has been created. You can modify the table's tag, the table data tags, or the table row tags. To modify a tag, click a point within the table. Notice that WebObjects Builder visually represents the tag that contains your cursor (see Figure 3.14). All tags up to the <BODY> tag are also represented.

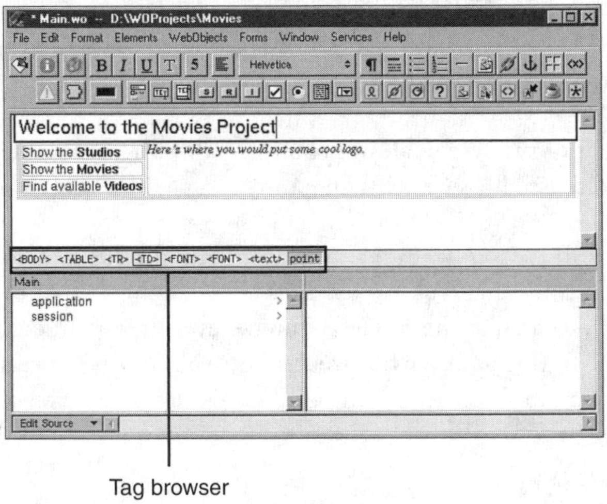

Tag browser

Figure 3.14
The nested tags in WebObjects Builder.

To display the inspector for these tags, you can either click the Inspector button or right-click the tag and select Inspect *<tag>* from the pop-up menu (see Figure 3.15). On Macs, the pop-up menu is activated by holding down the Control key when clicking the tag.

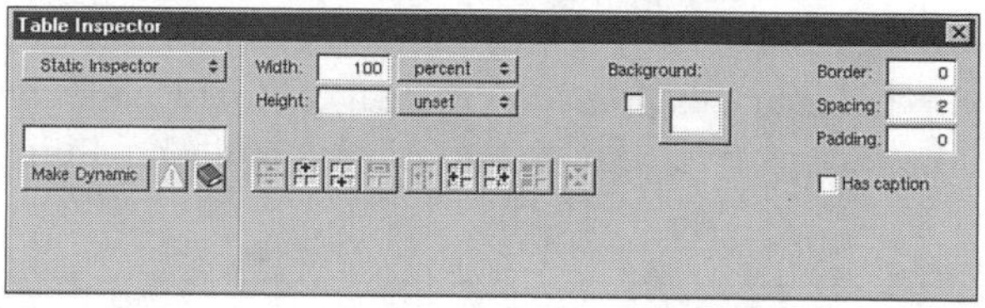

Figure 3.15
The Table Inspector dialog box.

The table inspector allows you to change the structure of the table by adding and removing rows and columns (see Figure 3.16). You can also set the table settings such as the background color and the width and height.

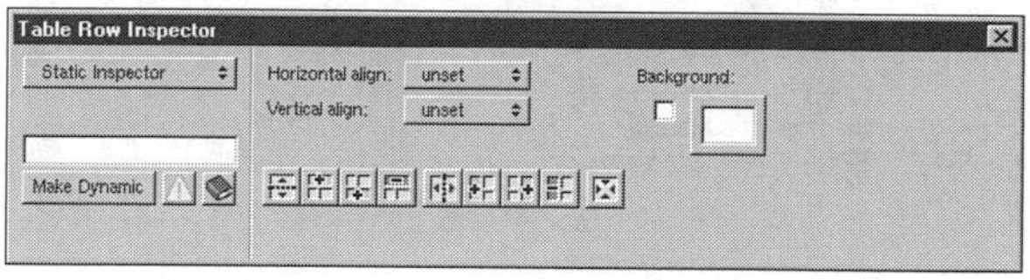

Figure 3.16
The Table Row Inspector dialog box.

Inspecting a table row allows you to change the settings for an entire row such as the background color and the horizontal and vertical alignment (see Figure 3.17).

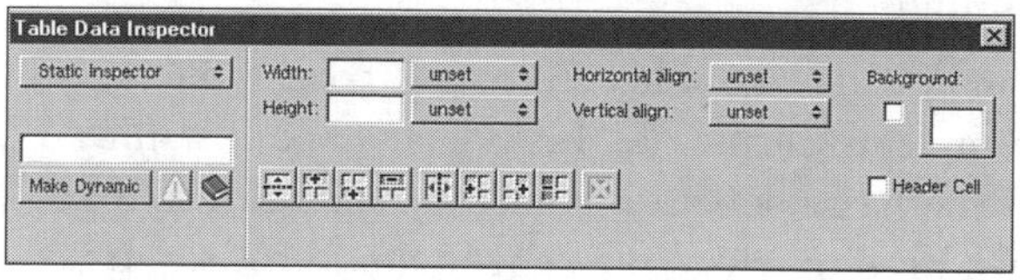

Figure 3.17
The Table Data Inspector dialog box.

The most atomic part of the table is the table cell tag, <TD>. (*TD* actually stands for *Table Data*.) When inspecting the table data tag, you not only can set the background color the same as the others, but also the horizontal and vertical alignment.

Tip
For almost all table cells, the vertical alignment should be set to top. The default value, center, is unappealing to most.

Back to the Movies...

It would be a good idea at this point to create a cool first page for your movies application. Make sure to save your changes in WebObjects Builder (see Figure 3.18).

Tip

You can tell if a document in WebObjects Builder is saved based on the name displayed in the title bar. If the name has an asterisk in it, it isn't saved.

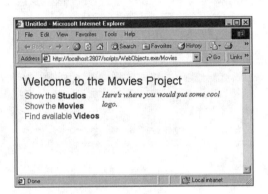

Figure 3.18
WebObjects Builder with a sample first page. The formatting is done with a number of tables.

Building and Running

Your project can now be built and run from Project Builder in the same way you built and ran the example in Chapter 1, "Introducing and Installing WebObjects." The HTML for the main component is loaded dynamically, so if you make a change to the HTML, you just need to reload the page in your browser. If you change any Java code, however, your application will need to be rebuilt.

WebObjects Components

A component consists of an HTML file, a Java class file, and something called a WebObjects definition file. The HTML file provides all the static HTML elements for your component along with tags for the dynamic elements. Dynamic elements do not resolve themselves until runtime. In contrast, static HTML elements are exactly the same as when they were created by the developer. You can mix static and dynamic elements in a WebObjects component.

In this part of the chapter, we will start a new project to experiment with building components that contain dynamic elements. So set the Movies project aside for a while; we will get back to it in the next chapter.

Dynamic Elements

Dynamic elements contain certain attributes that are bound to Java variables and methods. When it comes time for these dynamic elements to resolve themselves, they use Java objects to determine how to display their content. A number of Dynamic Elements come with WebObjects; the more commonly used ones are displayed in Table 3.4.

Table 3.4

Common Dynamic Elements

WOString	The most common dynamic element, it represents dynamic text.
WOConditional	Dynamically displays its contents depending on a conditional value.
WORepetition	Repeats its contents dynamically.

There are also dynamic elements for forms, including text fields, lists, pop-up buttons, check boxes, and radio buttons. One of the biggest challenges of learning WebObjects is mastering the usage of all the dynamic elements. These will be covered throughout this book.

Attributes

Dynamic elements contain *attributes* that govern how the dynamic element will behave, and every dynamic element has a different set of attributes. These attributes are "bound" to values that are relative to the component that contains the dynamic element. These bindings use key-value coding, which is described later, to resolve their values. One of the easiest ways to understand how these bindings work is to go through an example, and a good dynamic element to start with is the WOString.

WOString

The WOString displays dynamic text. The WOString is used to display the contents of one of your variables. It's almost the WebObjects equivalent to printf, only in HTML. The way a WOString works is that when the time comes for it to be displayed, it will display the contents of its value binding.

Using WOString, an Example

The following steps show how to use the WOString by building an application that displays a random number:

1. Create a new WebObjects application project called RandomNumbers.

2. Edit the Main.java file in Project Builder. This is the Java file for the Main component. Add a method called randomNumber() that returns a random integer between 0 and 100. The code for Main.java is in Listing 3.1.

Listing 3.1

The randomNumber() *Simply Returns a Random Number between 0–100*

```
import com.apple.yellow.foundation.*;
import com.apple.yellow.webobjects.*;
import com.apple.yellow.eocontrol.*;
import com.apple.yellow.eoaccess.*;

public class Main
    extends WOComponent
{
    public int randomNumber()
    {
        return (int)(Math.random()*100.0);
    }
}
```

3. Modify the Main component in WebObjects Builder. Type **The random number is** in the graphical display.

4. With the cursor at the end of the sentence you just wrote, add a WOString by clicking the WOString icon.

5. Now bind randomNumber to the WOString's value attribute. This is done by clicking randomNumber in the lower part of the WebObjects Builder window and dragging it to the center of the WOString as shown in Figure 3.19. If you do not hit the center of the WOString, a pop-up menu will appear with all the WOString attributes, and you can select the value attribute. Save your component.

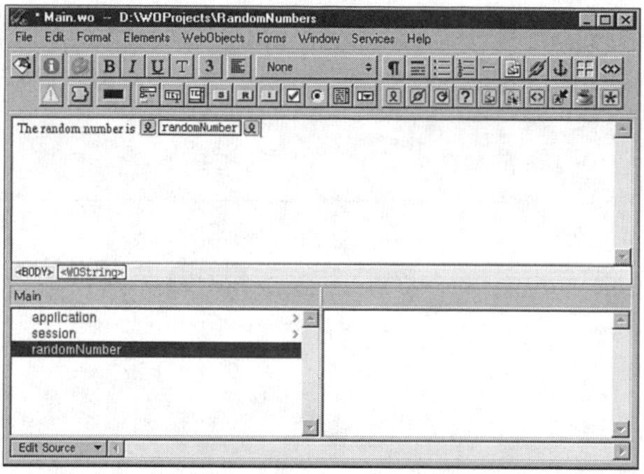

Figure 3.19
Click the `randomNumber` *value in the Main component and drag it to the* `WOString` *to create a binding.*

6. Build and run your application from Project Builder. The result is shown in Figure 3.20.

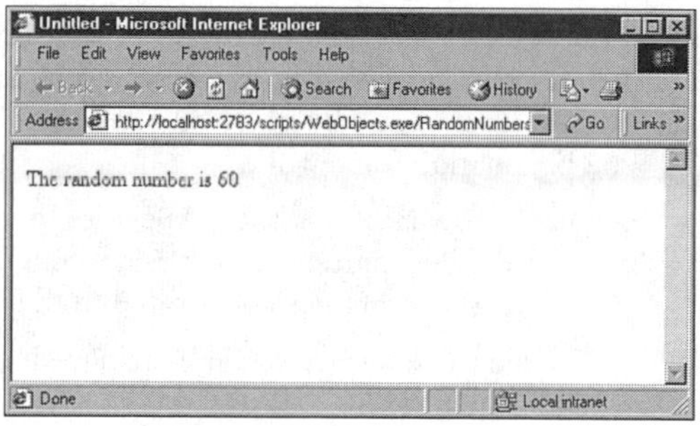

Figure 3.20
The finished random number application. Click the Refresh button to display a new number.

WOString Bindings

`WOString` does more than simply display text in an HTML component; the `WOString` can format your number or date, among other options. Table 3.5 contains a list of `WOString` bindings. The bindings for a particular dynamic element can be determined by inspecting the element. Figure 3.21 shows the inspector for a `WOString`. Documentation about the dynamic element can be displayed by clicking the Book icon in the inspector.

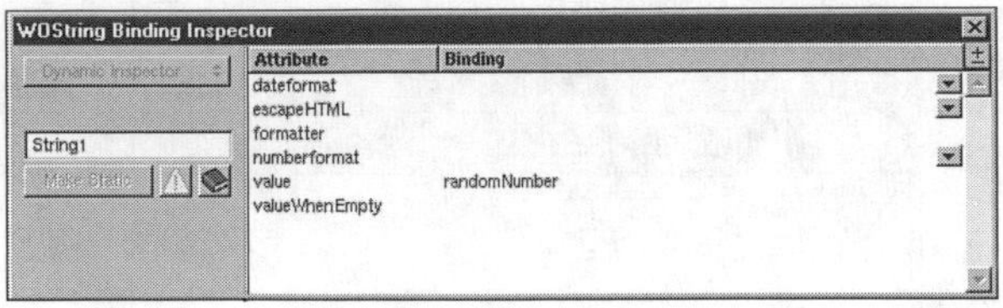

Figure 3.21
The Dynamic Inspector shows a list of the available bindings.

Table 3.5

WOString *Attributes*

Attribute	Description
dateFormat	If the value binding is to a NSGregorianDate object, the dateFormat will determine how the date is displayed. The available formats are documented in the NSGregorianDateFormatter class in the Foundation framework.
escapeHTML	Bound to true (YES) or false (NO), this binding determines how the value will be displayed if it contains HTML control characters. If true, the HTML control characters will be escaped out, meaning that they will be explicitly displayed. If this is false, any HTML tags will be rendered normally.
formatter	If you are displaying data of a custom type, you can also specify a custom formatter. This must be a subclass of NSFormatter, located in the Foundation framework.
numberFormat	Similar to the dateFormat, this specifies how numbers are to be presented. The appropriate values are found in the documentation for the NSNumberFormatter class, located in the Foundation framework.
value	The value to be displayed. Non-string values are converted using the toString method.
valueWhenEmpty	Allows another value to be substituted when the value binding is null. This is useful when the WOString is placed in an HTML table. Instead of an empty table cell, you could set this binding to " ", which is HTML's non-breaking whitespace. This would need to be done in conjunction with the escapeHTML binding being set to NO.

In the WOString inspector, the dateFormat, numberFormat, and escapeHTML bindings all use pop-up lists to assist in setting values. The two format bindings have lists of common formats that allow you to get the formatting done a bit faster. The escapeHTML binding allows you to select YES or NO.

Bindings Behind the Scenes

These bindings that are being discussed are saved with the component. Every component has a directory containing up to three files: The HTML, WOD, and WOO files. The HTML file is the HTML template for the component, and contains place holders for the dynamic elements. The HTML file for the main component in the random numbers example is shown in Listing 3.2.

Listing 3.2

Main.html

```
<!DOCTYPE HTML PUBLIC "-//W3C//DTD HTML 3.2//EN">
<HTML>
    <HEAD>
        <META name="generator" CONTENT="WebObjects 4.5">
        <TITLE>Untitled</TITLE>
    </HEAD>
    <BODY BGCOLOR=#FFFFFF>
        <FONT FACE="Courier, Fixed">The random number is:
        <WEBOBJECT NAME=String1></WEBOBJECT></FONT>
    </BODY>
</HTML>
```

The HTML file associated with a component consists of mostly legal HTML. Apple has added the WEBOBJECT tag used by WebObjects. The WEBOBJECT tag is found in Listing 3.2. There is always one attribute of this tag, the NAME. This NAME resolves to a name in the associated WOD file, also found in the component directory.

The *WOD*, or *WebObjects definition* file determines how the bindings relate to the Java code associated with the component. The WOD file contains a separate entry for every WEBOBJECT tag contained in the HTML file. The first line of the entry contains the name and type of the tag. For example, in Listing 3.2, the NAME specified in the WEBOBJECT tag was String1, which is also the name supplied on the first line of Listing 3.3. The WOD file also specifies that String1 is a WOString. The bindings are specified between the opening and closing braces, each with a key-value pair and ending with a semicolon.

Listing 3.3

Main.wod

```
String1: WOString {
    value = randomNumber;
}
```

Binding Resolution

You might have noticed that some bindings are surrounded by double quotes and some are not. For example, in the last tutorial, the `value` for the `WOString` was bound to `randomNumber`. A valid number format would be `"###,##0"`. A value is resolved differently depending on whether it is in double quotes.

If a value is in double quotes, it is evaluated as a literal string. In the number format example, the value is always the string `"###,##0"`.

If a value does not contain double quotes, it is resolved at runtime based on the contents of the Java code that is associated with the component. This resolution is done according to a process called *key-value coding*. The method `valueForKey()` is called with the key from the binding being passed in as an argument. The default for a `WOComponent` is to resolve this according to the key-value coding process, which means that the Java reflection API will be used to introspect the component, looking for certain methods or instance variables.

get Access Method

If the class has a non-private method with the same name as the binding with a prepended `get`, that method is called. The method must have no parameters and return something other than `void`. For example, a method with the signature `public int getRandomNumber()` would be called to resolve the `randomNumber` binding.

Java developers will recognize this naming convention as the appropriate convention for Java access methods.

Other Access Methods

The next point of search for the appropriate resolution is to look for a method that contains the same signature as the binding. For example, the method containing the signature `public int randomNumber()` would be used if `getRandomNumber()` was not found. This is the naming convention used by Objective-C, and is also supported by Java.

Caution
The access methods you provide must be non-private. If you provide a private method, the WebObjects framework will determine that it exists and then try to call it, resulting in a runtime error.

Instance Variable

If no method access method exists, the class is searched for a non-private instance variable with the same name as the binding.

> **Tip**
> The binding names must begin with a lowercase letter in order for that binding to be resolved properly, as is the convention for method names and instance variables.

A couple of other methods are searched with the same signature as the previous methods—with an underscore at the beginning. The order of the methods searched to resolve a binding is as follows:

1. get access method; that is, `getRandomNumber()`

2. access method; that is, `randomNumber()`

3. get private access method; that is, `_getRandomNumber()`

4. private access method; that is, `_randomNumber()`

5. Instance variable, that is, `randomNumber` and then `_randomNumber`.

For more information about key-value coding, take a look at the `EOKeyValueCoding` interface, located in WOInfoCenter under Reference, Enterprise Objects Framework, EOControl Reference(Java), EOKeyValueCoding.

Using Images

So, what good is a Web page without some images? I say the key to a good looking Web site is to go heavy with the tables, and then pile on the KBs of images. (But then, I haven't won any awards for Web site design, so you probably shouldn't take that advice…)

There are a few ways to add images to your components. One way is to make the images part of your application and display them using a `WOImage` dynamic element. For most situations, this is appropriate method.

Another way is to bind the URL for the image to one of the `WOImage` bindings. This is useful if you are reusing images that already exist on a HTTP server.

It's fairly easy to add images to your application. The first thing you need to do is add the images to your Web Server Resources suitcase. This is done by either double-clicking the suitcase or by dragging the images from the file viewer and dropping them in the suitcase (see Figure 3.22). Next, you can drag the image from Project Builder to WebObjects Builder.

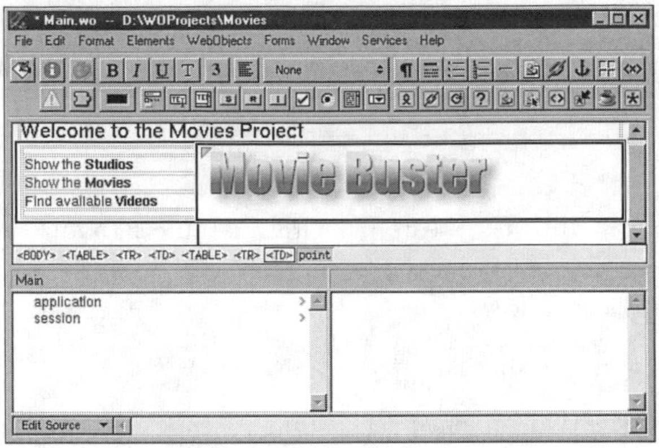

Figure 3.22

Drag an image to your component from Project Builder to WebObjects Builder to create a WOImage dynamic element.

Dragging or dropping the image from Project Builder to WebObjects Builder will create a WOImage dynamic element, with the filename bound to the name of the image. Table 3.6 lists the bindings for a WOImage.

Table 3.6

WOImage *Attributes*

Attribute	Description
data	This should be bound to an instance of NSData, which is a class that stores a blob of data. This binding is used when the images are either retrieved from disk or database or are created dynamically. If this is bound, the mimeType binding must also be specified.
filename	Specifies a filename for a file in the Web Server Resources suitcase or in the framework specified by the framework binding.
framework	If the image is in a WebObjects framework, it is the name of the framework. Frameworks will be discussed in Chapter 11, "Creating Reusable Components."
key	When using the data binding, the WebObjects Resource Manager will cache the data according to the key specified in this binding. If this is used, the application will be able to use the cached data rather than reload it.
mimeType	The mime type of the image; that is, image/gif, image/jpg, and so on. This is required if the data tag is specified.
otherTagString	What is displayed if the browser cannot display the image.
src	The URL of the image. This is useful if the images for your application are stored on an existing HTTP server.

In general, there are three ways to use a WOImage: binding the data, binding the src, or binding the filename. If two of those bindings are set for a WOImage, it will be invalid.

WOImage data **Binding Example**

One of the ways to use a WOImage is to bind the data attribute to an instance of an NSData. *NSData* is a class in the Foundation kit that stores a blob of data as an array of bytes. This gives you a lot of flexibility: You can store and retrieve image data from the database, you can manipulate image data, or you can generate images on-the-fly, similar to the way the Street Mapping Web sites work.

NSData has only a few methods (see Table 3.7), mainly because the purpose if the class is to provide an object-oriented interface to an array of bytes.

Table 3.7

Common NSData Methods

Method	Description
NSData(java.net.URL)	Creates an NSData object using the contents of the URL provided.
NSData(byte [])	Creates an NSData object using the array of bytes.
NSData(java.io.File)	Opens the file and creates an NSData object using the contents of the file.
public byte[] bytes()	Returns the contents of the NSData object as an array of bytes.
public int length()	Returns the length, in bytes, of the contents of the object.

An example of using the NSData class is modifying the Random Numbers example to display a random image. Assume that there are six images in a dice directory. The images are shown in Table 3.8. These images are available at the book's Web site: www.wowack.com.

Table 3.8

The Dice Images

Image	Filename
	one.jpg
	two.jpg

Table 3.8
Continued

Image	Filename
	three.jpg
	four.jpg
	five.jpg
	six.jpg

We need to create a method that will return an NSData object that represents one of the random images every time. The easiest way to do this is to create an array of filenames, and randomly choose a file to load and display. The code for this component is given in Listing 3.4.

Listing 3.4

The Main Component for the RandomDice Application

```
import com.apple.yellow.foundation.*;
import com.apple.yellow.webobjects.*;
import com.apple.yellow.eocontrol.*;
import com.apple.yellow.eoaccess.*;
import java.io.*;

public class Main
    extends WOComponent
{
    String [] filenames={ "one.jpg", "two.jpg",
                          "three.jpg","four.jpg",
                          "five.jpg","six.jpg"};
    String basePath="d:\\WOProjects\\dice\\";

    public int randomNumber()
    {
        return (int)(Math.random()*6.0);
    }

    public NSData randomImage()
    {
```

Listing 3.4

Continued

```
        String filename = basePath+filenames[this.randomNumber()];
        File file = new File( filename );
        return new NSData(file);
    }
}
```

The `filenames` instance variable stores the filenames, and the `basePath` instance variable stores the location where the files are stored. Replace this with the actual location of the files. The double backslashes are used because the filename is a string, and the backslash is an escape character. Therefore, \\ represents one backslash. If you're specifying a path on the Mac, you simply need to use the forward slash. For example, if the dice directory is in your home directory under the images, the `basePath` instance variable would be set as follows:

```
String basePath="~/images/dice/";
```

For complete cross-platform compatibility, get the `file.separator` Java system property using:

```
System.getProperties().getProperty("file.separator");
```

Another change in Listing 3.4 is the `randomNumbers` method. It now returns a random number between `0` and `5`.

The biggest change is the addition of the `randomImage` method. This method returns an NSData object that represents one of the filenames specified in the instance variable array. The complete filename is calculated based on the `basePath` and `filenames` variables, and then the `File` object is created. This can be used to construct the `NSData` object that is returned. After we have this code, displaying the data will be easy.

Add a `WOImage` to the Main component in WebObjects Builder, and bind the values according to Table 3.9. Save the component and the code, and build your application.

Table 3.9

`WOImage` *Bindings for the Dice Example*

Binding	Value
data	randomImage
mimeType	"image/jpeg"

Where Are the Web Server Resources?

WebObjects does a good job of handling the resources such as images and text files for you. This is extremely useful most of the time because you are freed from the mundane task of keeping track of files and directories. However, it can get in the way sometimes, such as when you want to retrieve the image for a different reason, or if you want to find the relative path to another resource.

Resources Versus Web Server Resources

Resources that are not going to be sent to the client can be installed anywhere on the server. Examples of this type of resource are the model file, lookup files, configuration files, and so on. Resources that are to be served to the clients must be installed in a location within the Web Server's document root directory. When your application is built, it is placed in a `.woa` directory. Two directories are inside that directory: Resources and WebServerResources. The application executable is placed inside the `.woa` directory. Figure 3.23 displays the directory structure for the RandomDice application.

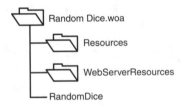

Figure 3.23
The directory structure for the RandomDice application.

When the application is installed, the contents of the WebServerResources directory are copied into a directory within the document root of the Web server. This is set in the WebServerConfig.plist, which is found in the `\Apple\Library\WebObjects\` `Configuration` directory on Windows and the `/System/Library/WebObjects/` `Configuration` directory on Macs. An example of this file is given in Listing 3.5.

Listing 3.5
The WebServerConfig.plist

```
{
    //** This configuration file is used by WOF
    //** to compute startup parameters.
    DocumentRoot = "d:/inetpub/wwwroot/";
    WOAdaptorURL = "http://localhost/scripts/WebObjects.exe ";
}
```

Programmatic Access to Resources

It's common to want to have access to the resources within the project. There's a need to access these resources through the file system and another need to access resources by providing URLs. The WOResourceManager is used to retrieve the files either way.

To retrieve the WOResourceManager, use the WOApplication's `resourceManager()` method:

```
public WOResourceManager resourceManager()
```

The WOResourceManager contains two methods that are used to return file paths: `urlForResourceNamed()` and `pathForResourceNamed()`.

urlForResourceNamed()
The declaration for the `urlForResourceNamed()` method is as follows:

```
public String urlForResourceNamed(
        String fileName,
        String frameworkName,
        NSArray laguageList,
        WORequest request )
```

The `urlForResourceNamed()` returns a path on the Web server to the resource given in the filename argument. The resource name is the name as it appears in the suitcase in Project Builder. If the resource is contained in a framework, give the framework name in the second argument; otherwise use `null`. You can also specify a language list for multilingual applications, or `null` for a single-language application. And, you will need to pass in the current request so the URL can be generated correctly. The URL returned can then be used in a hyperlink.

pathForResourceNamed()
The declaration for the `pathForResourceNamed()` method is as follows:

```
public String pathForResourceNamed(
        String fileName,
        String frameworkName,
        NSArray laguageList )
```

This method returns the absolute file path to the resource given the name of the resource. Similar to `urlForResourceNamed()`, this method can compute the path given a framework and list of languages. Unlike `urlForResourceNamed()`, a `WORequest` is not required.

Summary

In this chapter, you learned how to create and modify a WebObjects application project. You used WebObjects Builder to modify the Main component's HTML, WOD, and class file. You also learned how to use HTML tables and add dynamic images. In the next chapter, you will learn how to use WOHyperlinks to navigate between components and WOForms to receive data from the user.

Q&A

Q I've got some files in my non-project files suitcase that I want to get rid of. How do I do that?

A Even though these files will not affect the build of your project and are not a permanent part of your project, it can be annoying to see files in this suitcase that you do not intend on using. They will be removed when you exit the project. However, you can remove them manually by selecting them and the File, Close menu items.

CHAPTER 4

ADDING NAVIGATION

In 1989, Tim-Berners Lee created the first Web Server and browser, along with the HTTP protocol and HTML on a NeXT machine. His reason was simple: to simplify the viewing of documents that are spread across multiple machines. HTML is a stripped down version of SGML, and Mr. Lee added one significant tag: the anchor, or *hyperlink*. When the hyperlink is clicked, the document that it points to is displayed in the browser window.

Today the Web is a lot different, but the anchor tag is still an important part of HTML. Simply linking to another page is fairly easy and can be done with static HTML or by using some of the WebObjects Builder features. What's more interesting and complicated is binding a hyperlink to a method, allowing you to perform some operation when the hyperlink is clicked. This is also done relatively easily using WebObjects Builder.

In addition, an important part to any Web application is using forms to enter data. This chapter discusses how to use static and dynamic hyperlinks and forms in a WebObjects application. The following topics are discussed:

- Using static and dynamic hyperlinks
- Using forms to enter data
- WebObjects component architecture

Navigation with Hyperlinks

The hyperlink is really considered the anchor tag. Everything contained inside the anchor tag is blue and underlined by default. An example of the anchor tag is

```
<A HREF="http://www.wowack.com">Learn WebObjects</a>
```

This displays the text Learn WebObjects in blue, underlined.

Static Hyperlinks

To create a static hyperlink, open a component in WebObjects Builder, highlight some text and click the Add Link icon; then inspect the anchor tag and enter the URL, as described in Figures 4.1 and 4.2.

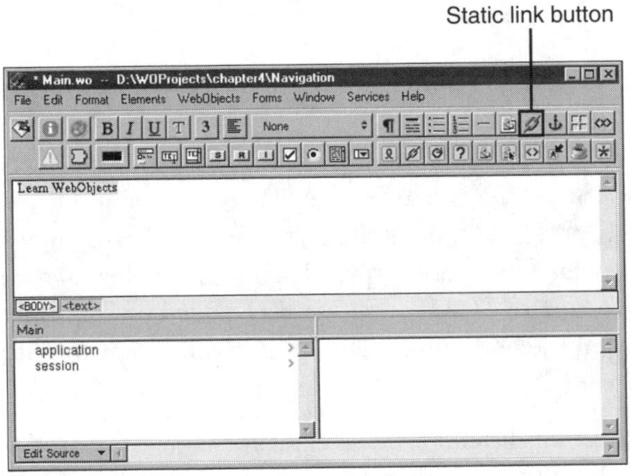

Figure 4.1
To create a static link in WebObjects Builder, highlight the text you want to turn into a link and click the Add Link icon.

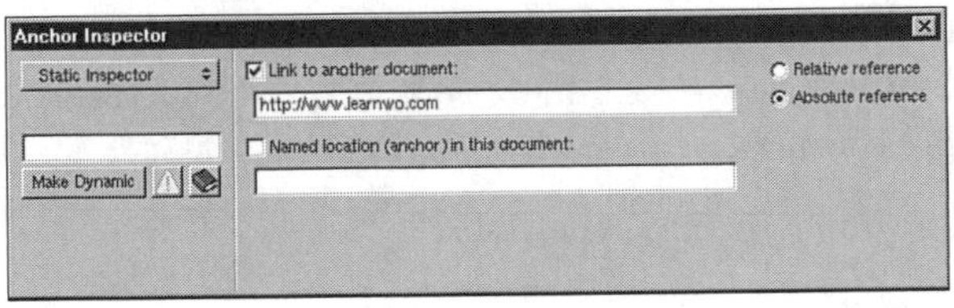

Figure 4.2
The reference is edited in the Anchor Inspector window.

Adding this type of link does not create a dynamic element and the reference cannot change. Also, using this type of link, it's difficult to navigate to another WOComponent.

Navigating to Components

The WOHyperlink dynamic element is used to navigate to another WOComponent. The process of creating the WOHyperlink is similar to creating the static link, where you highlight some text and click the WOHyperlink icon. The difference is that the

WOHyperlink is a dynamic element, and the reference is generated on-the-fly. Similar to the other dynamic elements, the WOHyperlink has certain bindings that are used to determine the actual anchor tag that is generated.

WOHyperlink

The WOHyperlink can be used for a number of purposes, as displayed by the number of potential bindings (see Figure 4.3). WOHyperlinks can be used to call direct actions, to display regular components, to call action methods, or to link to a URL that you specify. Direct actions are discussed in Chapter 12, "Using Statelees Transactions," but the rest is discussed right here.

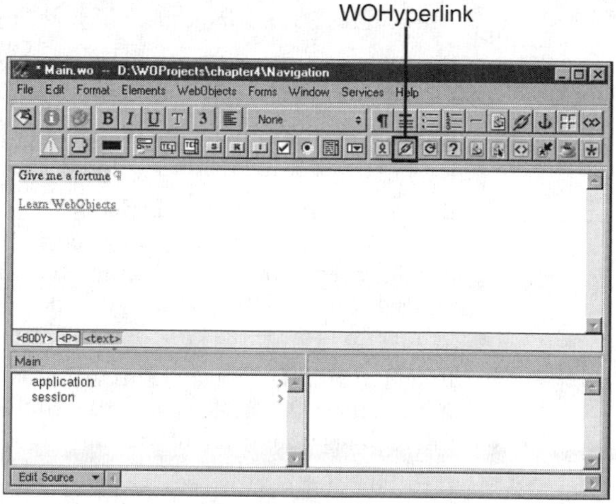

Figure 4.3

To create a dynamic hyperlink, highlight some text and click the WOHyperlink icon.

WOHyperlink Bindings

There are three distinct ways to use a WOHyperlink, and the bindings that you choose to use will determine the way the hyperlink is used.

Table 4.1

WOHyperlink Attributes

Attribute	Description
action	This method in the component will be called when the hyperlink is clicked. This method is expected to return a WOComponent that will provide the response.
actionClass	Used with direct actions, this is the class in which the directActionName method is located.

Table 4.1

Continued

Binding	Description
directActionName	Used with direct actions, this is the name of the direct action that is executed when the hyperlink is selected. Direct actions are discussed in Chapter 12.
disabled	If this binding resolves to true, the contents of the hyperlink are displayed, but there is no hyperlink. Otherwise, the hyperlink is displayed as normal.
fragmentIdentifier	This indicates the part of the page to initially display. Anchor tags can be placed throughout an HTML document without the href attribute to indicate different anchors in the document. The fragmentIdentifier indicates which anchor to jump to.
href	Bind this to a string that is an absolute URL.
otherTagString	Not used for the WOHyperlink. This binding is included in all dynamic elements that represent an HTML tag. This binding is used to add a string that is not a key-value pair.
pageName	Bind the pageName to a string that represents the name of the WOComponent to navigate to when the hyperlink is clicked. A new instance of the component indicated by the binding will be created when this hyperlink is clicked. This new component will be used to provide the response.
queryDictionary	Bound to a NSDictionary. This will place the dictionary's key-value pairs in the URL to be passed to the next page as form values. This is most useful with direct actions.
string	If this binding is provided, the string will be used as the contents of the WOHyperlink. This binding will not wrap the WEBOBJECT tag around some text, but provides the display name for the hyperlink dynamically.
target	Used with frames, this specifies the target frame for the response. Frames are discussed in Chapter 10, "Advanced UI."

There are some complex rules for which bindings you can set, and some are mutually exclusive, meaning that if you provide one of these bindings, you cannot provide any of the other bindings. Table 4.2 lists the mutually exclusive WOHyperlink bindings.

Table 4.2

WOHyperlink Mutually Exclusive Bindings

Binding	Related Bindings
action	None
pageName	None

Table 4.2

Continued

Binding	Related Bindings
directActionName	actionClass, queryDictionary
href	queryDictionary

This does not mean that providing one of these bindings excludes the use of any other binding, it simply means that it excludes the use of the other mutually exclusive bindings.

Example: Using a WOHyperlink

The easiest way to start using a WOHyperlink is to use it in conjunction with the pageName binding. In the following example, you will create a WOComponent called FortunePage that will eventually display an ever-changing fortune message.

1. In Project Builder, create a new WOComponent called FortunePage. This is accomplished by selecting the Web Components suitcase (see Figure 4.4) and selecting the File, New In Project menu items.

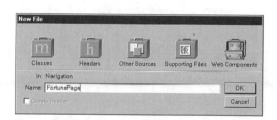

Figure 4.4

When creating a new WOComponent, make sure that the Web Components suitcase is opened.

2. When creating a new component, the WebObjects Component Wizard dialog will be displayed (see Figure 4.5). This allows you to create a component with some pre-generated code and select the language to be used. Make sure Java is selected as the language and the type of assistance is None, and then click the Finish button. This creates the FortunePage Web component and FortunePage.java class, placed in the appropriate suitcases.

3. Modify the new component in WebObjects Builder. You will eventually display a fortune on this page. For now, just insert the following text:

```
Here is your fortune:
You are going to have a great day.
```

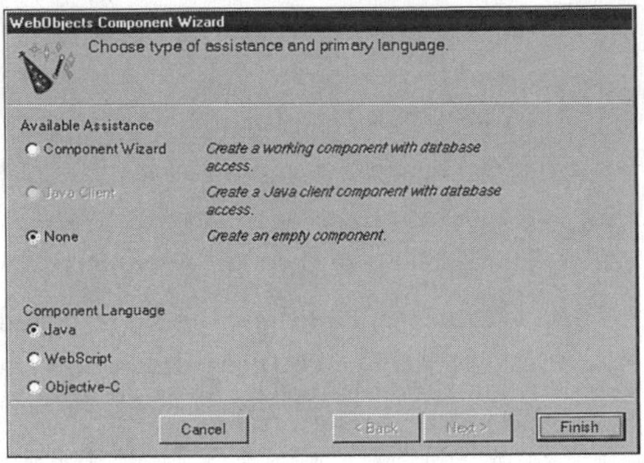

Figure 4.5
The WebObjects Component wizard.

4. Modify the Main component in WebObjects Builder. Type the text **Give me a fortune**, highlight it, and click the WOHyperlink icon as shown in Figure 4.6.

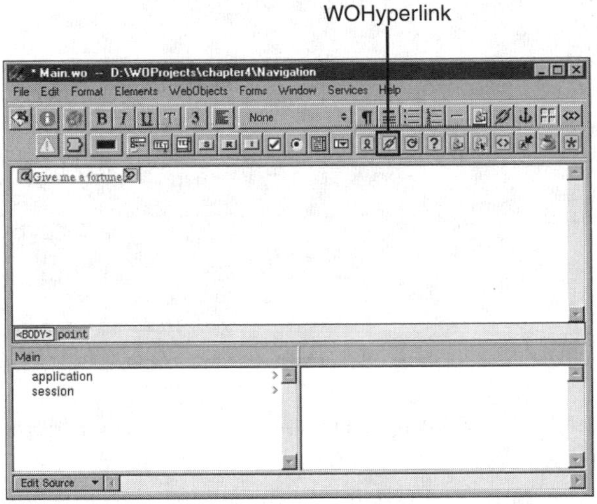

Figure 4.6
To create a WOHyperlink, highlight some text and click the WOHyperlink icon.

5. Inspect the WOHyperlink and set the pageName to "FortunePage". You can either type in the value or use the drop-down list as shown in Figure 4.7. Build and test your application.

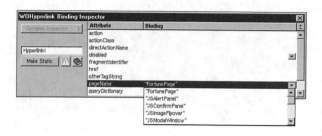

Figure 4.7

The pageName *binding allows you to select from the set of pages in the project using the drop-down list.*

Using the pageName binding is the easiest way to navigate between components. However it isn't used too much in production environments because it creates a new copy of the component every time the hyperlink is clicked. Also, it would be nice if you could get a hyperlink to call a method that was written by you.

Action Methods

Another way to use the WOHyperlink is to bind the action to an action method. This executes the method bound to this key when the user clicks on the hyperlink. The method must be an action method, which means that there are no parameters and the return value is a WOComponent. The component that is returned will be the next page. If null is returned, the same component will be displayed, only with updated information.

As it turns out, it's easy to create an action and bind it to a WOHyperlink. WebObjects Builder will generate template action code for you using the Add Action menu item under the Edit Source menu at the bottom left portion of the WebObjects Builder window.

In the next example, we will add the Rotating Fortune feature on the FortunePage. This will involve creating a Fortune class that loads a set of fortunes from disk and rotates the fortunes that are given out.

1. Create a new class in your project. To do this, select the Classes suitcase and select the File, New in Project menu item. You will be presented with the New File dialog. The Classes suitcase should be highlighted. If it is not, click it. Type **Fortune.java** in the text field and click the OK button. If you leave off the .java extension, an Objective-C class will be created for you (see Figure 4.8).

2. Edit the Fortune.java file in Project Builder to resemble Listing 4.1. This class stores a list of strings in a vector, and continuously gives out the next string in the nextFortune() method.

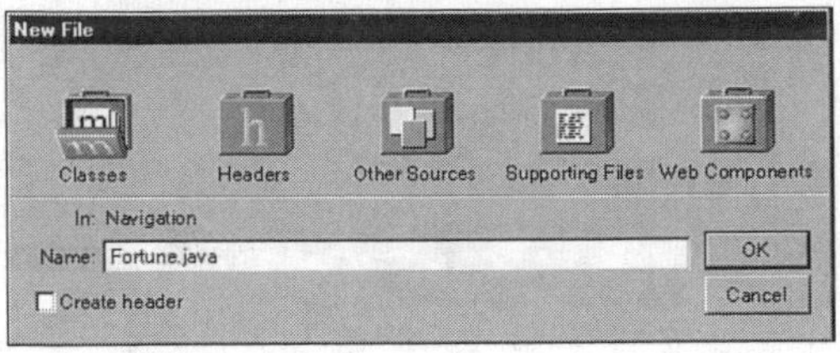

Figure 4.8

To create a Java class, you need to supply the .java extension. Otherwise an Objective-C class will be created.

Listing 4.1

Fortune.java

```java
import java.util.*;
import java.io.*;

public class Fortune
    extends Object
{
    private Vector fortunes = new Vector();
    private int currentFortuneIndex=0;

    public Fortune( String fileName )
        throws FileNotFoundException, IOException
    {
        FileReader file = new FileReader( fileName );
        BufferedReader reader = new BufferedReader( file );

        String line=null;
        do
        {
            line=reader.readLine();
            if ( line != null )
            {
                fortunes.addElement(line);
            }
        }while ( line != null );
        reader.close();
    }

    public String nextFortune()
    {
```

Listing 4.1

Continued

```
        String returnValue =
            (String)fortunes.elementAt(currentFortuneIndex);
        currentFortuneIndex ++;
        if (currentFortuneIndex >= fortunes.size())
        {
            currentFortuneIndex =0;
        }
        return returnValue;
    }
}
```

Notice that the constructor throws any exception that might be thrown during the execution of the method. This is common in WebObjects because a default error page is provided for you if an uncaught exception is thrown during the execution of your code.

Also notice that the nextFortune() method performs a Round Robin algorithm for returning the next fortune. currentFortuneIndex is incremented until it points past the end of the Vector; then it is set back to zero.

After you have entered the code for this class, it's a good idea to build your application and fix any syntax errors.

3. Create a new text file by selecting File, New Untitled and save it as **fortunes.txt** to the project directory. It doesn't matter what's in the file, as long as it contains a few lines of text. A sample is given in Listing 4.2.

Listing 4.2

fortunes.txt

```
You are going to have a great day.
Sometimes when the rock is turned over, there's dirt underneath.
A long lost relative will ask you for money.
You will will be a WebObjects developer someday.
Those who save have more money than those who spend it.
You are feeling very sleepy.
```

4. Now add the fortunes.txt file to the Resources suitcase. This can be done by double-clicking the Resources suitcase and opening the file.

5. Edit the FortunePage.java file; add a Fortune instance variable called fortune and a constructor that creates a new Fortune object using the fortunes.txt file. The FortunePage.java class is given in Listing 4.3.

Listing 4.3

FortunePage.java

```
import com.apple.yellow.foundation.*;
import com.apple.yellow.webobjects.*;
import com.apple.yellow.eocontrol.*;
import com.apple.yellow.eoaccess.*;
import java.io.*;

public class FortunePage extends WOComponent
{
    Fortune fortune;

    public FortunePage()
        throws IOException, FileNotFoundException
    {
        fortune = new Fortune("fortunes.txt");
    }

}
```

Notice that the `FortunePage` constructor throws the same exceptions that were thrown in the Fortune constructor. This is so they can be caught by the WebObjects framework. Also notice that the instance variable is non-private. This allows the WebObjects framework to access it, and it will be displayed in WebObjects Builder.

6. Edit the `FortunePage` component in WebObjects Builder. Add a WOString where the static fortune was, and bind its value to `fortune.nextFortune` (see Figure 4.9).

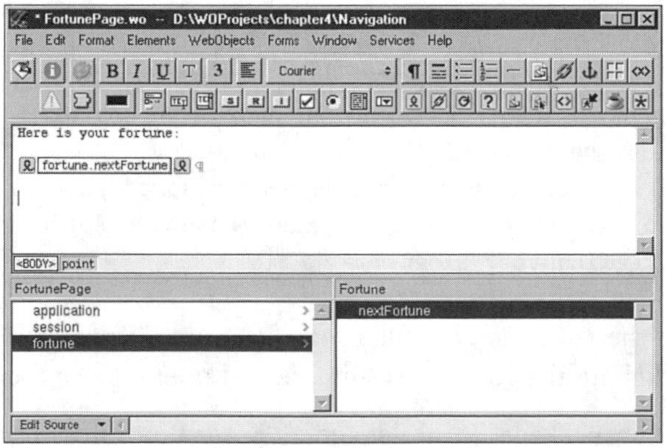

Figure 4.9
To access a key in a child object, traverse the key path in WebObjects Builder.

7. Add the text `Get another fortune` to the bottom of the page, and add a WOHyperlink around the text.

8. While still editing the FortunePage component, click the Add Action method in the Edit Source menu at the bottom left part of the window (see Figure 4.10), which will display the Add Action dialog box.

Code generation menu

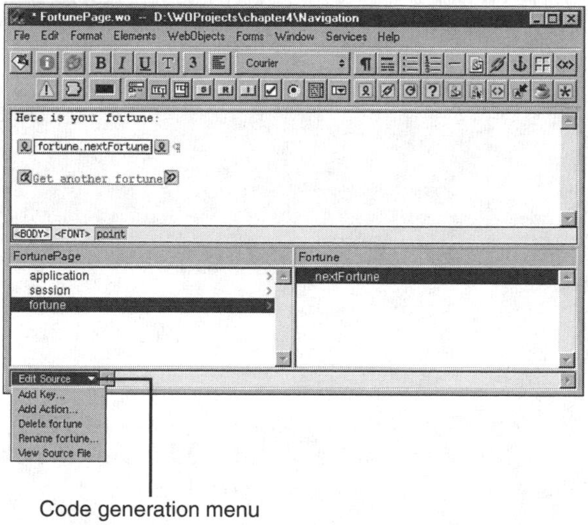

Figure 4.10
To modify the Java class, click the Edit Source menu at the bottom left part of the WebObjects Builder window.

9. In the Add Action dialog box (see Figure 4.11), enter `getNewFortune` into the Name text field and leave the Page returned text field's value `null`. This will create a method in the `FortunePage.java` file called `getNewFortune` that returns `null`.

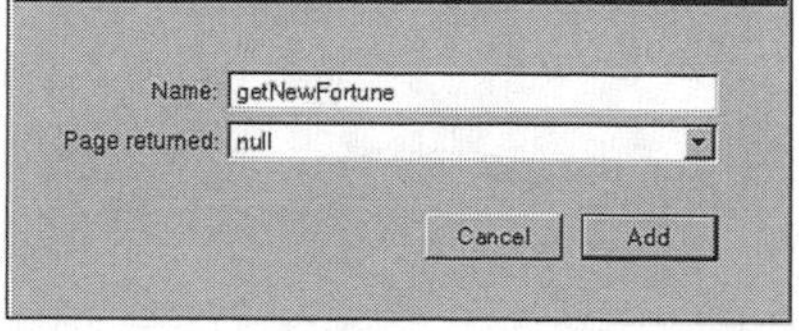

Figure 4.11
When adding an action, you can specify the action name and the page returned.

10. Add the text **Main** at the bottom of the page with a WOHyperlink around it. Set the pageName of this hyperlink to Main so that it returns the main page. Build and test your application (see Figure 4.12).

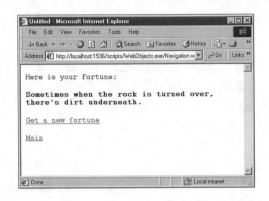

Figure 4.12
The finished fortune application.

At this point you should be able to use the Get a New Fortune hyperlink to refresh the Fortune page. When the fortune page is refreshed, the nextFortune() method is called in the Fortune object, which gets the next fortune.

There is a peculiar behavior with the application that is related to the Main hyperlink. Notice that if you go back to the main component and then back to the FortunePage component, the first fortune is displayed, no matter what fortune was next from the previous fortune page. This is because the FortunePage is created using the pageName binding in the WOHyperlink in Main. Reusing common components will be discussed in the "Component Architecture" section of this chapter.

Using WOHyperlinks with Images

For a more professional look, many Web sites use images as navigation rather than text. To do this in WebObjects, add an image to the component as described in Chapter 3, "WebObjects Components." Then select the image in WebObjects Builder and click on the WOHyperlink icon, creating a hyperlink around the image (see Figure 4.13).

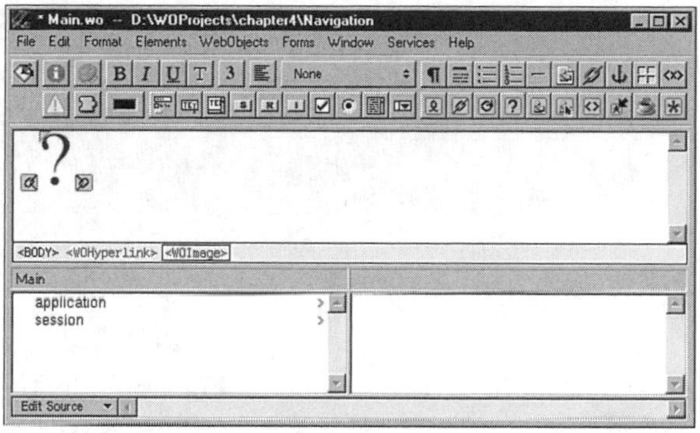

Figure 4.13
A WOImage can be placed inside a WOHyperlink.

The output might be what you were looking for, but probably not. At this point the blue hyperlink line will be displayed around your image when the application is executed (see Figure 4.14). This can be fixed by setting the border to zero in the static inspector.

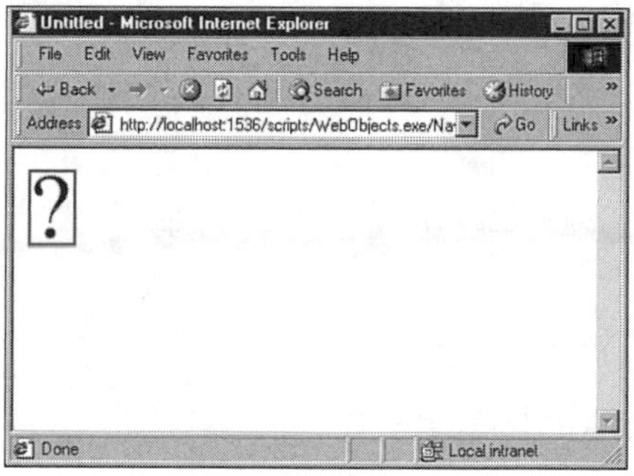

Figure 4.14
Without setting the image border to zero, the blue hyperlink line appears around the image.

A number of dynamic elements have static and dynamic inspectors. Both inspectors are displayed in the same window. The Image Inspector dialog box alternates between being a static and dynamic inspector by clicking the Dynamic Inspector or Static Inspector toggle button, accordingly (see Figure 4.15).

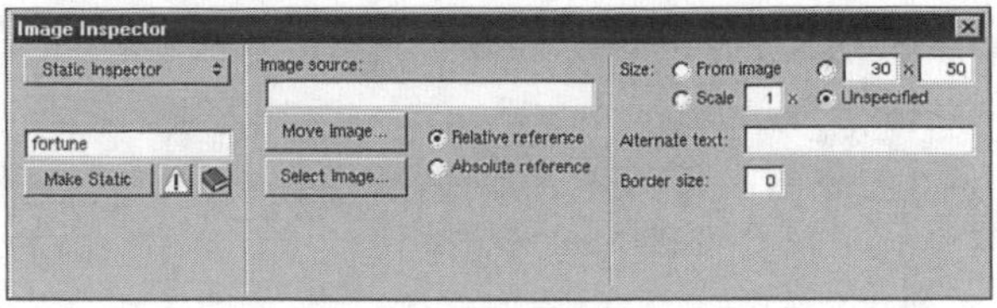

Figure 4.15
The WOHyperlink static inspector.

Some of the values overlap these two inspectors. For example, the source of a WOImage can be set in the Image Source text field that is part of the static inspector. It can also be set in the `src` binding, which is part of the dynamic inspector. This actually causes a conflict in the WOImage, as switching between the static and dynamic inspectors places an empty string in the `src` binding. This needs to be removed before you build and run your application (see Figure 4.16).

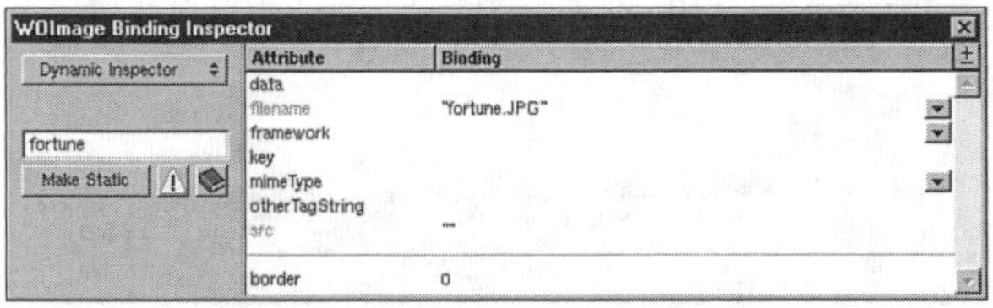

Figure 4.16
The WOHyperlink dynamic inspector. Remove the empty string, "", from the `src` binding for the image to display properly.

Entering Data Using Forms

Most applications that you write will require some sort of user data entry, even if it's simply a string to search for. Retrieving this data from the HTTP request is somewhat troublesome; however, this is taken care of for us in the WebObjects framework. WebObjects handles retrieving what the user entered from the HTTP request and placing it in instance variables in your code.

WOForm

The first thing you need is an HTML form. Everything that the user types into must be inside the form. For now, the only WOForm binding to be concerned with is `multipleSubmit`. If you have more than one submit button in a form, this must be set to YES.

WOTextField

The The basic data entry control is the text field, which is represented by the WOTextField dynamic element. This dynamic element is linked to a key in one of your classes. When the text field is displayed, it displays the contents of the key; and when the form is submitted, it updates the contents of the key.

WOTextField Attributes

The main binding to be concerned with is the `value`. This is bound to the key in your class that will be modified by the text field. The WOTextField attributes are shown in Table 4.3.

Table 4.3

WOTextField Attributes

Attribute	Description
dateFormat	If the `value` is a NSGregorianDate, this format will be applied.
formatter	Allows you to create a formatter for the value.
name	The HTML name for the text field. If this is not bound, WebObjects will create a unique name. It could be necessary to set this name if the page contains some JavaScript that would need a name to access this text field.
numberFormat	If the `value` is a number, the `numberFormat` will be applied.
value	The object bound to `value` will be retrieved to display the WOTextField and set when the user enters a value in the WOTextField.

WOSubmitButton

A WOSubmitButton is used to set the values for the form controls. Only the controls in the same form as the submit button will be submitted. Each submit button is associated with an action method, and there can be more than one submit button in a form, each with its own action method. If there is more than one submit button for a form, the `multipleSubmit` binding on the WOForm must be set to YES.

WOSubmitButton Attributes

The most important binding for the WOSubmitButton is the `action` attribute. This specifies the action method that is called when the form is submitted. Another useful attribute is the value, which specifies the text that will be displayed on the button. The WOSubmitButton attributes are listed in Table 4.4.

Table 4.4

WOSubmitButton Attributes

Attribute	Description
action	Bind this to an action method. This method is called when the button is pressed.
value	Bound to a string; the value is the text that will appear on the button.
disabled	If this is true, the button appears but does not work.
name	The HTML name for the button. If this is not bound, WebObjects will create a unique name.

Forms Example

The previous example will be modified to display a different fortune depending on a name that's entered by the user. This involves determining which fortune to display depending on an arbitrary string, and displaying that in the WOString.

1. Modify the Fortune.java, add a method called fortuneForName() that takes a string for the name and returns a String fortune. This method should return a different fortune depending on the name supplied, but the fortune should be the same for any given name that is supplied more than once. The code for this method is given in Listing 4.4.

Listing 4.4

The fortuneForName() Method in Fortune.java

```
public String fortuneForName( String name )
{
    int fortuneIndex = name.hashCode()%fortunes.size();
    return (String)fortunes.elementAt(fortuneIndex);
}
```

This method uses String's `hashCode()` method and the modulus operator (%) to determine the fortune for a particular name. The `hashCode()` method will return a different number based on the contents of the `name` string, which will be different for each string. The modulus operator returns the remainder when the number is divided into the `hashCode()`. If the size of the vector is given, we will end up with a number from 0 to the size of the Vector -1.

2. Open the FortunePage in WebObjects Builder. Add a WOForm, WOTextField, and WOSubmitButton as shown in Figure 4.17.

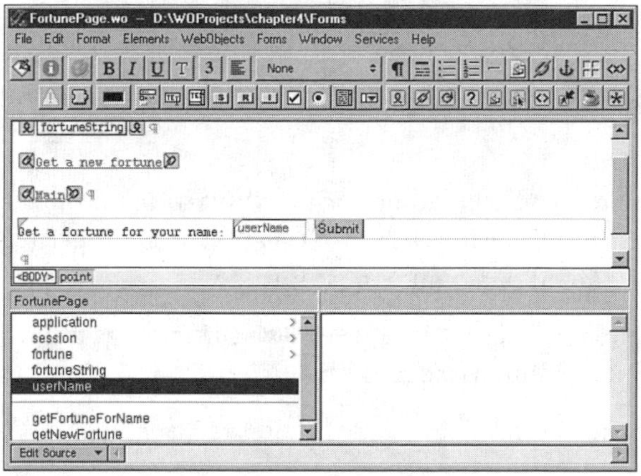

Figure 4.17
The Fortune Page in WebObjects Builder.

3. Now add a key to the component called `fortuneString`. This is done by selecting the Edit Source, Add Key menu items. The Edit Source menu is located in the lower left corner of the window. This will bring up the Add Key dialog box (see Figure 4.18). Make the name `fortuneString` and keep the type as `java.lang.String`. It is not necessary to create `set` and `get` methods, but you can if you want to. When you're ready, click the OK button. This will add a `String` instance variable called `fortuneString` to your component class.

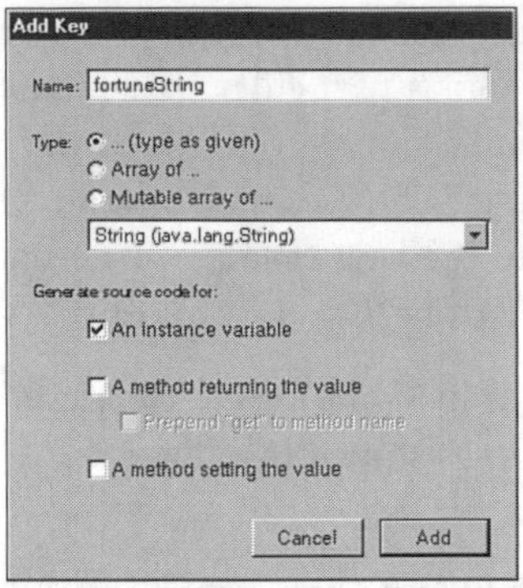

Figure 4.18
The Add Key window allows you to add a new key and associated access method to your component class.

4. Now change the value binding for the WOString on the component to `fortuneString`. You will set the `fortuneString` appropriately, either from the username entered or from the next fortune.

5. Add an action called `getFortuneForName` that returns `null`. Bind this method to the WOSubmitButton's `action` binding.

6. Add a `String` key called `userName`. Bind `userName` to the WOTextField's `value` binding.

7. Modify both action methods in `FortunePage.java`. `getNextFortune` should set `fortuneString` to the next fortune. `getFortuneForName` sets `fortuneString` to the fortune for the name entered. The code for these two methods is given in Listing 4.5. After you're finished entering these methods, build and test your application.

Listing 4.5
The Action Methods in `FortunePage.java`

```java
public WOComponent getNewFortune()
{
    fortuneString = fortune.nextFortune();
    return null;
}

public WOComponent getFortuneForName()
{
```

Listing 4.5

Continued

```
        fortuneString = fortune.fortuneForName(userName);
        return null;
}
```

Component Architecture

At this point, you should have some questions about what's going on. If you have any experience with writing dynamic Web applications, you have probably begun to realize the amount of magic that's going on behind the scenes. This part of the chapter is dedicated to sorting out some of the details about the underlying architecture along with describing some other methods that can be used to change the behavior of your application.

Important Objects

There are a few really important objects involved during a transaction: the `WOAdaptor`, the `WOApplication`, the `WOSession`. These objects work together along with the components you write to respond to the requests that come in to the application.

WebObjects Adaptor

The WebObjects Adaptor is software that interfaces directly with the Web Server (see Figure 4.19). The goal of the WebObjects Adaptor is to convert any requests for a WebObjects application to WORequest objects and send them to the appropriate application. Adaptors are written specifically for different Web servers. Currently, there are adaptors for Microsoft, Netscape, and Apache Web servers, along with a generic CGI-bin adaptor.

When a client submits an HTTP request, the Web server passes it to the WOAdaptor. The WOAdaptor converts the request to a WORequest object and sends it to the application. The application will then process the request and return a WOResponse object, which is converted to HTML and sent back to the user.

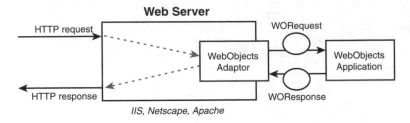

Figure 4.19
The relationship between the Web Server, WebObjects Adaptor, and the Application.

When the application is finished processing the request, a WOResponse object is sent back to the adaptor. The WOResponse object contains the HTML that will be returned to the client.

WOApplication

The class of the object that receives the WORequest from the adaptor is a subclass of WOApplication. The default is that this object is an Application object (see Figure 4.20). You have the ability to modify the code for this object by changing `Application.java`.

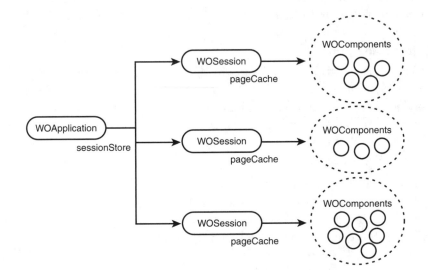

Figure 4.20
The WebObjects architecture.

There is one Application object per application instance. Any data that could be shared across the entire application could be stored here. Be careful, however, because depending on your installation, there could be more than one application instance. In this case, instance variables would not be shared across instances.

The Application object is available from every component by calling the `application()` method. It is even available from WebObjects Builder in the bindings section.

An example of how to use the Application instance would be to move the `Fortune` instance variable from `FortunePage.java` to `Application.java`. You would also have to change all the bindings. The change that this causes is subtle, but important. Remember that before this change, every time the user navigates from the Main component to the FortunePage component, the `nextFortune` would be the first one. This is because a new FortunePage is created every time.

If the `Fortune` is moved into the `Application` class, there would be only one `Fortune` object, and any component that accesses it will modify the current fortune. A good way to test this is to load the start page in two browsers and continually select the Get Me a New Fortune hyperlink on the Fortune page, alternating browsers. In this case, both browsers will be modifying the same Fortune object, and changes in one browser will affect what is displayed in the other.

WOSession

Sometimes you want the data segregated by user. For example, you would not want one user to be able to affect another user's shopping cart. This segregation is accomplished using the Session class, which is a subclass of WOSession. Every browser that hits your site will start a new session. Each session contains a *page cache* that contains all the components for that session.

Even though WebObjects keeps track of your session for you, it is a bit trickier than described. HTTP is a *stateless* protocol, meaning that there is no long-term state stored between the client and server. HTTP does sit on top of TCP on the network stack, which simply means that it is a somewhat reliable and connection oriented. The connection is per transaction, however, and storing state between transactions is where the tricks start happening.

WebObjects uses a common method for storing state between HTTP transactions, the Session ID. When a session is created, a unique number is created called the Session ID. This ID is added to every hyperlink that is sent down to the client, so when the client requests another page from the server, the ID is transmitted back up. The Session ID eventually appears in the URL (see Figure 4.21), or it can be stored in a cookie.

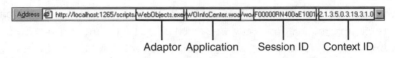

Figure 4.21
The WebObjects URL Dissected.

All the sessions are stored in the application's session store. If there are no transactions for a session after a certain period of time, the session will timeout and be unavailable. The default session timeout period can be set using the WOApplication method `setSessionTimeOut()`. The timeout for a particular session can be set using the WOSession method called `setTimeOut()`.

Listing 4.6

Setting the Default Session Timeout in the Application Constructor

```
public Application()
{
    super();
    System.out.println("Welcome to " + this.name() + " !");
    /* ** put your initialization code in here ** */
    this.setSessionTimeOut( new Integer(300) ); // 5 minutes
}
```

The session is available from a component using the `session()` method.

Request/Response Loop

When a WORequest comes in to an Application object, the request/response loop for that application begins. Different methods are called at different times throughout the loop. You have the ability to provide custom behaviors by overriding these methods. The methods that are called during the request/response loop are

`awake()`—Called on all objects that are going to be involved in the transaction.

`takeValuesFromRequest()`—Called when the transaction involves a form submission.

`invokeAction()`—Called when navigation between components is performed.

`appendToResponse()`—Called on all objects that will be responsible for responding to the current request.

`sleep()`—After the request is sent back to the client, all objects that received an `awake()` message will also receive a `sleep()` message.

These methods are called on the WOApplication, WOSession, and all associated WOComponents during the transaction.

awake()

At the beginning of the request/response loop, every object that will be participating in this transaction will receive the awake() method. This method allows you to initialize some variables in preparation to receive the request. It is sent to the WOApplication, WOSession, and WOComponent objects. You have not received the request at the time that the awake() method is called, so you cannot act on any variables that would be populated from a form submission. Listing 4.7 gives a sample awake() method that could be put in any WOApplication, WOComponent, or WOSession subclass. Notice that super.awake() is called first; this is required by the specification.

Listing 4.7

Sample awake() *Method*

```
public void awake()
{
    super.awake();
    // put your initialization code here
}
```

takeValuesFromRequest()

The next stage in the request/response loop is for any form values to be set. This is done in the takeValuesFromRequest() method. This method is called to populate any values from the request. It is usually not necessary to override this method; however, this is the first method that allows you to access the WORequest object directly. This could be useful if you are interested in retrieving some of the header information. The available header information is generally dependent on the adaptor. For example, the direct connect adaptor that is used in the development environment does not give very much header information at all.

Direct Connect Adaptor
The direct connect adaptor allows clients to directly connect to the application. You can tell that you're using the direct connect adaptor when an obscure port number appears next to localhost in the URL. For example, when running your application, the URL might be something like http://localhost:3891/.... 3891 is the port number, and this usually indicates that you are using the direct connect adaptor. Also, this port number changes every time you run the application in order to avoid any potential conflicts.

The headers are key-value pairs in which both the keys and values are strings. The header keys can be obtained using the `headerKeys()` method, and the values can be obtained using the `headerForKey()` method. A sample `takeValuesFromRequest()` method is given in Listing 4.8. Part of the output is shown in Listing 4.9.

Listing 4.8

Retrieving the Headers in the `takeValuesFromRequest()` *Method*

```
public void takeValuesFromRequest( WORequest request, WOContext context )
{
    super.takeValuesFromRequest( request, context );
    NSArray keys = request.headerKeys();
    for ( int index=0; index<keys.count(); index++ )
    {
        String key = (String)keys.objectAtIndex(index);
        String value = request.headerForKey( key );
        System.out.println( key+"="+value );
    }
}
```

Listing 4.9

A Partial Listing of the Output When Running the Code in Listing 4.8

```
Accept-Language=en-us
Accept-Encoding=gzip, deflate
HTTP_CONNECTION=Keep-Alive
ProgramFiles=D:\Program Files
x-webobjects-request-method=GET
x-webobjects-remote-host=127.0.0.1
PATH_TRANSLATED=d:\inetpub\wwwroot\Forms.woa\wo\qT6000bZ400C54003\0.2
USERPROFILE=D:\Documents and Settings\Default User
x-webobjects-server-port=80
...
```

invokeAction()

The turning point of the request/response loop is the `invokeAction()` method. This is where the loop stops being a request loop and starts being a response loop. The `invokeAction()` method will call the appropriate action method based on the request. It is expected that whatever method is called will return a WOComponent. That component will be sent the `awake()` method (if it has not already been awoken), and will be responsible for the response part of the request/response cycle. If this method returns null, the same component that was responsible for the request will be liable for the response.

If an action method is required to create a new instance of a page, the WOComponent's pageWithName() method must be used. Using this method ensures that the page created will be stored in the WOSession's page cache appropriately. The code created for you by WebObjects Builder when creating an action that returns a particular page is a good template to start with (see Listing 4.10).

Listing 4.10

An Action Method Created by WebObjects Builder

```
public FortunePage showFortunePage() {
    FortunePage nextPage = (FortunePage)pageWithName("FortunePage");

    // Initialize your component here

    return nextPage;
    }
```

The code in Listing 4.10 simply creates a new page and returns it. Notice that there is room to initialize the component before returning it. For example, the FortunePage component could be initialized with a default userName or with a different fortune.

Also, nothing says that you have to create a new component on every action method; that's just the default implementation. As stated earlier in the chapter, it could get quite expensive to create a new component for every action, and that behavior should be avoided. It is quite common to create a set of components that are used repeatedly. These components could be stored in the Session class (see Listing 4.11).

Listing 4.11

Storing the FortunePage *Object in the* Session.java *Class*

```
import com.apple.yellow.foundation.*;
import com.apple.yellow.webobjects.*;
import com.apple.yellow.eocontrol.*;

public class Session extends WOSession
{
    private FortunePage fortunePage;

    public FortunePage fortunePage()
    {
```

Listing 4.11

Continued

```
        if ( fortunePage == null )
        {
            WOComponent page = this.context().page();
            fortunePage = (FortunePage)page.pageWithName("FortunePage");
        }
        return fortunePage;
    }
}
```

In Listing 4.11, the FortunePage object is stored as an instance variable in the Session class. An access method is created that will create the object associated with the instance variable if necessary. The object is created by using pageWithName() if the instance variable is null. The WOSession class does not have direct access to a WOComponent or a pageWithName method, so it must retrieve the current page that is processing the request/response loop using the associated WOContext. The WOContext is retrieved using the WOSession's context() method, and the current page is retrieved using the WOContext's page() method. At that point, the instance variable can be set using the pageWithName() method.

Now the action method in the Main.java file needs to be modified to use the new method in Session.java.

In Listing 4.12, the first task is to retrieve the Session object. This is done by calling the WOComponent's session() method. The return value for this method is WOSession. However, WebObjects makes sure that Session objects are created rather than WOSessions, so the return value from the session() method is cast to Session.

Listing 4.12

The showFortunePage() *Method in* Main.java

```
public FortunePage showFortunePage()
{
    Session session=(Session)this.session();
    return session.fortunePage();
}
```

The last line simply calls the fortunePage() method in your Session class, which will create a FortunePage object or simply return the one that exists.

appendToResponse()

The last method to be called before the response is sent to the adaptor is `appendToResponse()`, which is sent to the `Application` and `Session` objects. The object that is returned from the action method will also receive the `appendToResponse()` method. The default implementation for this method is to create the appropriate HTML in the response object. This is where all the dynamic elements resolve their bindings, so hopefully all your variables have the correct information. This method is used as a last chance to change anything before the response is generated.

Typically, when this method is overridden, the superclass method is called after any variables are set. If the superclass method is called before the variables are modified, the modifications will not be represented in the response. Listing 4.13 can be used as a template for overriding `appendToResponse()`.

Listing 4.13

Template for Overriding `appendToResponse()`

```
public void appendToResponse( WOResponse response, WOContext context )
{
    // put your code here
    super.appendToResponse( response, context );
}
```

sleep()

After the response has been sent to the adaptor, the `sleep()` method is called for all objects involved in the transaction. This is a good place to put any cleanup that is required after the transaction is complete. Because the `sleep()` method is called after the response has been sent, you don't need to worry about raising the response time by performing a lengthy cleanup.

The `sleep()` method is more useful in the Objective-C implementation than it is in Java. In Objective-C, `sleep()` is used to clean up memory that was allocated during the request/response cycle. Java has automatic garbage collection, however, and there is little need for this type of memory cleanup.

Summary

This chapter discusses a number of topics that are crucial to WebObjects programming. Here is a summary of the major highlights:

- The WOHyperlink dynamic element is used to provide a link to action methods and other WOComponents.

- Use the WOTextField, WOForm, and WOSubmitButton to retrieve text from the user.

- For your application, there is one instance of the Application object for every application instance.

- There is a separate instance of the Session object for each browser that requests information from your application.

For more information about the topics in this chapter, take a look at the WebObjects developers guide in the WOInfoCenter under the Books, WebObjects hyperlinks. In particular, the sections titled "What is a WebObjects Application?," "Dynamic Elements," and "Common Methods" are good supplemental reading for this chapter. Also, take a look at `http://www.wowack.com` for the latest exercises, examples, questions, and answers for this book.

PART II

USING THE ENTERPRISE OBJECTS FRAMEWORK

CHAPTER

CHAPTER 5

USING DISPLAY GROUPS

Up to now, you have built a WebObjects project, modeled your application, sketched out a site map, and built some components. Now is where the fun begins: accessing the database. As discussed in Chapter 2, "Creating a Model," EOF provides a great object-to-relational mapping system, and you have already used EOModeler to create a model. There are a number of ways to access the *enterprise objects*, or *EO*s, from your application. One would be to use a number of EOF classes and write some code to retrieve objects from the database. This method is necessary in certain situations and will be discussed in Chapter 6, "Retrieving Objects." Another way to access these objects is to use a WODisplayGroup. The purpose of a WODisplayGroup is to provide an easy way for the user interface components to access enterprise objects. In order to use the WODisplayGroup, you will need to learn about some additional classes and dynamic elements.

This chapter introduces the WODisplayGroup along with some new dynamic elements: WOConditional and WORepetition. All these new items will help you build WOComponents that display data out of your relational database. By the end of this chapter, you will be able to:

- Use a WODisplayGroup to display objects and send queries to the database.

- Use a WORepetition to display a NSArray of objects.

- Use a WOConditional to conditionally display HTML.

- Create a detail WODisplayGroup that contains a master object.

Foundation

The WODisplayGroup uses some classes from the Foundation framework (see Figure 5.1). The Foundation framework contains classes that are used throughout the rest of the Apple frameworks and contains some functionality that duplicates what is found in the standard Java packages. For example, the NSMutableArray is extremely similar to the `java.util.Vector`. If you're thinking "Why didn't they just use the Vector class," there's a good reason. These frameworks were originally written in Objective-C a few years before Java was released in 1995. Most of the classes in the Foundation framework (`com.apple.yellow.foundation`) have had the same API since the first release. Because the Foundation framework contained core classes that were used in the rest of the frameworks including EOF and WebObjects, Apple engineers decided to continue to use these classes when they wrote the Java wrappers for the Objective-C classes rather than use the standard Java classes. Replacing these core classes would require a bit of work. The good news is that these classes work well and are easy to use if you are accustomed to the standard Java classes.

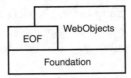

Figure 5.1

All Apple frameworks depend on the Foundation framework, and some dependencies exist between the WebObjects Framework and EOF.

NSArray

The `NSArray` is located in the `com.apple.yellow.foundation` package and provides functionality similar to the `java.util.Vector`. The major difference besides the different APIs is that the `NSArray` is a *nonmutable* class. This means that after you create an instance of `NSArray`, it cannot be modified. There is a modifiable version of `NSArray` called `NSMutableArray`. Table 5.1 contains some useful `NSArray` and `NSMutableArray` methods.

Table 5.1

Common NSArray and NSMutableArray Methods

NSArray/NSMutableArray Method	Description
`public NSArray( Object [] objects )`	Constructs a `NSArray` that contains the array of objects specified.
`public int count()`	Returns the size of the array.
`public Object objectAtIndex( int index )`	Returns the objects at the specified index. Indexes range from 0 to the array count-1.
`public boolean containsObject( Object object )`	Returns true if the object is contained in the array.

Table 5.1
Continued

NSArray/NSMutableArray Method	Description
`public int indexOfObject( Object object )`	Returns the index for the specified object. If the object is in the array more than once, the lowest index is returned. If the object does not exist in the array, `NSArray.NotFound` is returned.
`public void addObject( Object object )`	Adds the object to the end of the array. Available only in `NSMutableArray`.
`public void removeObject( Object object )`	Removes all references to the object from the array.

`NSDictionary` and `NSMutableDictionary`, another pair of foundation classes, will be discussed later in the chapter.

Display Groups

Display groups are used a lot by WebObjects developers to quickly create user interfaces that access database records. The best way to think about the `WODisplayGroup` class is that it is a conduit from the user interface objects to the database objects. The engineers at Apple realized that there exists a certain set of functionality that almost every Web application is expected to do:

- Query the database
- Display the results
- Batch the results into separate pages

This functionality has been built in to the `WODisplayGroup` (see Figure 5.2). In addition, display groups are also used to help with the display of to-many relationships.

A `WODisplayGroup` is based on an Entity. The entity name is the first item that you configure on a `WODisplayGroup`. The display group has the ability to run queries against the entity table or simply display all the objects that exist for that entity. Objects for other entities can also be displayed through relationships that you have defined in EOModeler.

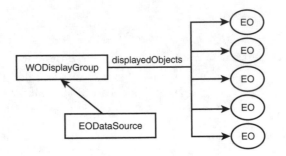

Figure 5.2
The WODisplayGroup *retrieves the database records from an* EODataSource. *When the* WODisplayGroup *receives the records, they are Enterprise Objects, or EOs.*

The WODisplayGroup retrieves all the data through the EODataSource, which is an abstract class located in the com.apple.yellow.eocontrol package. WODisplayGroup uses either EODatabaseDataSource or EOEODetailDataSource objects, which are concrete subclasses of EODataSource. EODatabaseDataSource retrieves its data from the database, EODetailDataSource retrieves its objects from a master object. Using an EODetailDataSource will be discussed later in the chapter. You can also create your own data source by implementing the few methods in EODataSource; however, the need for this is rare. Also, you rarely need to access the EODataSource directly, it's mostly done through accessing WODisplayGroup methods. All you really need to know about data sources at this point is that the WODisplayGroup uses two types of them; one retrieves records from the database and one doesn't.

The records are fetched from the database when the qualifyDataSource method is called on the WODisplayGroup. When qualifyDataSource is called, the records are placed into either the allObjects or the displayedObjects arrays. The allObjects array stores all the objects associated with that entity, displayedObjects stores the objects returned from a query based on the queryMatch, queryMin, and queryMax settings. Also, if batching is enabled, displayedObjects stores the objects for the current batch. The WODisplayGroup uses NSArrays for allObjects and displayObjects and NSDictionarys for queryMatch, queryMin, and queryMatch.

Using the WODisplayGroup

Enough of the background: Let's get to work! Creating the WODisplayGroup is extremely easy, and it requires no code. You need to make sure that the EOModel you want to use is in your project, and then you need to decide what you want to display. An example of displaying the Studio objects will be used to demonstrate the WODisplayGroup features throughout this chapter. A WODisplayGroup is added to a

WOComponent, creating a WODisplayGroup instance variable in the component's class. Here are the steps for adding a WODisplayGroup representing the Studio entities to a component:

1. Add the EOModel you created in Chapter 2 to your project. You can either create a new project or use one from a previous chapter. The EOModel is added to the project by dragging the EOModel directory from the file viewer and dropping it in the Resources suitcase in Project Builder. Alternatively, you could double-click the Resources suitcase and navigate to the EOModel file in the file dialog box.

2. Create a new component, StudioListPage. As you already know, that can be created in Project Builder by selecting the File, New in Project menu items.

3. Open the EOModel for your project in EOModeler by double-clicking it in the Resources suitcase. Also open your new component in WebObjects Builder by double-clicking the StudioListPage icon in Project Builder.

4. Drag the entity you want to display (Studio, for example) from EOModeler to WebObjects Builder as depicted in Figure 5.3. This will create a WODisplayGroup for you.

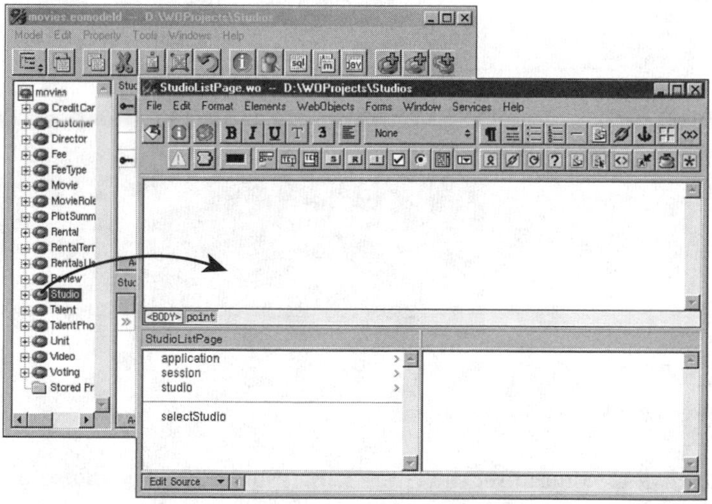

Figure 5.3
Adding a WODisplayGroup to a WOComponent.

5. You will be prompted for the name of the instance variable to be used in your class: The default name is usually appropriate. The name of the variable is usually DisplayGroup appended to the name of the entity with a lowercase first letter. A display group representing the Studio entity would be referenced by an instance variable called `studioDisplayGroup`. The options you have at this point are to Add the display group or Add and Configure. You might as well pick Add and Configure to use the display group configuration dialog.

6. Select the Fetches on Load check box as shown in Figure 5.4 and click the OK button to add the Display Group to the component.

Configuring the Display Group

Display groups are configured using the Display Group Options dialog box as shown in Figure 5.4. This is displayed when selecting Add and Configure for a new display group or by double-clicking a display group in WebObjects Builder.

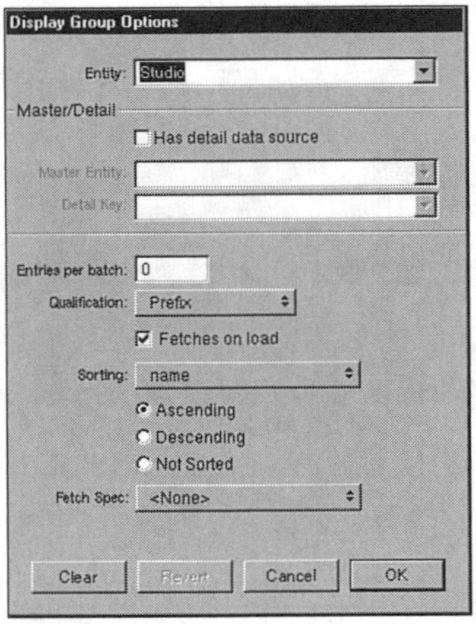

Figure 5.4
Display Group Options dialog box.

Using this dialog, you can set the entity name, sort ordering, and some of the batching options, among other things. Table 5.2 lists the basic settings.

Table 5.2

Basic `WODisplayGroup` *Settings*

Setting	Description
Entity	The name of the entity associated with the display group.
Entries per batch	When setting up a display group to page through a large resultset, this specifies how many objects to display on each page. To turn off batching, set the value to zero.
Qualification	Specifies the default string match operator. The options are Prefix, Contains, and Suffix.
Fetches on load	A check box that specifies whether to fetch the data for the display group when the page is loaded. If this is not checked, the data will only be loaded by calling another method in the display group such as `qualifyDataSource`. If this is left checked, it could result in unnecessary trips to retrieve database data.
Sorting	Specifies the key that will be used to order the objects and whether to sort the objects ascending or descending.
Fetch Spec	If a fetch specification has been created in the model for this entity, it can be specified here to filter the data.

Other `WODisplayGroup` values can be set; however, setting these involves writing code. Some of these options will be discussed later in the chapter.

If you are adding a `WODisplayGroup` for the first time, it is important to click the Fetches on Load check box, which causes the display group to automatically fetch data when loading the page.

So where is the `WODisplayGroup` configuration information stored? If you look at the class file for the component, the only change is the addition of a `WODisplayGroup` instance variable. If you examine the HTML and WOD files, you will notice nothing about the display group. Initially all the configuration information is being stored in memory for the currently executing WebObjects Builder application. When the WebObjects Builder window representing the component is closed, a file with the extension `woo` is created in the component's directory. This file contains the values that you set in the configuration dialog.

Okay, now that we have added the display group to the component, we need to have some way to display the objects.

WORepetition

The WORepetition is a dynamic element used to repeat a set of HTML. Everything between the beginning and closing WORepetition's <WEBOBJECT> tag is repeated, including static HTML along with other dynamic elements and components.

There are two ways to use a WORepetition, the most popular method is to bind a NSArray to the list attribute. Figure 5.5 shows what a WORepetition looks like when the list and item attributes are bound (although your window will not look like this yet). Using this approach, the WORepetition will repeat its contents once for every object in the NSArray. The object bound to the WORepetition's item will be replaced with an object from the array each time the WORepetition repeats. This works well for datasets that are represented by a NSArray. If you have a dataset that is represented by something different, such as a java.util.Vector, you should use the count binding, which is discussed later in this chapter. As it turns out, using the list binding works really well for WODisplayGroups because WODisplayGroups use NSArrays to represent their data.

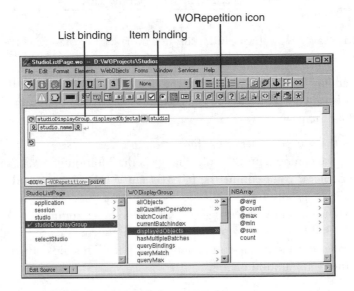

Figure 5.5
Using a WORepetition.

WORepetitions **and** WODisplayGroups

Using a WORepetition with a NSArray is quite easy. You will need to add a key to your component and bind some attributes. The following steps will guide you through adding a WORepetition to the StudioListPage.

1. Add a key to your component of the same class as the objects that are contained in the NSArray. For example, if you are displaying studios, create a key called studio of type Studio.

2. Place your cursor at the location in your document where you want the WORepetition to go and click on the WORepetition icon as highlighted in Figure 5.5. Make sure that you are in graphical editing mode before doing this.

3. Bind the WORepetition's list and item attributes to the NSArray and the key that you just created, respectively. This could be done through the binding inspector or by binding the keys to the two little boxes on the graphical representation of the dynamic element as pointed out in Figure 5.5. Continuing with the studio example, you would bind the list attribute to studioDisplayGroup. displayedObjects and the item attribute to the studio key that you created earlier.

4. The final step involves displaying something in the WORepetition. The easiest thing to do is to place a WOString followed by a line break, and bind the WOString's value to an attribute of the key you added earlier. Remember, the item will be changed every time the WORepetition repeats its contents. To display the studio names, you would bind the WOString's value to studio.name.

After you've completed these steps, it's time to build your project and test it. If you have created this as a new component, you might want to put a WOHyperlink on the Main component that loads your new page.

WORepetitions **and HTML Tables**

Database data is best displayed in HTML tables, with the columns lined up, the numbers right-justified, and so on (see Figure 5.6). The typical table would have a header row at the top with the second row repeating once for every record returned.

This is accomplished with a repetition around the table row, which is a bit tricky to configure. To understand this better, consider the sample table HTML in Listing 5.1.

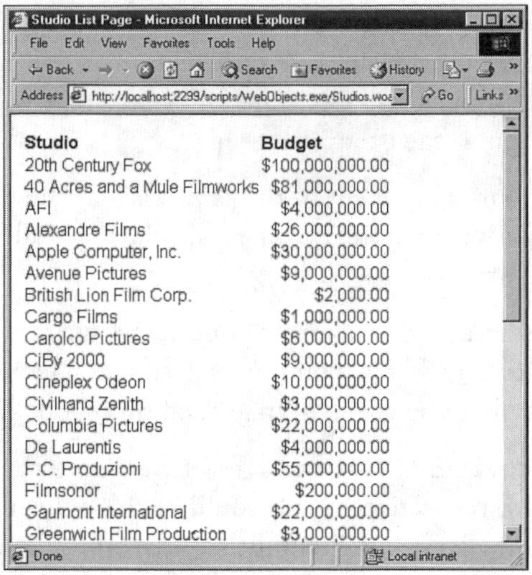

Figure 5.6
Displaying database data in an HTML table.

Listing 5.1

Sample HTML for a Table

```
<TABLE CELLPADDING=0 CELLSPACING=2 BORDER=0>
    <TR>
        <TD>Studio</TD>
        <TD>Budget</TD>
    </TR>
    <TR>
        <TD> The name goes here </TD>
        <TD ALIGN=RIGHT> The budget goes here </TD>
    </TR>
    </TABLE>
```

The second <tr> tag should be repeated once for every object in the resultset, and
WOStrings should be placed inside the <td> tags it contains. Listing 5.2 adds the
WORepetition and WOStrings to the HTML table.

Listing 5.2

The Proper Arrangement for Repeating Table Rows

```
<TABLE CELLPADDING=0 CELLSPACING=2 BORDER=0>
    <TR>
        <TD>Studio</TD>
        <TD>Budget</TD>
    </TR>
    <WEBOBJECT NAME=Repetition1>
        <TR>
            <TD><WEBOBJECT NAME=String1></WEBOBJECT></TD>
            <TD ALIGN=RIGHT><WEBOBJECT NAME=String7></WEBOBJECT></TD>
        </TR>
    </WEBOBJECT>
</TABLE>
```

Chances are that you will not have to code this HTML by hand; there are a few ways to create this using WebObjects Builder. However, if it doesn't seem to be working right, you can always switch to source editing mode and make the appropriate edits by hand. Here are the steps for creating a table in WebObjects Builder for displaying studio names and budgets:

1. Remove the current WORepetition by selecting it and pressing the Delete key.

2. Create a new table using the table icon. This will bring up the New Table dialog box as shown in Figure 5.7. Choose two columns and two rows. At this point, you can also select the Second Row Is Wrapped in a WORepetition check box in the lower left corner. This will automatically create the WORepetition the way we want it. Now select OK.

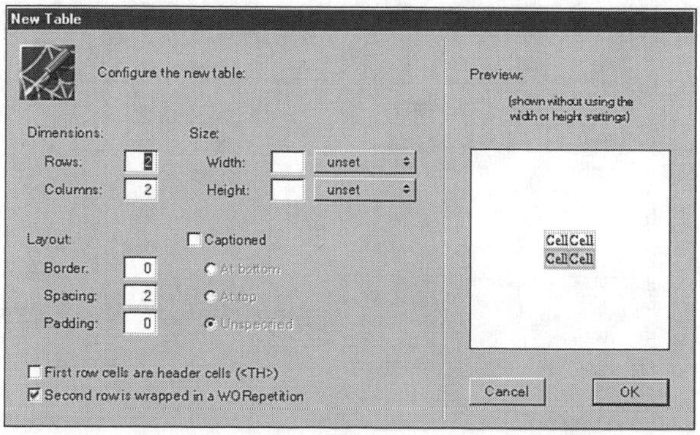

Figure 5.7

The New Table dialog box.

> **HTML Table Setup**
> The number of columns that you choose depends on the number of attributes in the entity you're displaying. No matter what data you're displaying, you always choose two rows. The first row contains header fields, and the second will be repeated.

3. You will now see an HTML table on your page. Change the contents of the top two cells to Studio and Budget, respectively. For added polish, make these bold as well.

4. Recreate the bindings to the WORepetition that you had before, binding list to studioDisplayGroup.displayedObjects and item to studio. It is not obvious where the WORepetition is located at this point. Notice that the second row has a shaded background (it will be shaded blue on your screen). This indicates that it is wrapped in a dynamic element, which happens to be the WORepetition. There are two ways to create bindings for the repetition:

   • Drag the binding to the WORepetition. Be careful to select the WORepetition and not one of the WOStrings. You will know when the WORepetition is selected when a dark outline goes around the entire row.

   • Select an area within one of the cells inside the WORepetition. Notice that the bar in the middle of the page displays the elements nested inside one another. You should see the <WORepetition> tag; and you can drag bindings directly to this tag.

5. Recreate the WOStrings inside the cells in the second row of the table, as shown in Figure 5.8.

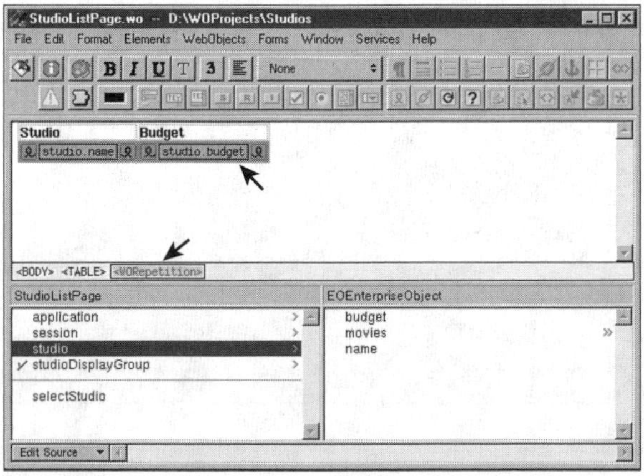

Figure 5.8
A WORepetition inside an HTML table. There are two places for binding keys to the WORepetition.

Now build and run the project. The output for the table view should now be formatted in an HTML table.

The Count

The other method of using a WORepetition is to assign a value to the count binding. The contents of the repetition will be repeated as many times as is set in the count binding. This method is useful if you are storing information in some object that is not a NSArray, such as a java.util.Vector or a standard Java array. The drawback of using the count binding is that you have to write code to keep track of where you are in the array.

Detail Display Groups

This chapter's introduction discussed the WODisplayGroup's data source. It was said that the data source is an instance of a concrete subclass of EODataSource, usually EODatabaseDataSource. Up to now, you have been using an EODatabaseDataSource, whether you know it or not. A WODisplayGroup can also be set to use an EODetailDataSource, which allows the easy display of a to-many relationship, given the source object. The EODetailDataSource fetches only the records that are available as part of a to-many relationship for a given object. This object is called the *master* object, and the detail data source will need to know the master object, the object's entity name, and the to-many relationship used. All the operations that are performed on an EODatabaseDataSource can also be performed on an EODetailDataSource (see Figure 5.9), including batching, sorting, and querying.

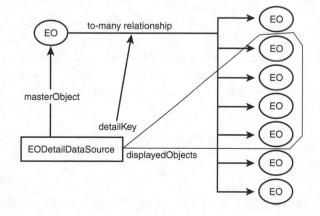

Figure 5.9
The EODetailDataSource.

For an example on using the EODetailDataSource, let's say that you want to modify the StudioDisplayPage to display the studio names as hyperlinks (see Figure 5.10). When a studio is selected, you want to display the set of movies produced by that studio. If you have a to-many relationship from Studio to Movie (and you should), you can set this up fairly easily using a pair of WODisplayGroups.

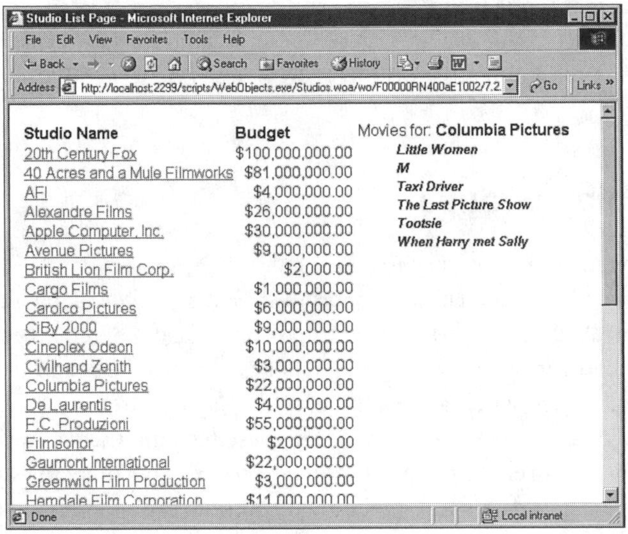

Figure 5.10
Enhancing the Studio List Page to display movie information.

Here are the steps for making this enhancement:

1. Open the StudioListPage component in WebObjectsBuilder and create a WODisplayGroup for the Movie entity called movieDisplayGroup. When configuring the display group, check the Has Detail Data Source check box, set the Master Entity to Studio, and set the Detail Key to the name of the one-to-many relationship from Studio to Movie. Make sure that Fetches on Load is checked.

2. Create a WORepetition to display the set of movies and set the necessary bindings. This will require adding a key called movie to the component. Also, create a WOString inside the repetition to display the Movie's title, and bind movie.title to the value attribute.

3. Create an action called studioSelected that returns null. This action should set the master object for the movieDisplayGroup to the object associated with the hyperlink. This is easier than it sounds; the value associated with the WORepetition's item binding will contain the appropriate object when the action method is called. The code for this action method can be found in Listing 5.3.

Listing 5.3

The studioSelected *Method*

```
public WOComponent studioSelected()
{
    movieDisplayGroup.setMasterObject( studio );
    return null;
}
```

4. Create a hyperlink around the WOString that contains the Studio's title. This can be done by selecting the WOString and then clicking on the WOHyperlink icon. Bind the hyperlink's action to studioSelected. After you complete this, you can build and run your project.

Batching Resultsets

Being an avid Web surfer, I have noticed that the coolest sites on the Web batch large query resultsets into separate pages. The query result page displays the total number of matches for your query along with hyperlinks for the next and previous pages. This has become so common that sites unwilling to deliver this piece of functionality are considered out of date. Lucky for us, this is built in to the WODisplayGroup (see Figure 5.11).

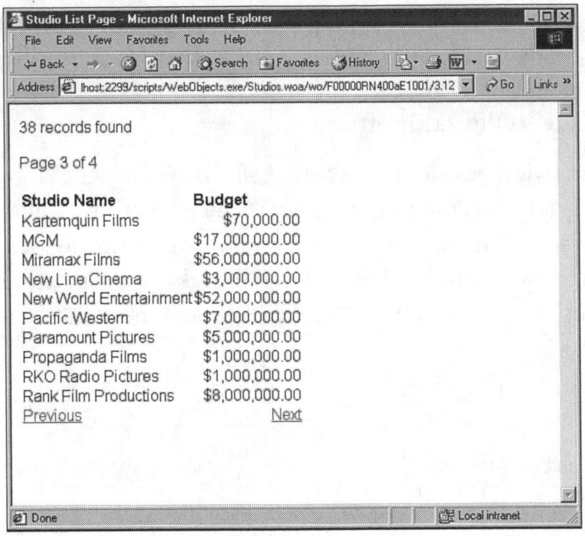

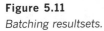

Figure 5.11
Batching resultsets.

To turn on batching, pull up the display group configuration dialog by double-clicking the display group's name in WebObjects Builder and enter a number in the Entries Per Batch field. After clicking the OK button in the display group configuration dialog, your display group will batch the resultset.

You will need to add hyperlinks to display the next and previous batches along with WOStrings to display the total number of records returned, the number of records displayed, the page number, and the total number of pages. Table 5.3 lists the keys in the display group that are used for these bindings.

Table 5.3
WODisplayGroup Batching Bindings

Common Term	WODisplayGroup key
Page Number	`currentBatchIndex`
Number of pages	`batchCount`
Action to return the next page	`displayNextBatch`
Action to return the previous page	`displayPreviousBatch`
Total number of records found	`allObject.count`

So, setting a pair of WOHyperlinks' action bindings to displayNextBatch and displayPreviousBatch will cause the page to be redisplayed with either the next or previous batches when selected.

Searching for the Right Match

The next thing that you can do with a WODisplayGroup is search, or *query* records in the database. This is accomplished by setting the WODisplayGroup's query bindings, and then fetching the data by calling the qualifyDataSource method. The query bindings are NSMutableDictionarys, so a brief introduction to the NSDictionary and NSMutableDictionary classes is necessary.

NSDictionary **and** NSMutableDictionary

Similar to NSArray and NSMutableArray, NSDictionary and NSMutableDictionary are classes located in the Foundation Framework, com.apple.yellow.foundation. Also similar to their array counterparts, NSDictionary objects are nonchangeable after their creation and NSMutableDictionary objects are changeable. The NSMutableDictionary is similar in functionality to the java.util.Hashtable class. These classes store objects that are retrievable by certain keys. When you add an object to a NSMutableDictionary, you have to specify a key. Table 5.4 lists commonly used dictionary methods.

Table 5.4

Common NSDictionary *and* NSMutableDictionary *Methods*

NSDictionary/NSMutableDictionary Method	Description
public Object objectForKey (Object key)	Returns the object for that key.
public NSArray allKeys()	Returns an array of the dictionary keys.
public int count()	Returns the number of items in the dictionary.
public void setObjectForKey (Object value, Object key)	Sets the object for the specified key. If the key exists in the dictionary, the object provided replaces the one in the dictionary; otherwise a new entry is added. Available only in NSMutableDictionary.
public void removeObjectForKey (Object key)	Removes the entry specified by the key. Available only in NSMutableDictionary.

Search Bindings

The search bindings for a WODisplayGroup consist of four NSDictionarys that specify how a search is to be constructed: queryMin, queryMax, queryMatch, and queryOperator. Each dictionary contains key value pairs in which the keys are identical to the entity keys, and the values are the items to query on. The where clause for the select statement is computed based on the values in these dictionaries. If these dictionaries are empty, they are ignored. If a particular key for a dictionary is empty, it's ignored. Values in each of the dictionaries create different types of queries. For example, values in the queryMin dictionary will result in greater than items in the where clause. Items in the queryMax dictionary will result in less than where clause specifications.

This is best described with an example. Assume that we want to display studios where the budget is between $10,000,000 and $20,000,000. We would have a key in the queryMin dictionary for budget with the value of 10000000.00 and a budget key in the queryMax dictionary with the value of 20000000.00.

Example of querying for studios with budgets between $10,000,000.00 and $20,000,000.00.

The queryMin Dictionary
budget	10000000.00

The queryMax Dictionary
budget	20000000.00

The queryMatch dictionary attempts to match the values. For numbers and dates, an is equal match is performed. For strings, a string match is performed based on the defaultStringMatchFormat and the defaultStringMatchOperator. The default is for a match to be performed using the like operator to match the first few letters of the string. The defaultStringMatchFormat is a string that represents the format of the like statement, and the default for the string is "%@*". The %@ part of the format specifies where the object should be placed, and the asterisk is a literal. For example, if a queryMatch key is bound to the String "A", "A" would replace the %@ in the defaultStringMatchFormat. The format for the like statement would be "A*". The defaultStringMatchFormat can be changed in the display group configuration dialog using the Qualification pop-up. The default value is Prefix, with the other options being Contains and Suffix.

Example of defining a query for studios with names starting with the letter "A":

The `queryMatch` Dictionary	
name	"A"

Using Query Values in WebObjects Builder

Assigning these values in WebObjects Builder is as easy as creating the form to enter the values and binding the `value` of each `WOTextField` to the appropriate key in one of the query binding dictionaries (see Figure 5.12). The submit button for the form is then assigned to the display group's `qualifyDataSource` method.

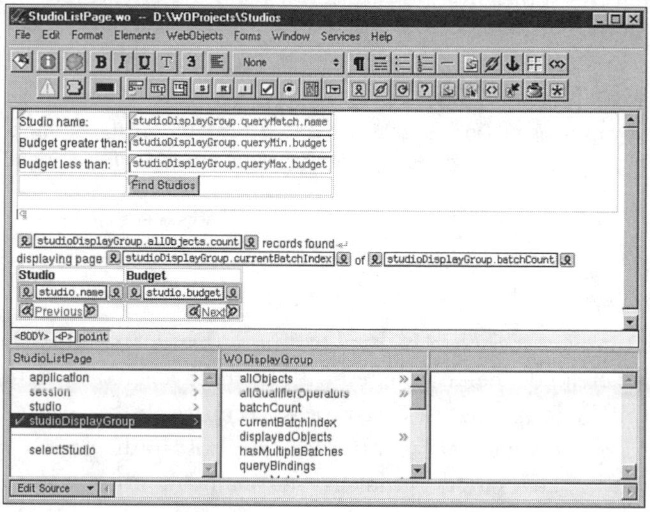

Figure 5.12
Adding a query form to the `StudioListPage`.

Here are the steps for adding a form to the `StudioListPage` that will allow the user to provide query values:

1. Add a `WOForm` to the component before the `WORepetition` of studios. Inside the form, add WOTextFields for the studio's name, budget greater than, and budget less than. Also add a submit button.

2. Bind the form values to items in the `studioDisplayGroup` according to Table 5.3.

3. Uncheck Fetches on Load for the `studioDisplayGroup` in the Display Group Options dialog box. According to the bindings in Table 5.5, the data will be loaded when the submit button is pressed.

Table 5.5

Display Group Query Bindings for the StudioListPage

Form element	Binding
Submit Button action	studioDisplayGroup.qualifyDataSource
Studio name text field value	studioDisplayGroup.queryMatch.name
"Budget greater than" text field value	studioDisplayGroup.queryMin.budget
"Budget less than" text field value	studioDisplayGroup.queryMax.budget

When running the application, notice that if you leave a text field blank, the value is ignored in the query.

> Notice that if you're using OpenBaseLite, the like operator for the studio's name is not case sensitive. This is a side effect of using OpenBaseLite; all likes in that database are not case sensitive.

Query Operators

The queryMatch dictionary can be used for more than matching strings; all sorts of queries can be created when combined with the queryOperator dictionary. The queryOperator dictionary defines the type of comparison that is used with the queryMatch keys and values. If an entry does not exist in the queryOperator dictionary for a particular key that's used in the queryMatch dictionary, the default operator is used for that key's type. The queryOperator values are different based on the type of the key being compared. The WODisplayGroup has three arrays that define the appropriate operators for each type of key: relationalOperatorQualifiers, stringQualifierOperators, and allQualifierOperators. The operators usable for string comparisons are found in the stringQualifierOperators array. Operators for all other datatypes are found in the relationalQualifierOperators. Tables 5.6 and 5.7 contain the value found these arrays.

Table 5.6

Contents of the stringQualifierOperators *Array*

Operator
starts with
contains

Table 5.6
Continued

Operator
ends with
is
like

Table 5.7
Contents of the relationalQualifierOperators *Array*

Operator
=
<>
<
<=
>
>=

Using the queryOperator dictionary allows for finer control over the query. You could, for example, display all talents in which the first name starts with "Hu" and the last name ends with "art".

The queryMatch Dictionary

firstName	"Hu"
lastName	"art"

The queryOperator Dictionary

firstName	"starts with"
lastName	"ends with"

Because the query operators are defined in arrays, it would be easy for us to provide a way for the user to select the operator for a query item using a WOPopupButton. Simply place a WOPopupButton in the form and bind the attributes as described:

```
list            studioDisplayGroup.stringQualifierOperators
selection       studioDisplayGroup.queryOperator.name
```

The WOPopupButton will now display the list of available String qualifier operators.

One of the disadvantages of using the queryOperator dictionary is that a key cannot be entered twice. For example, it would be impossible to specify "budget > $10,000,000.00 and budget < $20,000,000.00" using only the queryOperator and queryMatch dictionaries. The queryMax and queryMin dictionaries are provided for this because these type of range queries are so common.

WOConditional

Our Studio List page is almost complete, but have you noticed that it's sort of sloppy when first presented? One thing that really kills me is when an application displays a dialog that says "1 file(s) deleted". Okay, so how hard is it for a developer to code "if 1 file is deleted, leave off the 's'"? The answer, in any language, is "not that hard." It just takes some attention to detail (see Figure 5.13).

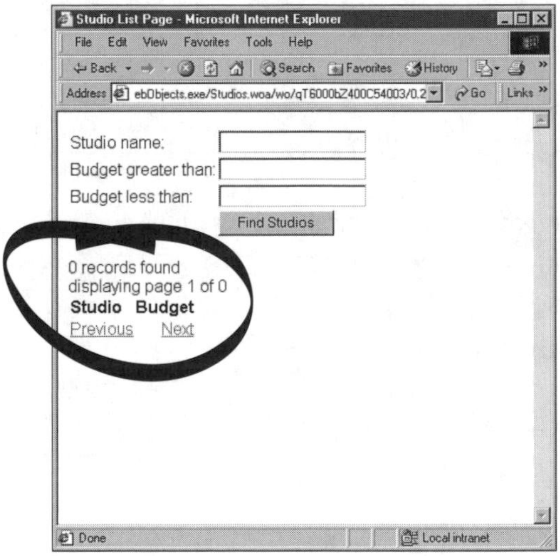

Figure 5.13
Unnecessary and distracting text.

As our application stands right now, we fall into the same boat as the lazy developers who don't bother to fix the grammar on their dialogs. This is easily remedied by using the WOConditional dynamic element (see Figure 5.14). There are two bindings for a WOConditional: condition and negate. If condition resolves to true or YES, the contents of the WOConditional are displayed; otherwise the contents are not displayed. If negate resolves to true or YES, the functionality is reversed (the contents are displayed if condition resolves to false or NO).

Condition binding   WOConditional icon

WOConditional
dynamic element
display

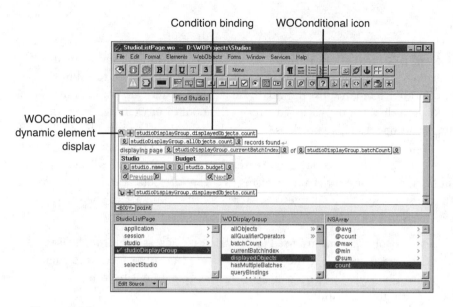

Figure 5.14
Using the WOConditional.

To fix our page is relatively simple. Add a WOConditional around the repetition of studios and all the associated controls. Highlight the conditional area and select the WOConditional icon as shown in Figure 5.11. The condition for this WOConditional is studioDisplayGroup.allObjects.count. If the count is zero, anything inside the WOConditional will not be displayed. You can set the condition binding directly in the graphical representation of the WOConditional as shown in Figure 5.11. The + symbol next to the WOConditional's question mark denotes that it is a positive conditional. This means that if condition resolves to true the contents are displayed. This also means that negate is either not set or resolves to false. Clicking on the + symbol will turn the dynamic element into a negative conditional and the negate binding will then become true.

A similar conditional can be placed around the list of movies (if they are displayed on the same page), with condition bound to movieDisplayGroup.allObjects.count. Now when you execute the application, you will only see the form on the StudioListPage to begin with. After you query for objects, you should see the list of studios, but not the list of movies. When you select a studio, you should then see the list of movies.

Summary

In one sense, we've covered a lot of ground this chapter. You should now have an application that accesses the database, displays records, and allows you to submit queries. On the other hand, it's just the tip of the iceberg. There are some limitations to WODisplayGroups that will be discussed later in the book. For example, in all the query bindings and operators, an or clause cannot be specified. We introduced methods for modifying data, but a lot of considerations need to be made that were not discussed. Also, as versatile as display groups are, they are not useful in all situations, and you will be forced to use other mechanisms to access the database. In other words, you've learned just enough to be dangerous. Here's a brief summary of the topics covered in this lesson:

WODisplayGroup—Display groups are used to provide easy access from the display objects to the database objects. Use the displayedObjects array to access the data. A WODisplayGroup can be added to a WOComponent by dragging an entity from EOModeler to WebObjects Builder.

Querying data—Data can be queried by setting values in WODisplayGroup's queryMatch, queryMin, and queryMax dictionaries.

NSArray and NSMutableArray—These classes in the com.apple.yellow.foundation package store arrays of objects. NSArray objects are "*nonmutable*;" that is, they cannot be changed after they are created. NSMutableArray objects can be changed after creation. A number of EOF and WebObjects classes use NSArrays and NSMutableArrays.

NSDictionary and NSMutableDictionary—Again, classes in the foundation framework. These classes store key-value pairs, where both the keys and values are objects. Similar to NSArray and NSMutableArray, these classes are used by a number of WebObjects and EOF classes.

WORepetition—A dynamic element that repeats a set of HTML. The primary bindings for WORepetitions are the list and item bindings.

WOConditional—A dynamic element that conditionally displays HTML. A WOConditional will display HTML depending on the resolution of its condition binding.

Q&A

Q When I display a set of data, it's all on one large line. How can I get the data on separate lines?

A Put a line break (Shift+Enter) inside the WORepetition immediately after the last WOString.

Q I followed along with the Movie List Page example and my movies are not ordered properly. What's going on?

A In the Movie List Page example, *EOF Next Generation*, *Star WOB*, and *WOF The Next Big Thing* are the first three movies, in front of the movies that start with A! This is a problem with the data and not a bug in the framework; the titles for each of the out-of-order movies all begin with a space character.

Q I added the display group, but I don't see any data when I run the program.

A Bring up the Display Group Options dialog box and make sure that the Fetches on Load check box is checked.

CHAPTER 6

RETRIEVING OBJECTS

The WODisplayGroup uses the Enterprise Objects Framework to retrieve data through the use of the display group's datasource. However, there are many situations that require the use of the Enterprise Objects Framework more directly, such as creating different types of queries and optimizations. Also, there are times when the WODisplayGroup cannot be used, such as when using DirectActions.

This chapter introduces the EOF's control layer, which is used for retrieving enterprise objects and keeping track of the changes to them. Retrieving objects using the control layer will also be covered in this chapter.

Editing Context

One of the more commonly used classes in EOF is the editing context, or EOEditingContext. This class is found in the EOControl layer. EOEditingContext objects keep track of all of the changes made to the enterprise objects that are retrieved from the database. There are methods in the editing context for retrieving, inserting, and deleting objects along with methods for saving and discarding any changes made to the objects.

There are also methods for undoing and redoing modifications made to the objects, using an instance of NSUndoManager, found in the Foundation framework. This feature should be avoided in WebObjects applications, however. Due to the nature of Web applications, it might be unclear to the user which operation is being undone at any given point. This has the potential to create some unexpected results. Because of this, it is a common practice to set the undo manager for the editing context to null to reduce the associated overhead.

Retrieving Data

The EOEditingContext can be used to retrieve enterprise objects from the database. The exact objects to retrieve are determined by the contents of the EOQualifier object that is used. The order in which the objects are retrieved is determined by an NSArray of EOQualifier objects. This can also be specified using raw SQL, but a good bit of the power that EOF provides is given up at that point. So, to retrieve enterprise objects using an EOEditing context, the following are required:

- An EOQualifier that specifies the objects to be retrieved

- An NSArray of EOSortOrdering objects that specifies the order in which to retrieve the objects

- An EOFetchSpecification that uses the qualifier and sort orderings

- An EOEditingContext

To facilitate the explanation of these topics, a simple application will be used that searches for records in the customer table, given the first few letters of the first and last names. This example uses the Movies and Rentals database that was installed in Chapter 1, "Introducing and Installing WebObjects." A page from this application is shown in Figure 6.1.

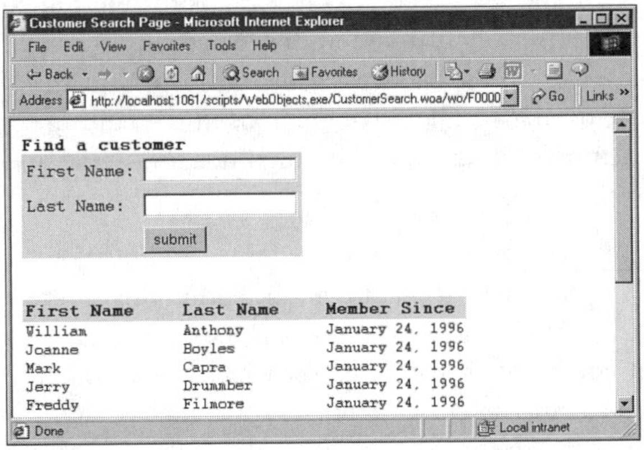

Figure 6.1
The Customer Search Application.

To follow along with the book, you can either create a new application and add the movies.eomodeld file to the Resources suitcase, or add to an existing project that contains the EOModel.

EOQualifier

The EOQualifier specifies exactly which rows should be retrieved from the database. It is essentially the "where" clause without the logical joins. There are a few different types of EOQualifiers, and they are structured together to perform complex projections. Each different type of qualifier is a subclass of EOQualifier.

The most basic type of EOQualifier is the EOKeyValueQualifier. This qualifier compares a key in the enterprise object to some value. Two or more of any qualifiers can be combined using an EOAndQualifier or an EOOrQualifier. An EONotQualifier can be used to negate any qualifier, and if all else fails, you can use the EOSQLQualifier to specify an absolute SQL statement.

There are a number of different ways to create the exact "object graph" of qualifiers. The easiest way to create a qualifier programmatically is to use the EOQualifier static method called qualifierWithQualifierFormat. This method takes two parameters: a qualifier format string and a parameter array. A qualifier format string is very similar to the "where" part of a SQL query. Some sample qualifier formats are

```
lastName = 'Jones'
customerSince > '1/1/2000'
firstName like 'G*' and lastName like 'R*'
```

The keys specified (firstName, lastName, and customerSince) must be attributes in the entity that will be specified in the EOFetchSpecification. The qualifierWithQualifierFormat method will automatically generate the correct qualifiers based on the string supplied.

The parameter array provides values for substitution in the qualifier format string. Similar to the C function printf(), these values are substituted into the format string at runtime to create a new one. The values are all objects, and are substituted into the qualifier format for each %@ symbol. Listing 6.1 demonstrates creating a qualifier format for a date object.

Listing 6.1

Creating a Qualifier Using a Qualifier Format

```
NSArray qualifierBindings = new NSArray( new Object[]{searchDate});
EOQualifier memberSinceQualifier =
    EOQualifier.qualifierWithQualifierFormat(
        "memberSince > %@", qualifierBindings);
```

To demonstrate this, create a new WOComponent called CustomerSearchPage with two text fields for the first and last names. You will need to retrieve the values entered in the TextFields to create the EOQualifier properly. To do this, create two String instance variables called `firstName` and `lastName` in the component, and bind them to the `value` attributes of the `WOTextFields` as shown in Figure 6.2.

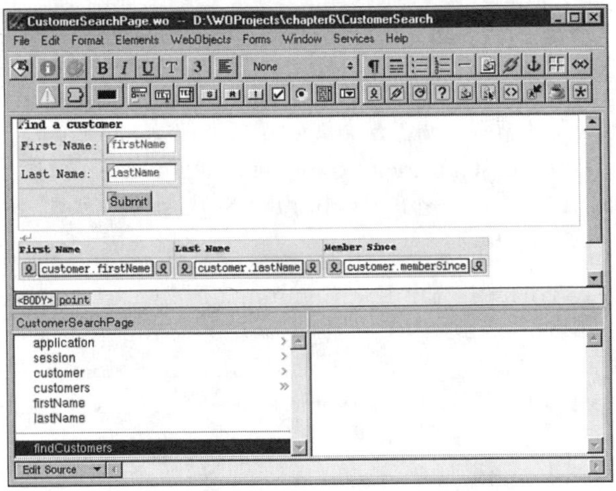

Figure 6.2
The customer search page in WebObjects Builder.

To support the retrieval of this data from the database, a number of keys must be created. Those keys are listed in Table 6.1.

Table 6.1
Keys Required to Support the `CustomerSearchPage`

Key	Type
firstName	String
lastName	String
customer	Customer
customers	NSArray of Customer

In addition, an action called `findCustomers`, which returns `null`, is required. This should be bound to the Submit button's `action` attribute.

The code for creating the qualifier for the first and last names is given in Listing 6.2.

Listing 6.2

Creating the Qualifier for the First and Last Names

```
public WOComponent findCustomers()
{
    String firstNameString = "*";
    String lastNameString = "*";

    if ( firstName != null )
    {
        firstNameString = firstName+"*";
    }

    if ( lastName != null )
    {
        lastNameString = lastName+"*";
    }

    NSArray bindings =
        new NSArray( new Object [] { firstNameString, lastNameString } );

    EOQualifier qualifier =
        EOQualifier.qualifierWithQualifierFormat(
        "firstName like %@ and lastName like %@", bindings );
    return null;

}
```

At this point, add a WORepetition to the component in WebObjects Builder, and bind the list attribute to customers and the item attribute to customer. You can then add WOStrings inside the WORepetition to display parts of the Customer objects.

This is a bit more complicated than the first example. The firstName and lastName variables are String instance variables that are bound to WOTextFields. Because the user enters the first few letters of the person's name, we want to use a like qualifier. The * symbol is used as a wildcard, and means "any number of characters." So, to find the people with the first name starting with G, the like value is G*. This is the reason for appending * to the end of whatever is entered by the user. If the user does not enter a value into these text fields, the variables are null, so you must also check these variables for null values.

It is important to append the wildcard values before the variable is substituted into the qualifier format. It might be tempting to create a qualifier such as "firstName like %@*", but that will not work. If firstName is G, the qualifier will resolve to "firstName like 'G'*", and it will probably result in a SQL error. The asterisk should be inside the single quotation marks with the letter, which is what happens when it is appended before the substitution.

EOSortOrdering

Almost every time multiple objects are retrieved from the database, order is important. If the order is not specified, the rows are usually returned based on the database table's clustered index. If the developer has a reasonable knowledge of the underlying table and if the table's order is the desired order, it might not be necessary to supply the sort ordering, but it's still a good idea. More than likely, the presentation order will be different than the clustered index, and you don't want to rely on something that is database-dependent to display your data. So, you probably will have to supply a sort ordering for every one of your queries that returns multiple rows.

When describing the sort order to objects, a few things must be specified. The attribute to sort by is the first requirement, and then whether to sort the objects in ascending or descending order. Also, if some objects contain identical values for the first attribute, you must specify the second attribute by which they should be ordered, and so on.

EOSortOrdering objects are used to specify how to order the result set. These objects are created using the static sortOrderingWithKey() method. This method takes two parameters: the key to order by and a value representing the ascending or descending order. The two appropriate values for this parameter are EOSortOrdering. CompareAscending and EOSortOrdering.CompareDescending. An example of creating a sort ordering to order the result set by the lastName and firstName attributes is given in Listing 6.3.

Listing 6.3

Creating the Sort Orderings

```
EOSortOrdering lastNameSortOrdering =
    EOSortOrdering.sortOrderingWithKey(
        "lastName", EOSortOrdering.CompareAscending);
EOSortOrdering firstNameSortOrdering =
    EOSortOrdering.sortOrderingWithKey(
        "firstName", EOSortOrdering.CompareAscending);
NSArray sortOrderings =
    new NSArray( new Object[]{lastNameSortOrdering, firstNameSortOrdering} );
```

The EOSortOrdering objects are then combined in an NSArray that defines the priority of orderings. The result set order will be based on the order of the objects in the sort orderings array.

EOFetchSpecification

At this point, all the work has been done for the creation of the qualifier and sort orderings array. The next step is to create a fetch specification that combines the completed work with the entity name. The easiest way to construct an EOFetchSpecification is to use the constructor:

```
EOFetchSpecification fetchSpec =
    new EOFetchSpecification(
        "Customer", memberSinceQualifier, sortOrderings );
```

The parameters for the EOFetchSpecification constructor are the entity name, the EOQualifier, and the sort orderings array. At this point, you are ready to retrieve the objects from the database.

EOEditingContext

As stated earlier, the editing context can be used to retrieve enterprise objects from the database. Every WOSession object has a default editing context that can be retrieved by using the defaultEditingContext() method. After an EOEditingContext is retrieved, the objects can be retrieved from the database using the objectsWithFetchSpecification() method. Listing 6.4 demonstrates these final two steps.

Listing 6.4

Using the Editing Context

```
EOEditingContext ec = this.session().defaultEditingContext();
customers = ec.objectsWithFetchSpecification(fetchSpec);
```

So, the steps for programmatically retrieving enterprise objects are to define the qualifier and sort orderings, combine them with a fetch specification, and use the session's default editing context to retrieve the objects. To finish the customer search page, we need an action method that is called when the user submits the first and last names. This method will retrieve the records from the database and place them in an NSArray called customers. The full listing for the component class is given in Listing 6.5.

Listing 6.5

The Complete Listing for the CustomerSearchPage *Component*

```
import com.apple.yellow.foundation.*;
import com.apple.yellow.webobjects.*;
```

Listing 6.5

Continued

```
import com.apple.yellow.eocontrol.*;
import com.apple.yellow.eoaccess.*;

public class CustomerSearchPage extends WOComponent {

    /** @TypeInfo Customer */
    protected EOEnterpriseObject customer;

    /** @TypeInfo Customer */
    protected NSArray customers;
    protected String firstName;
    protected String lastName;


    public WOComponent findCustomers()
    {

        String firstNameString = "*";
        String lastNameString = "*";

        if ( firstName != null )
        {
            firstNameString = firstName+"*";
        }

        if ( lastName != null )
        {
            lastNameString = lastName+"*";
        }

        NSArray bindings =
            new NSArray( new Object [] { firstNameString, lastNameString } );

        EOQualifier qualifier =
            EOQualifier.qualifierWithQualifierFormat(
                "firstName like %@ and lastName like %@", bindings );

        EOSortOrdering lastNameSortOrdering =
            EOSortOrdering.sortOrderingWithKey(
            "lastName", EOSortOrdering.CompareAscending);
        EOSortOrdering firstNameSortOrdering =
            EOSortOrdering.sortOrderingWithKey(
```

Listing 6.5

Continued

```
            "firstName", EOSortOrdering.CompareAscending);
        NSArray sortOrderings =
            new NSArray( new Object[]
            {lastNameSortOrdering, firstNameSortOrdering} );

        EOFetchSpecification fetchSpec =
            new EOFetchSpecification( "Customer", qualifier, sortOrderings );

        EOEditingContext ec = this.session().defaultEditingContext();

        customers = ec.objectsWithFetchSpecification( fetchSpec );

        return null;
    }

}
```

A WORepetition is used to display the first and last names along with the Member Since attributes for all the customers returned, as shown in Figure 6.3.

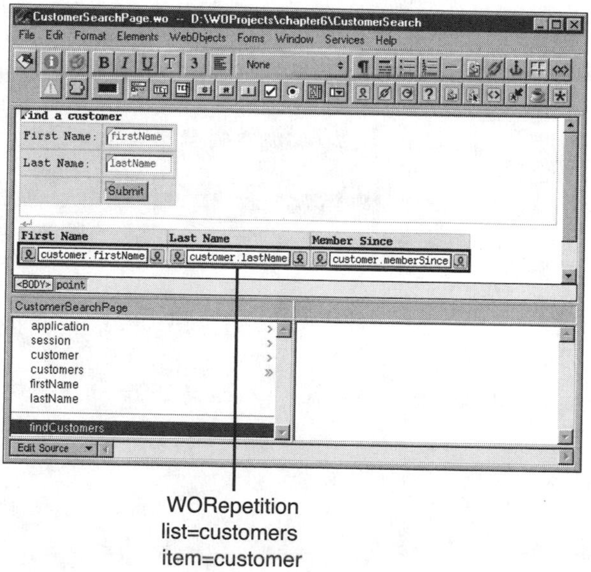

WORepetition
list=customers
item=customer

Figure 6.3

The WORepetition *for the* CustomerSearchPage.

Model-Based Fetch Specifications

As much fun as it is to code, sometimes it's better to let a tool do some of the job for you. It is important to understand the relationship between the editing context, fetch specification, and qualifiers, but it is not necessarily important to code it by hand every time.

Using EOModeler, fetch specifications can be created as part of the model. The big advantage this brings is that the developer now has a tool to aid in the creation of these fetch specifications.

Creating a Fetch Specification Using EOModeler

Fetch specifications are associated with entities in EOModeler. For the customer search example, the programmatically created fetch specification could be replaced with one that was created in the model. This is done by selecting the Customer entity in EOModeler and clicking the New Fetch Specification button as shown in Figure 6.4, or by selecting the Property, Add Fetch Specification menu item.

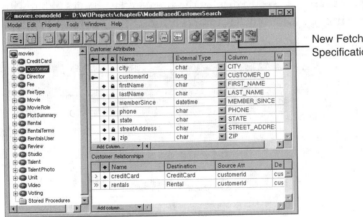

Figure 6.4
Use the New Fetch Specification button to add a fetch specification to an Entity.

The first thing that you will want to do is to change the name of the qualifier. In Figure 6.5, the name has been set to firstNameLastNameFetchSpec. This is a finicky part of the EOModeler; you must make sure to press the Enter key after changing the qualifier name. If you don't, the name will not be saved.

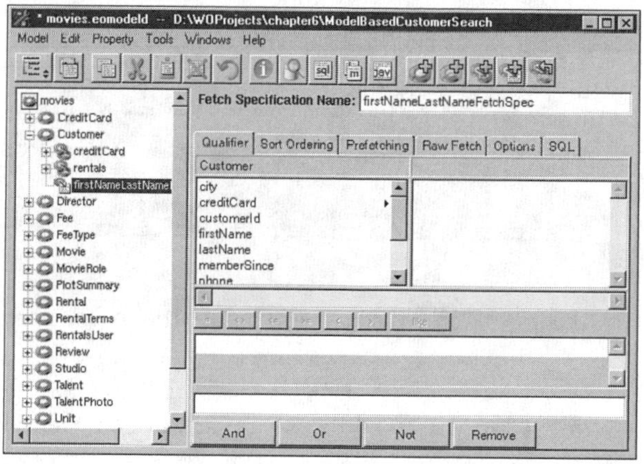

Figure 6.5
The fetch specification editing panel.

Modifying the Qualifier

The qualifier can be modified by associating attributes with operators and values in EOModeler. Complex qualifiers can be created by clicking on the And, Or, and Not buttons. For example, to specify a qualifier in which the last name is like R*, double-click the lastName attribute, click the Like button, and then type in 'R*'. For this to work correctly, you must click on the top line in the bottom part of the window before double-clicking attributes and operators.

When creating more complex queries that include And and Or operators, EOModeler will add parentheses appropriately, as shown in Figure 6.6. To end editing, click anywhere else in EOModeler.

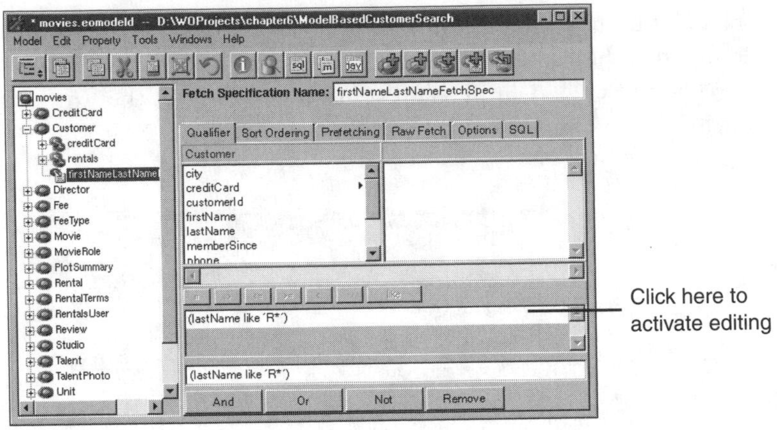

Click here to
activate editing

Figure 6.6
*Editing the qualifier of a model-based fetch specification. The parentheses will be automatically
added.*

There's hardly a time when you would want to hard-code a value like R*; this is usually
entered at runtime. As when using the qualifierWithQualifierFormat method in code,
substitution items can be specified in EOModeler's qualifiers. However, instead of
specifying an NSArray of values to be substituted, an NSDictionary is specified. To
specify a placeholder for substitution, use a dollar sign in front of a term. In Figure 6.7,
notice the text lastName like $lastNameValue. This indicates that an NSDictionary
containing a key equal to the string "lastNameValue" will be provided at runtime. The
qualifier will use the value associated with that key to qualify the statement.

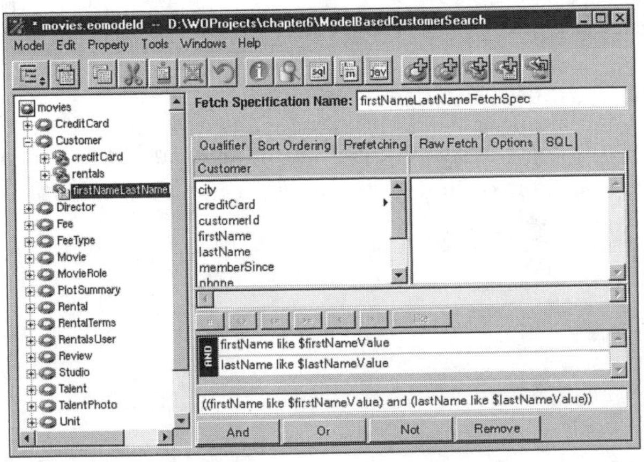

Figure 6.7
Using substitution values in a model-based fetch specification.

Modifying the Sort Ordering

Click the Sort Ordering tab to modify the sort ordering. Double-click on attributes to add them to the sort ordering, as shown in Figure 6.8.

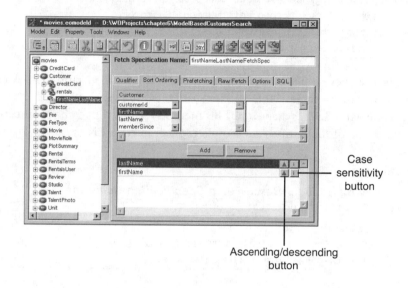

Figure 6.8

The type of ordering can be set to ascending or descending, along with the case sensitivity.

As you might notice, there are a number of other options for creating fetch specifications. These options are covered in different parts of the book.

Retrieving the Fetch Specification

The goal of this exercise is to reduce the amount of work done on the coding side. A fetch specification that is created in EOModeler is represented by an EOFetchSpecification object. This object is located inside the EOF object graph, so it will require some work to retrieve and use. The fetch specification is located in the EOEntity object that is associated with the entity that contained the fetch specification. In the previous example, this entity was the Customer entity. The EOEntity object can be retrieved from the EOModel object, which stores all the information in the model that you have been updating in EOModeler. It is actually easier to retrieve the entity directly from the EOModelGroup. An EOModelGroup object is created for your application because a project can store multiple models, and the model group contains these models. The code for retrieving a model-based fetch specification is given in Listing 6.6.

Listing 6.6

Retrieving a Model-Based Fetch Specification by Using the Model Group and Entity Classes

```
EOModelGroup group = EOModelGroup.defaultGroup();
EOEntity entity = group.entityNamed("Customer");
EOFetchSpecification fetchSpec =
    entity.fetchSpecificationNamed( "firstNameLastNameFetchSpec" );
```

Luckily, there are multiple ways to retrieve the fetch specification. Another way is to use a static method in the `EOFetchSpecification` class called `fetchSpecificationNamed()`. This method returns the fetch specification when given the name of the entity. An example is given in code Listing 6.7.

Listing 6.7

Retrieving a Model-Based Fetch Specification Using the `fetchSpecificationNamed()` *Method*

```
EOFetchSpecification fetchSpec =
    EOFetchSpecification.fetchSpecificationNamed(
    "firstNameLastNameFetchSpec", "Customer" );
```

Binding in Code

After the fetch specification is retrieved, the bindings for the substitution values must be made using an `NSDictionary`. This can be done by creating an `NSMutableDictionary` that contains keys with the same names that you supplied in the fetch specification, but without the dollar sign. To substitute these values, use the `fetchSpecificationWithQualifierBindings()` method in the `EOFetchSpecification` class to create a new fetch specification with the correct bindings. Listing 6.8 demonstrates creating an `NSMutableDictionary` that can be used for the `firstNameLastNameFetchSpec`.

Listing 6.8

Substituting Values in a Model-Based Fetch Specification

```
NSMutableDictionary queryBindings = new NSMutableDictionary();

if ( firstName != null )
{
```

Listing 6.8

Continued

```
    queryBindings.setObjectForKey(firstName+"*", "firstNameValue");
}

if ( lastName != null )
{
    queryBindings.setObjectForKey(lastName+"*", "lastNameValue");
}

fetchSpec = fetchSpec.fetchSpecificationWithQualifierBindings( queryBindings );

EOEditingContext ec = this.session().defaultEditingContext();
customers = ec.objectsWithFetchSpecification( fetchSpec );
```

Notice that if the user does not enter values for the first and last names, the key-value pair is left out of the dictionary. This causes that part of the qualifier to be dropped, which is what we want. There are certain cases that you want all substitution values to be supplied, and that can be set in EOModeler. In the Options tab for the fetch specification, select the Require All Variable Bindings to require all variable bindings to be supplied. Again, this isn't desirable here based on the type of search we are using.

Binding Using WOBuilder

The steps for creating an `NSMutableDictionary` and populating it from instance variable are still somewhat cumbersome, but there is an alternative. If the dictionary is an instance variable and is created as part of the component's constructor, the substitution keys can be bound directly in WebObjects Builder. An example of this is given in Listing 6.9.

Listing 6.9

Using the Query Bindings as an Instance Variable

```
import com.apple.yellow.foundation.*;
import com.apple.yellow.webobjects.*;
import com.apple.yellow.eocontrol.*;
import com.apple.yellow.eoaccess.*;

public class CustomerSearchPage extends WOComponent {
```

Listing 6.9

Continued

```
/** @TypeInfo Customer */
protected EOEnterpriseObject customer;

/** @TypeInfo Customer */
protected NSArray customers;
protected String firstName;
protected String lastName;

NSMutableDictionary queryBindings;

public CustomerSearchPage()
{
    queryBindings = new NSMutableDictionary();
}

public WOComponent findCustomers()
{

    EOFetchSpecification fetchSpec =
        EOFetchSpecification.fetchSpecificationNamed(
        "firstNameLastNameFetchSpec", "Customer" );

    fetchSpec =
        fetchSpec.fetchSpecificationWithQualifierBindings( queryBindings );

    EOEditingContext ec = this.session().defaultEditingContext();
    customers = ec.objectsWithFetchSpecification( fetchSpec );

    return null;
}
}
```

Because WebObjects uses key-value pairs to resolve bindings, an NSMutableDictionary can be used, but the keys must be entered manually. For example, one of the keys for the dictionary is the lastNameValue. If the dictionary is called bindingsDictionary, the WOTextField's value binding is set to bindingsDictionary.lastNameValue (see Figure 6.9).

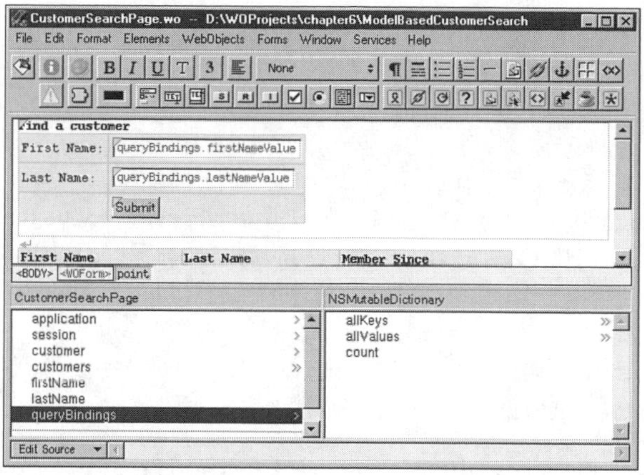

Figure 6.9
Setting the WOTextField's *value bindings to the* queryBindings *dictionary keys.*

The action method at this point would be smaller than previously described. The complete code for the component class at this point is given in Listing 6.9.

Note that this slightly changes the functionality of the component. The user is now required to enter the asterisk because it is not manually appended. It is not desirable for this query because it uses the like operator, but this technique would work for other operators, such as =, >, and <.

Also notice that the like operator for OpenBase Lite is a case-insensitive like, whereas the like operator for most other relational databases is case sensitive.

Using EOUtilities

Another way to retrieve the fetch specification is through the EOUtilities class, which contains a set of static methods that are essentially convenience methods for common functionality.

One method that is applicable for this example is objectsWithFetchSpecificationAndBindings(). This method requires the editing context, entity name, fetch specification name, and the bindings dictionary as parameters. This replaces some of the code that was previously written, and reduces the action method to two lines, as shown in Listing 6.10.

Listing 6.10

Using an `EOUtilities` *Method to Execute the Fetch Specification*

```
public WOComponent findCustomers()
{

    EOEditingContext ec = this.session().defaultEditingContext();
    customers = EOUtilities.objectsWithFetchSpecificationAndBindings(
        ec, "Customer", "firstNameLastNameFetchSpec", queryBindings );

    return null;
}
```

The `EOUtilities` class contains a number of methods that can be used in place of more cumbersome methods. Note that the `EOUtilities` class is in the `com.apple.yellow.eoaccess` package. You will probably need to import that package at the top of your file.

In-Memory Ordering

Have you ever this point, you know enough about qualifiers, editing contexts, and ordering arrays to make that happen. However, what if you do not want to make another trip to the database? What if you just want to reorder the items in memory? The `EOSortOrdering` class contains methods either to sort an array in place or to return an ordered array based on the initial array. Both these methods use `EOSortOrdering` objects, so you can reuse the ones created by hand.

The `EOSortOrdering.sortedArrayUsingKeyOrderArray()` method creates an `NSArray` that contains a set of ordered objects based on an existing `NSArray`. This method requires two parameters: the first parameter is the array to be ordered, and the second is an `NSArray` of `EOSortOrderings`. The method returns an ordered `NSArray` that contains the same objects as the `NSArray` that was given.

The `EOSortOrdering.sortArrayUsingKeyOrderArray()` method is similar, except the array is ordered in place. The first parameter is an `NSMutableArray` that will be ordered after the method completes. The second parameter is the `NSArray` of `EOSortOrdering` objects that will determine how the mutable array is to be ordered.

To demonstrate how this could work, you can add `WOHyperlinks` to the column headers for the table of customers, as shown in Figure 6.10. Clicking a column header will reorder the array based on the column clicked.

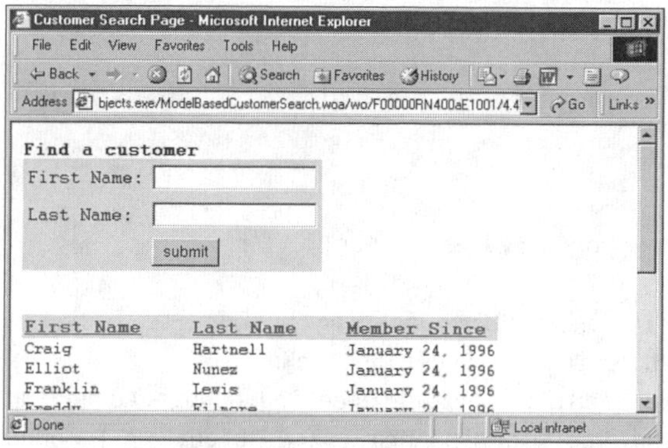

Figure 6.10
The column headers are now hyperlinks. Clicking one will reorder the resultset.

Three action methods will also be created and bound to the action bindings for the hyperlinks. Each action method will reorder the array of customers appropriately and redisplay the page. The code for these three action methods is given in Listing 6.11.

Listing 6.11
The Action Methods to Reorder the Customer Resultset

```
public WOComponent orderByFirstName()
{
    EOSortOrdering firstNameOrdering =
        EOSortOrdering.sortOrderingWithKey(
        "firstName", EOSortOrdering.CompareAscending);
    NSArray orderings = new NSArray( new Object [] { firstNameOrdering } );
    customers =
        EOSortOrdering.sortedArrayUsingKeyOrderArray( customers, orderings );


    return null;
}

public WOComponent orderByLastName()
{
    EOSortOrdering lastNameOrdering =
        EOSortOrdering.sortOrderingWithKey(
            "lastName", EOSortOrdering.CompareAscending);
    NSArray orderings = new NSArray( new Object [] { lastNameOrdering } );
    customers =
        EOSortOrdering.sortedArrayUsingKeyOrderArray( customers, orderings );
```

Listing 6.11

Continued

```
    return null;
}

public WOComponent orderByMemberSince()
{
    EOSortOrdering memberSinceOrdering =
        EOSortOrdering.sortOrderingWithKey(
            "memberSince", EOSortOrdering.CompareAscending);
    NSArray orderings = new NSArray( new Object [] { memberSinceOrdering } );
    customers =
        EOSortOrdering.sortedArrayUsingKeyOrderArray( customers, orderings );

    return null;
}
```

As you can see, ordering objects in memory opens up a number of possibilities.

Fetching Raw Rows

Sometimes, the standard fetch specification operators and qualifiers just will not work. For example, there's no way to specify a database aggregation such as sum, avg, max, or min. These aggregations can be determined in memory after retrieving all the records, but that might be unnecessarily costly, especially if you're only interested in the aggregations and not the underlying data. Also, the standard fetch specifications do not allow for common SQL statements such as group bys, nested queries, and distinct queries. For these types of queries, we need to use a "raw row" fetch specification.

A raw row fetch specification enables you to specify part of the entity to be returned. For example, you could return only the first and last names, if that's all that you are interested in. Also, a raw row fetch specification enables you to specify SQL directly, allowing you to write any SQL query that is supported by the underlying database. The disadvantage is that after you start placing SQL in your application, you are tied to the underlying database, and you must port your application if you want to change databases.

Another difference of raw row fetching is that the objects returned are not enterprise objects. An NSArray of NSDictionarys is now returned. Each entry in the NSArray represents a row in the database as an NSDictionary. The keys of the NSDictionary for a row represent the columns from the select statement, and the values represent the values returned.

The objects returned can be used as read-only objects only; you cannot change their contents. This is an advantage in that the overhead associated with creating enterprise objects is reduced. This overhead is discussed in Chapter 7, "Writing Enterprise Objects Classes."

So, to use a raw row fetch specification, the first step is to create the fetch specification in EOModeler. Select the Raw Fetch tab to see the fetch specification options.

Note

A programmatically created fetch specification can also be configured to return raw rows, but it's easier to create one in EOModler.

The Raw Fetch tab has three options that are self-explanatory: Fetch Enterprise Objects, Fetch All Attributes as Raw Rows, and Fetch Specified Attributes as Raw Rows. For example, to display the distinct ratings for the Movie entity, select the Fetch Specified Attributes as Raw Rows option, and remove all the attributes except rated, as shown in Figure 6.11.

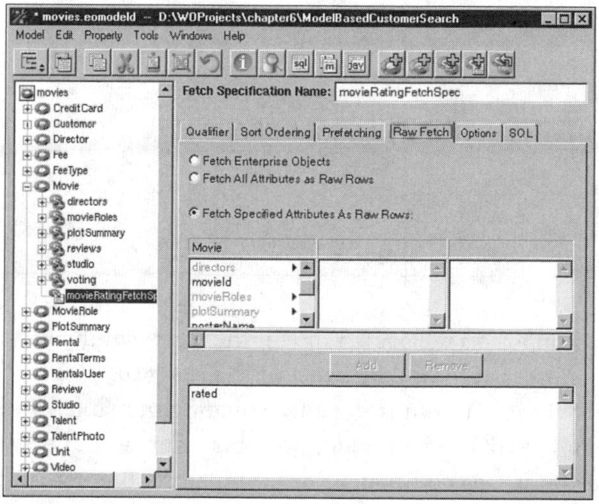

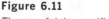

Figure 6.11
The raw fetch specification options.

To make the fetch a distinct fetch, select the Options tab, and enable the Fetch Distinct Rows check box as shown in Figure 6.12.

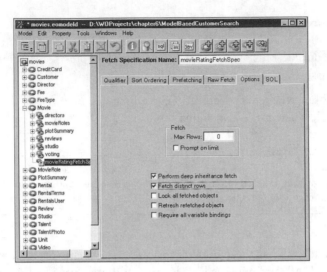

Figure 6.12
Selecting distinct rows.

These distinct movie ratings will be displayed in a new component called
`DistinctMovieRatingPage`. To support the fetch, a few keys will be required. Table 6.2
lists the required keys and their types.

Table 6.2
Keys Required to Display Distinct Movie Ratings

Key	Type
rating	NSDictionary
ratings	NSArray of NSDictionarys

These keys are bound to a `WORepetition` on the page. `rating` is bound to `item`, and
`ratings` is bound to `list`. Also, the value of the `WOString` inside the `WORepetition` is
bound to `rating.rated`. You must type this binding in manually because `rating` is an
`NSDictionary` and WebObjects Builder does not know what keys to display for it. The
`DistinctMovieRatingPage` component in WebObjects Builder is shown in Figure 6.13.

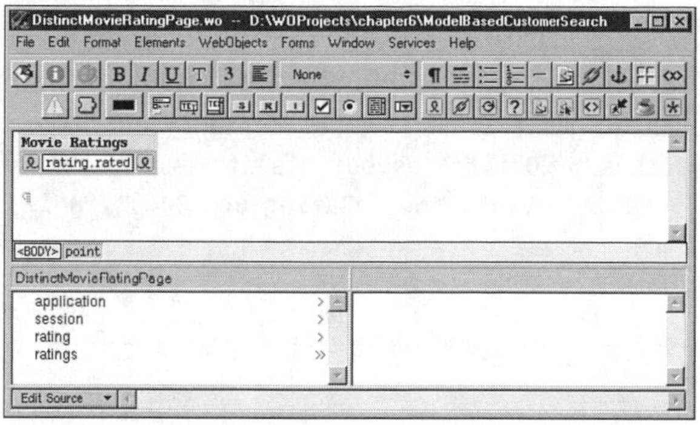

Figure 6.13

The DistinctMovieRatingPage *in WebObjects Builder.*

The code to retrieve these ratings is similar to the previous code; the difference is that it is placed in the awake() method. Because you don't want to retrieve these records every time the component is sent the awake() method, the objects are retrieved only if the array is null. This forces the objects to be retrieved only the first time awake() is called. The code for this component is given in Listing 6.12.

Listing 6.12

The DistinctMovieRatingPage.java File

```
// Generated by the WebObjects Wizard Mon Nov 13 11:13:10 US/Eastern 2000

import com.apple.yellow.foundation.*;
import com.apple.yellow.webobjects.*;
import com.apple.yellow.eocontrol.*;
import com.apple.yellow.eoaccess.*;

public class DistinctMovieRatingPage extends WOComponent
{

    /** @TypeInfo com.apple.yellow.foundation.NSDictionary */
    protected NSArray ratings;
    protected NSDictionary rating;

    public void awake()
    {
        super.awake();

        if ( ratings == null )
        {
```

Listing 6.12

Continued

```
            EOEditingContext ec = this.session().defaultEditingContext();
            ratings = EOUtilities.objectsWithFetchSpecificationAndBindings(
                ec, "Movie", "movieRatingFetchSpec", null );
        }
    }
}
```

Summary

So, now you know a couple of different ways to retrieve objects from the database. Display groups are useful for a number of different situations, but there are many times when they cannot be used. You will find that the information in this chapter will be useful in the upcoming chapters.

CHAPTER 7

WRITING ENTERPRISE OBJECTS CLASSES

A *pattern*, by definition, is something that has been recognized to repeat. This could be by design—for example, the pattern of waiting in line at a bank for the next teller—or it could be by cause and effect. Regardless, patterns are found everywhere we look, and the recognition of these patterns help us through life.

A *design pattern* can be defined as an observed occurrence of types of classes that fit into a pattern. The advantage of using a design pattern is that it represents a recognized, familiar, and effective way to solve a problem. A few design patterns are used heavily throughout the Apple frameworks: Delegation, Notification, and especially the Model-View-Controller patterns are used frequently.

This chapter discusses the *Model* part of the Model-View-Controller pattern, and how to implement this model using EOF.

Model-View-Controller

The Model-View-Controller design pattern designates three types of classes that are used in an application: the Model, View, and Controller classes. The View classes deal only with the user interface and have no knowledge of a specific domain. Sample view objects are the WOTextField, WOString, WORepetition, WOConditional, WOImage, and so on. The Model classes contain all the logic for a business domain, but have no knowledge of specific user interface objects. Sample Model classes for the Movies and Rentals database are Rental, Fee, RentalUser, and so on. These classes store code that contains specific business rules, such as charging a fee for a late rental, or determining that a rental is returned late. The controller objects connect the model and view objects. It is important to keep all the business logic out of the Controller classes. This is demonstrated in Figure 7.1.

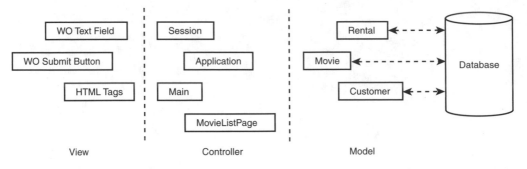

Figure 7.1
Model-View-Controller design pattern classes.

The advantage gained by using this design pattern is that the View and Model objects are reusable in different applications. For the most part, the Controller classes are not reusable, but some similarities in how views access models can be generalized. For more information on this and other design patterns, check out *Design Patterns: Elements of Reusable Object-Oriented Software* by Erich Gamma, et al, 1995 Addison-Wesley.

Writing Model Classes

EOModeler can be used to generate Java classes for your model. When you fetch rows from the database, the objects returned are instances of classes you write. Templates for these classes can be created in EOModeler.

Using EOModeler

To specify a custom class, open EOModeler and change the class name for an entity from EOGenericRecord to the class name of your choice. For example, change the class name for the Rental entity to Rental. At that point, click the Jav button in the toolbar to create the Java file as shown in Figure 7.2. You should be prompted for the directory to create the file, and if you place the file in the project directory, you will be asked whether you want to add the file to the project. At that point, click Yes and the file will be added.

The Class File

The class file that's generated contains accessor methods for all of the attributes that have the "class attribute" property set (the diamond in EOModeler). Also, methods are generated for all relationships. A sample class file is given in Listing 7.1.

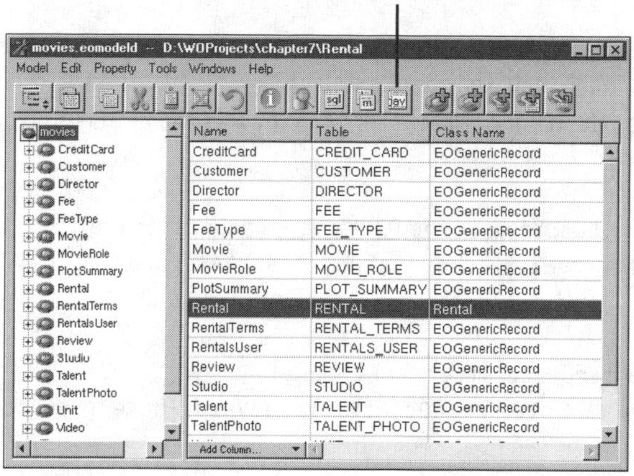

Create JavaFile icon

Figure 7.2
Setting the class for an entity.

Listing 7.1

The Generated Code for the Rental Class

```
// Rental.java
// Created on Tue Nov 14 10:44:50  2000 by Apple EOModeler Version 410

import com.apple.yellow.foundation.*;
import com.apple.yellow.eocontrol.*;
import java.util.*;
import java.math.BigDecimal;

public class Rental extends EOGenericRecord {

    public Rental() {
        super();
    }

    public NSGregorianDate dateOut() {
        return (NSGregorianDate)storedValueForKey("dateOut");
    }

    public void setDateOut(NSGregorianDate value) {
        takeStoredValueForKey(value, "dateOut");
    }
```

Listing 7.1

Continued

```
public NSGregorianDate dateReturned() {
    return (NSGregorianDate)storedValueForKey("dateReturned");
}

public void setDateReturned(NSGregorianDate value) {
    takeStoredValueForKey(value, "dateReturned");
}

public EOEnterpriseObject customer() {
    return (EOEnterpriseObject)storedValueForKey("customer");
}

public void setCustomer(EOEnterpriseObject value) {
    takeStoredValueForKey(value, "customer");
}

public EOEnterpriseObject unit() {
    return (EOEnterpriseObject)storedValueForKey("unit");
}

public void setUnit(EOEnterpriseObject value) {
    takeStoredValueForKey(value, "unit");
}

public NSArray fees() {
    return (NSArray)storedValueForKey("fees");
}

public void setFees(NSMutableArray value) {
    takeStoredValueForKey(value, "fees");
}

public void addToFees(EOEnterpriseObject object) {
    NSMutableArray array = (NSMutableArray)fees();

    willChange();
    array.addObject(object);
}
```

Listing 7.1

Continued

```
public void removeFromFees(EOEnterpriseObject object) {
    NSMutableArray array = (NSMutableArray)fees();

    willChange();
    array.removeObject(object);
}
}
```

In Listing 7.1, notice that the class that is created is a subclass of EOGenericRecord. The only requirement for this class is that it implements the EOEnterpriseObject interface, found in the EOControl framework. It is, however, much easier simply to subclass EOGenericRecord, inheriting all the basic utility functionality for key-value coding and the communication with the EOEditingContext.

Also, notice that the accessor methods for the attributes (dateOut and dateReturned) use the storedValueForKey() and takeStoredValueForKey() methods to set and retrieve the properties for these attributes. It is important that your accessor methods use these stored value methods and not the valueForKey() and the takeValueForKey() methods. The takeValueForKey() and the valueForKey() methods will eventually call your accessor methods, which has the potential for recursive disaster if you then use them in your accessor methods. The bottom line is this: Don't mess with the accessor methods that EOModeler generates.

The Template

The class file that is created uses a template for the general file format and the definition of the entity for the specific attributes that are added. The template file used is called EOJavaClass.template, and it is found in the Supporting Files suitcase. The majority of this file should not be modified, but additional comments that include copyright information and possibly Javadoc comments could be included. Also, a common modification is to change the naming convention for the "get" accessor methods to the standard Java convention. The default naming convention is for the "get" accessor methods to have the same name as the property; that is, the name property is correlated with accessor methods called setName() and name(). Listing 7.2 shows an example of these changes placed in the template file.

Listing 7.2

Partial Listing of Modified EOJavaClass.template File, with a Copyright at the Top, Set Methods Renamed, and Javadoc-Style Comments

```
##// TEMPLATEVERSION 1.25
##// You may customize this file to modify the
##// templates generated in this project.
// $entity.classNameWithoutPackage$.java
// Created on $date$ by Apple $eomVersion$
// Copyright 2000, Macmillan publishing
// The code in this book is to be used for
// the sole purpose of learning how to
// develop WebObjects applications and no
// warrenties are given, implied or otherwise

##loop $entity.classPackage$
package $property$;

##end
import com.apple.yellow.foundation.*;
import com.apple.yellow.eocontrol.*;
import java.util.*;
import java.math.BigDecimal;

public class $entity.classNameWithoutPackage$
    extends $entity.javaParentClassName$
{

    /**
     * Default constructor generated by EOModeler
     */
    public $entity.classNameWithoutPackage$()
    {
        super();
    }

##loop $entity.classAttributes$

    /**
     * Access method for retrieving the $property.name$ attribute.
     * Generated by EOModeler
     */
    public $property.javaValueClassName$ get$property.name$()
    {
```

Listing 7.2

Continued

```
            return ($property.javaValueClassName$)
                storedValueForKey("$property.name$");
        }


    /**
      * Access method for setting the $property.name$ attribute
      * Generated by EOModeler
      *
      * @param value    The value to set the attribute to.
      *                  After this method call,
      *                  the attribute will retain this value.
      */
    public void set$property.name$($property.javaValueClassName$ value)
    {
        takeStoredValueForKey(value, "$property.name$");
    }
##end
```

When making changes to the method names generated in the EOJavaClass.template file, remember to make changes to dependent methods. For example, the addTo<*to-many relationship*>() method uses the <*to-many relationship*>() method. So, if you change the name of the <*to-many relationship*>(), also change any references to that method.

Modifying the Class File

The goal is to customize your class files. By doing this, you are creating an environment in which the objects that are retrieved from the database are smart objects. Some examples of the types of changes that you would make to these files range from convenience methods that return concatenated strings to methods that calculate values based on intricate relationships. The main thing to remember when modifying the class files is to not include any references to Control or View classes.

The best way to describe adding this logic to enterprise objects is to illustrate an example. The example given is to write the business logic for checking in and out videos. This example starts by adding convenience methods and moves to adding more complex methods that require interaction between a number of different classes.

Adding a Constructor

One example is to modify the Rental class to add a constructor in preparation for adding check-out functionality to the application. It would be useful to have a constructor that creates a Rental given a Customer, Unit, and date out. The relationships for the Rental class are given in Figure 7.3.

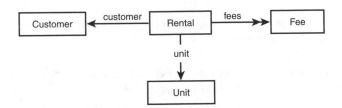

Figure 7.3
Relationships for the Rental class.

The Customer is the person who rents the video; the Unit is the actual videotape. There is a to-one relationship between Unit to Video, and another to-one relationship from Video to Movie. The code for the constructor is given in Listing 7.3.

Listing 7.3

Adding a Constructor to the Rental Class

```
public Rental( Customer customer, Unit unit, NSGregorianDate dateOut )
{
    this.setCustomer( customer );
    this.setUnit( unit );
    this.setDateOut( dateOut );
}
```

This constructor assumes that classes for Customer and Unit have also been created. If they have not been, this would still work by setting the type or both parameters to EOEnterpriseObject. This constructor would qualify as a convenience method; it doesn't really give us anything we couldn't do otherwise.

Other Convenience Methods

It is common to create other convenience methods for your class. For example, the Rental's title and video objects must be retrieved a number of times. It would be good to create access methods for these objects, and the code for this is given in Listing 7.4.

Listing 7.4

Other Convenience Methods for the Rental Class

```
public String movieTitle()
{
    return (String)this.valueForKeyPath( "unit.video.movie.title" );
}

public Video video()
{
    return (Video)this.valueForKeyPath( "unit.video" );
}

public Number price()
{
    return (Number)this.valueForKeyPath( "unit.video.rentalTerms.cost" );
}
```

These methods use the `valueForKeyPath()` method, which uses key-value coding to traverse relationships. This is the same method that is used to resolve bindings in WebObjects Builder.

Calculating Fees

A number of fees are associated with the Rental application, which are represented by Fee objects. The fees include a to-one relationship to `FeeType`, and there are two types of fees: Rent and Late. The Fee objects are associated with a Rental object through a to-many relationship. These relationships are shown in Figure 7.4.

Figure 7.4

Rental class relationships.

The first thing to do is to create methods that return Fee objects. These would be created as static methods in the Fee class called `lateFeeForRental()` and `rentalFeeForRental()`. Given a Rental object, these fees return an appropriate Fee object. Both of these methods must go to the database to get the appropriate `FeeType` object and associate it with the Fee before returning it. Listing 7.5 gives an example of the `feeTypeForString()` method that will return a FeeType object.

Listing 7.5

The `feeTypeForString()` *Method in the Fee.java Class*

```
public final static String RENTAL_FEE_TYPE="Rent";
public final static String LATE_FEE_TYPE="Late";

public static FeeType feeTypeForString( EOEditingContext ec, String feeType )
{
    NSArray values = new NSArray( new Object[] { feeType } );
    EOQualifier qualifier =
        EOQualifier.qualifierWithQualifierFormat( "feeType=%@", values );

    EOFetchSpecification fetchSpec =
        new EOFetchSpecification( "FeeType", qualifier, null );

    NSArray results = ec.objectsWithFetchSpecification( fetchSpec );

    if ( results.count() > 0 )
    {
        return (FeeType)results.objectAtIndex(0);
    }
    return null;
}
```

Notice the static final Strings listed at the top of Listing 7.5. These are the same values that are found in the database and will be used by the other methods when calling the `feeTypeForString()` method. Also notice that the method takes an `EOEditingContext` as the first parameter. This is common practice for static methods, such as those found in `EOUtilities`, that access the database.

Now the static methods to return rental and late fees can be created. These are also static methods in the Fee class, and are given in Listing 7.6.

Listing 7.6

The `lateFeeForRental()` *and* `rentalFeeForRental()` *Methods in the Fee.java Class*

```
public static Fee lateFeeForRental( EOEditingContext ec, Rental rental )
{
    Fee fee = new Fee();
    fee.setRental( rental );
```

Listing 7.6

Continued

```
        fee.setFeeType( feeTypeForString( ec, LATE_FEE_TYPE ) );
        fee.setAmount( new Double(rental.price().doubleValue()*2.0) );

    return fee;
    }

    public static Fee rentalFeeForRental( EOEditingContext ec, Rental rental )
    {
        Fee fee = new Fee();
        fee.setRental( rental );
        fee.setFeeType( feeTypeForString( ec, RENTAL_FEE_TYPE ) );
        fee.setAmount( rental.price() );

        return fee;
    }
```

Adding these methods will make it easier to create the methods on the Rental class for checking in and out videos. To do this, we need to insert Fees into the database. The first step in doing this is to insert the object into the EOEditingContext. This is done by calling the editing context's insertObject() method. This method inserts the object into the editing context with a temporary primary key, but does not insert the object in the database. To complete the insertion, call the EOEditingContext's saveChanges() method. For an insert, the primary key will then be determined using the next available primary key, and the insert statement is generated and sent to the database. This is normally done in a controller class to allow the controller to determine when the data is actually made persistent. saveChanges() will be discussed later in the chapter.

Rental Check-Out/Check-In

The next step is to write the rental check-out method, which will create the associated Fee objects and insert them into the editing context. This code is given in Listing 7.7.

Listing 7.7

The checkOut() *Method in the Rental Class*

```
public void checkOut( NSGregorianDate checkOutDate )
{
    this.setDateOut( checkOutDate );
    Fee fee = Fee.rentalFeeForRental( this.editingContext(), this );
```

Listing 7.7

Continued

```
        this.editingContext().insertObject( fee );
        this.addToFees( fee );
}
```

The checkIn() method is similar, but contains the logic to determine whether a late fee should be created. This code is given in Listing 7.8.

Listing 7.8

The checkIn() *Method in the Rental Class*

```
public void checkIn( NSGregorianDate checkInDate )
        throws   java.lang.IllegalArgumentException,
                 java.lang.IllegalStateException
{
    // check for exception conditions
    if ( this.dateOut() == null )
    {
        throw new IllegalStateException(
            "The check-out date cannot be null when checking in a Rental" );
    }
    if ( checkInDate.earlierDate( this.dateOut() ) == checkInDate )
    {
        throw new IllegalArgumentException(
            "The check-in date cannot be before the check-out date" );
    }

    // retrieve the time difference
    NSGregorianDate.IntRef days = new NSGregorianDate.IntRef();
    checkInDate.gregorianUnitsSinceDate(
        this.dateOut(), null, null, days, null, null, null );
    int daysOut = days.value;

    // retrieve the RentalTerms
    RentalTerms terms = this.video().rentalTerms();
    int rentalLength = terms.checkOutLength().intValue();

    // determine fees
    if ( daysOut > rentalLength )
    {
```

Listing 7.8

Continued

```
        Fee lateFee = Fee.lateFeeForRental(this.editingContext(), this);
        this.editingContext().insertObject( lateFee );
        this.addToFees( lateFee );
    }


    // set the check-in date
    this.setDateReturned( checkInDate );
}
```

This method is doing quite a bit. First, it makes sure that the `checkOut` date is not `null`. If it is, the code throws an `IllegalStateException`. This is a standard exception that should be thrown if a method is called in an object in which the state is invalid. In our case, to check in a Rental, it must be checked out!

The second check is that the `checkIn` date is after the `checkOut` date. If not, an `IllegalArgumentException` is thrown. Again, this is a standard Java exception that should be thrown when the value of an argument is not valid.

This method makes heavy use of the `NSGregorianDate`, which is a subclass of the `NSDate`. The first method used is `earlierDate()`. This method is given an `NSGregorianDate` as a parameter and returns the object that represents the earlier date. In this case, if the `checkIn` date is earlier than the `checkOut` date, the method throws an exception.

The next method used is the `gregorianUnitsSinceDate()`, which is used to determine the number of days between the two dates. The first parameter is the date to compare, and the rest of the parameters represent the number of Gregorian units that differentiate the two dates. The first parameter is the number of years, the second is the number of months, and so on. Because the Java language does not support passing primitive types by reference, these parameters are instances of `NSGregorianDate`. `IntRef`, which is an inner class. This class has one public instance variable, called `value`, which will contain the value to be passed by reference. Because we are concerned with only the number of days that are different, only the third parameter is given.

The rest of this example involves creating a WebObjects user interface to modify these classes, which will be left as an exercise for the reader. The complete solution is located in the "Rental" project on the Web site for the book, `http://www.wowack.com`.

Changing the Model

Changes to the model could occur at any time during the development process. These changes could range from adding relationships or attributes to an existing entity to adding entities or changing the class for an entity. These changes must also be reflected in the code associated with the entity.

There are a couple of ways to change the code; one way is to modify the code by hand, based on the changes in the model. As you become more experienced, this might be how you will want to handle these changes. Another way is to regenerate the class files and compare them in FileMerge.

Using FileMerge

FileMerge is a utility that enables you to compare the contents of two files and choose what to keep and what to discard. FileMerge graphically displays the differences between the two files. When you generate a file from EOModeler that already exists, you have the option of overwriting the existing file, canceling the operation, or comparing the new and existing files in FileMerge as shown in Figure 7.5.

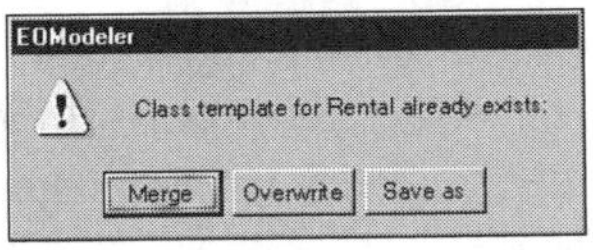

Figure 7.5
When trying to generate a class file that already exists in EOModeler, you are given the option to merge the files.

By selecting the Merge button, the new and existing files are then opened in FileMerge. The existing file appears on the right and the new file is on the left as shown in Figure 7.6.

The differences between the files are marked with a gray background, and have arrows that denote which version will be retained after the files are merged. Initially, all arrows point to the new file, and you must change this to keep the code you have written! You can change the side that is retained by selecting the difference (by clicking on the arrow) and choosing an operation from the drop-down menu at the bottom-right corner of the window. Table 7.1 lists the available operations.

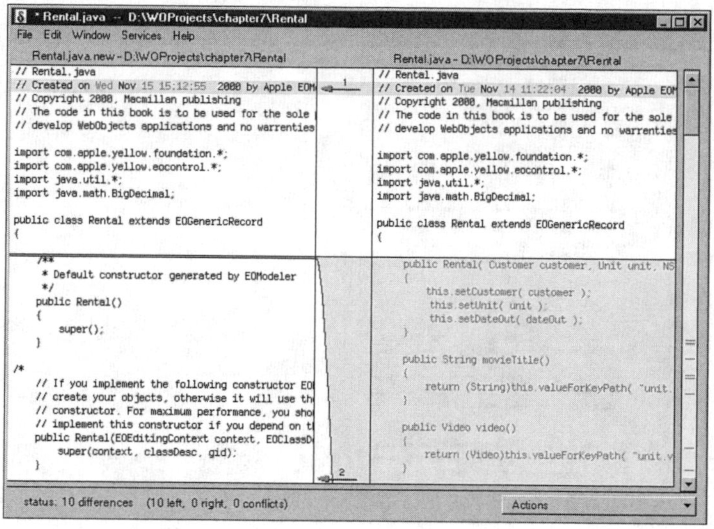

Figure 7.6

Two versions of the Rental class in FileMerge. The existing file is on the right, and the newly created file is on the left.

Table 7.1

FileMerge Operations

Choose Left	Keeps the contents in the left window for the selected difference; discards what is in the right window
Choose Right	Keeps the contents of the right window; discards what is in the left window
Choose Both (Left First)	Keeps both sides, but places the contents of the left side first
Choose Both (Right First)	Keeps both sides, but places the contents of the right window before the left window
Choose Neither	Discards the content from both sides

Make sure to select the correct difference for any code you have written. If you do not select the appropriate differences as highlighted in Figure 7.7, all the code written earlier in the chapter would be lost!

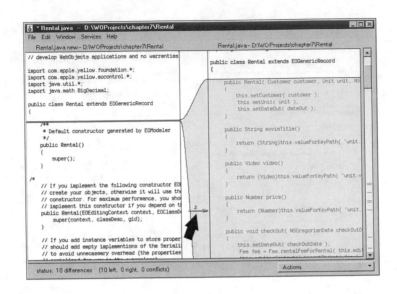

Figure 7.7
The code that was manually edited is selected.

After you're finished selecting the differences to keep, simply save the merge by selecting the File, Save menu item.

Specifying a Package

Most experienced Java developers are used to partitioning their classes into different package name spaces. A separate package is created for different projects, and within each project, packages are used to organize the model, view, and controller classes. So far, all our classes have been in the default package. This does not have to be the case for the Enterprise classes, however. To specify that your class is in a different package, simply place the fully qualified package name as the class of your entity as shown in Figure 7.8.

When the Enterprise class is created from EOModeler, the appropriate package syntax will be present, and accessing the class will require the package syntax. Unlike other Java IDEs, packages do not represent a directory structure until the code is built. In other words, all the classes are placed in the project directory regardless of the package name. When the application is built, the code is copied to the temporary folder (probably c:\temp on Windows) in the appropriate directory structure and then compiled and packaged as a jar file.

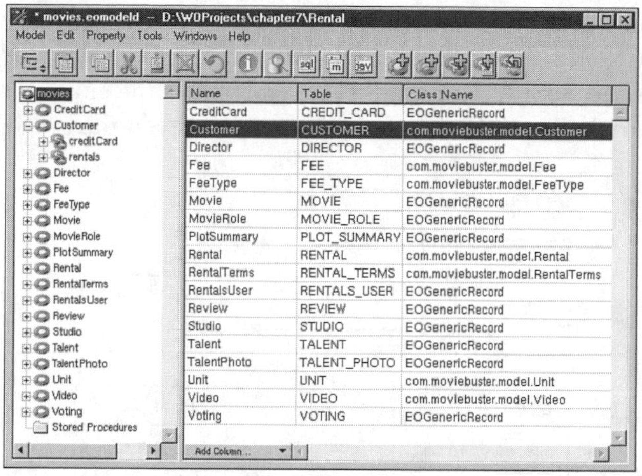

Figure 7.8
Placing the EO classes in a package.

EOF Relationships

One of the great features of EOF is the seamless integration of the mapping between relationships in the database and in code. The to-one relationships are simple attributes with "set" and "get" access methods. To-many relationships are mapped to an NSArray of objects, with access methods to add objects to the array and remove objects from the array, along with the "set" and "get" access methods. But before examining the code that is created for these types of relationships, it is important to understand the concept of faulting.

Faulting

Let's say that you are retrieving all objects for the Movie entity for the purpose of displaying the titles in a WODisplayGroup. Movie has a to-many relationship to the Director entity, which has a to-one relationship to the Talent entity. Given the description of the way relationships work, you can imagine that retrieving these Movie objects would, in turn, retrieve the Director objects, which would then retrieve the Talent objects. So, according to this scenario, half of the database would be retrieved into memory just to display the movie titles. This obviously is not how EOF works.

For the most part, objects are "lazily" retrieved from the database, meaning that they are retrieved when needed (see Figure 7.9). When the Movie objects are initially fetched, all the relationships are faults. These *faults* are simply placeholders for objects that are still in the database. For example, there is a relationship between the Movie entity and the Studio entity called studio. When the movies are fetched, each movie has a fault for the studio relationship. This fault stores the entity for the fault (Studio) and the primary key to use (taken from the foreign key in the movie).

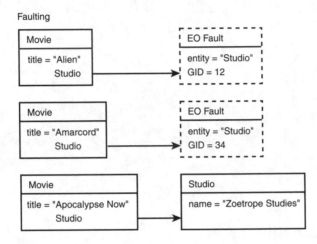

Figure 7.9
Objects for a relationship are lazily retrieved, or faulted.

When information is requested from the fault, EOF retrieves the appropriate object(s) from the database. This is known as *tripping* the fault.

Modifying Relationships

The relationships are accessed using the methods created when the class file was generated by EOModeler. An example can be found in Listing 7.1, earlier in the chapter.

The trick to modifying relationships is to keep any back-relationships intact. As given in an earlier example in this chapter, there is a to-one relationship from the Fee entity to the Rental entity called rental. There is also a to-many relationship from Rental to Fee called fees. When setting the value for one relationship, the other one should also be set. This maintenance was performed by both classes in the previous example. The Fee class sets the associated Rental in the `lateFeeForRental()` and `rentalFeeForRental()` static methods in Listing 7.6.

This could cause a potential problem if the model changes. Say, for example, the name of one of the relationships changes, or one of the relationships is removed. For example, if the relationship from Fee to Rental is removed, the code in Listing 7.6 would be invalid. It would be nice if a method existed that added an object to a relationship and set the back-relationship appropriately. There exists a method that is used for this purpose:

```
addObjectToBothSidesOfRelationshipWithKey()
```

This method takes the object to be added and the name of the relationship. For to-many relationships, the object is added to the key; for to-one relationships, the object is set. This method updates both sides of the relationship. For example, to add a Fee for a Rental, call this method on the Rental object, passing in the Fee object and the relationship name. The Rental object will be automatically set on the Fee. The `checkIn()` and `checkOut()` methods on the Rental class would be changed to accommodate this, as would the static methods in the Fee class. These modified methods are given in Listings 7.9 and 7.10.

Listing 7.9

Modified Versions of the Methods in the Fee Class. The Rental Is Not Being Set. This Assumes That It Will Be Set from the Rental Class

```
public static Fee lateFeeForRental( EOEditingContext ec, Rental rental )
{
    Fee fee = new Fee();
    fee.setFeeType( feeTypeForString( ec, LATE_FEE_TYPE ) );
    fee.setAmount( new Double(rental.price().doubleValue()*2.0) );

    return fee;
}


public static Fee rentalFeeForRental( EOEditingContext ec, Rental rental )
{
    Fee fee = new Fee();
    fee.setFeeType( feeTypeForString( ec, RENTAL_FEE_TYPE ) );
    fee.setAmount( rental.price() );

    return fee;
}
```

Listing 7.10

The New checkOut() *Method in the Rental Class Using*
addObjectToBothSidesOfRelationshipWithKey(), *Which Sets the Appropriate
Relationship in the Fee Object*

```
public void checkOut( NSGregorianDate checkOutDate )
{
    this.setDateOut( checkOutDate );
    Fee fee = Fee.rentalFeeForRental( this.editingContext(), this );
    this.editingContext().insertObject( fee );
    this.addObjectToBothSidesOfRelationshipWithKey( fee, "fees" );
}
```

If the name of the back-relationship changes or if the back-relationship is removed, the method will still work. For the most part, this method works fine. However, consider a case in which more than one relationship exists back to the source entity. Assuming that we are writing an application to schedule seminars for an organization, consider the example of an instructor and a seminar. For every seminar, there is an instructor and a backup instructor. There is a to-many relationship from Instructor to Seminar called seminars, and it represents the seminars that the instructor taught. There are two to-one relationships from Seminar to Instructor: instructor and backupInstructor, as shown in Figure 7.10.

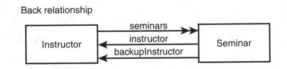

Figure 7.10
Sometimes the back-relationship is ambiguous.

When adding a seminar to the list of seminars that the instructor has taught, the instructor relationship should be set in the Seminar object. However, if the addObjectToBothSidesOfRelationshipWithKey() method is used, the relationship to be set is ambiguous.

The solution is to implement the inverseForRelationshipKey() method on the destination object. This method is used by addObjectToBothSidesOfRelationshipWithKey() method to determine the back relationship. In the instructor-seminar example, this method would be implemented in the Instructor class. If the seminars relationship key is given, the "instructor" string is returned. Otherwise, call the superclass method. This method will be used in the next example.

Maintaining Relationships

A number of user interface options can be used to maintain relationships. One approach is to create separate components to display the source and destination objects for a relationship. This would be somewhat cumbersome and confusing for the user to navigate. Another approach is to use drop-down and standard list boxes. This enables the user to select objects for a relationship from a set of existing objects, all on the same page, and works well for small resultsets.

Setting Up the Edit Page

The first step is to set up an Edit page for an entity. This involves creating a component that enables the user to select an object, and passing the object to another component to edit (see Figure 7.11).

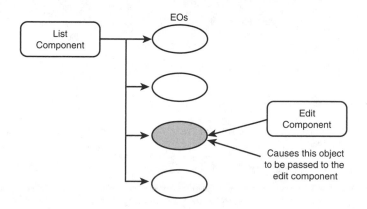

Figure 7.11
Passing an object from one component to another.

By now, you should know the fundamentals of creating a page that lists a set of objects from the database. You can refer to Chapter 5, "Using Display Groups," for information about using a WODisplayGroup to do this. The list component has one major difference from the components created in Chapter 5. This list component will have a WOHyperlink inside the WORepetition, as shown in Figure 7.12. The hyperlink will be used to select an object for modifying. The action for the WOHyperlink will be bound to an action that will pass the object to be modified to the edit component.

The trick in the action method is determining which hyperlink was selected. Remember that there will be many hyperlinks on the page due to the fact that the WOHyperlink is inside the WORepetition. As it turns out, the object associated with the hyperlink that was selected is the one bound to the WORepetition's item. In Figure 7.12, movie is bound to the WORepetition's item, so that is what is passed to the edit component in Listing 7.11.

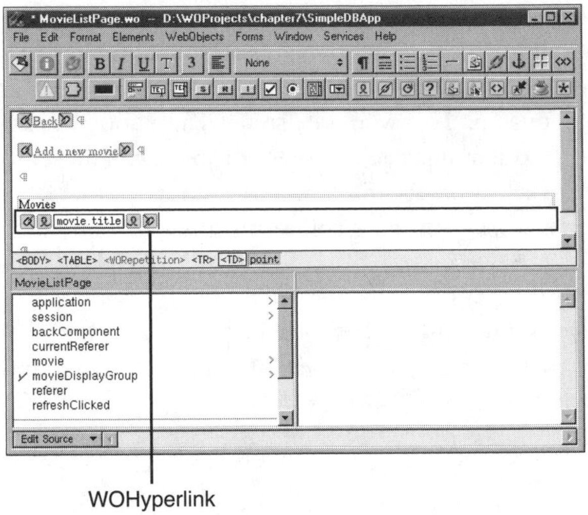

WOHyperlink

Figure 7.12

There is a WOHyperlink in the WORepetition around the title of the Movie.

Listing 7.11

The Action Method on the MovieListPage That Passes the Selected Movie to the MovieEditPage Component

```
public MovieEditPage movieSelected()
{
    MovieEditPage nextPage = (MovieEditPage)pageWithName("MovieEditPage");

    // Initialize your component here
    nextPage.setMovie( movie );
    nextPage.setBackComponent( this );
    return nextPage;
}
```

The back component is also set in the edit component. This gives the next component somewhere to go when the user modifies the data and clicks the Submit button. Setting the back component to this in this method returns the user to the list component.

The movie and backComponent keys must be added to the edit component for the code in Listing 7.11 to work. The movie key is a Movie, and backComponent is a WOComponent. At this point, the attributes can be bound to WOTextfields in the edit component. The edit component code is given in Listing 7.12, and the WebObjects Builder window is shown in Figure 7.13.

Listing 7.12

The Code for the MovieEditPage

```
// Generated by the WebObjects Wizard Sun Nov 05 20:26:28 US/Eastern 2000

import com.apple.yellow.foundation.*;
import com.apple.yellow.webobjects.*;
import com.apple.yellow.eocontrol.*;
import com.apple.yellow.eoaccess.*;

public class MovieEditPage extends WOComponent {
    protected Movie movie;
    protected WOComponent backComponent;

    public Movie movie()
    {
        return movie;
    }

    public void setMovie(Movie newMovie)
    {
        movie = newMovie;
    }

    public WOComponent backComponent()
    {
        return backComponent;
    }

    public void setBackComponent(WOComponent newBackComponent)
    {
        backComponent = newBackComponent;
    }

    public WOComponent submitChanges()
    {
        Session session = (Session)this.session();
        EOEditingContext editingContext = session.defaultEditingContext();
        editingContext.saveChanges();

        return this.backComponent();
    }
}
```

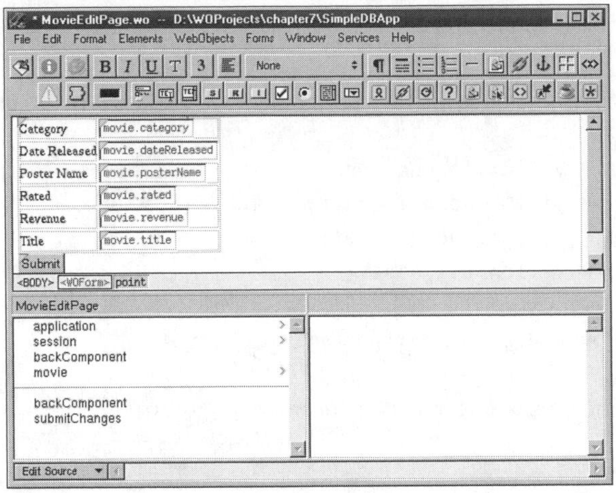

Figure 7.13
The MovieEditPage component in WebObjects Builder.

At this point, the data is not being saved in the database, it's just being modified in
memory. Note that the action for the Submit button is set to `backComponent`, which
will return the component that was set in Listing 7.11.

WOPopUpButton

After the edit page is setup, a `WOPopUpButton` can be added to give the users a set of
studios to choose from for the studio relationship. The `WOPopUpButton` dynamic
element is used to display a drop-down list, and it works similar to the `WORepetition`.
The `WOPopUpButton` uses an `NSArray` of objects for the list and a temporary variable to
hold each item. The `displayString` attribute specifies what will be displayed for each
object and the `selection` attribute holds whatever the user has selected. A complete
listing of attributes for the `WOPopUpButton` is given in Table 7.2.

Table 7.2

`WOPopUpButton` *Attributes*

Attribute	Description
list	Bound to an `NSArray`, the objects to be displayed.
item	Bound to a key of the same type as the objects in the `NSArray` bound to `list`. The key to which this is bound will reference each object in the list once during each of the request and response cycles.
displayString	What is to be displayed in the `WOPopUpButton`. This is usually an attribute of the object bound to the `item` binding.

Table 7.2

Continued

Attribute	Description
selection	The object is selected. This is used to display the current selection when appending to the response and it is also used to set the selection when the request is being processed.
selectedValue	Bound to a String, this is the String that the user selected.
name	The HTML name for the control.
disabled	Bound to a boolean, if it resolves to true, the WOPopUpButton is displayed; otherwise, it is not.
escapeHTML	Bound to a boolean, if it resolves to true, any HTML control characters are "escaped" out, meaning that the string appears in the browser exactly as it does in memory. Set this to false or NO if the data you are displaying contains HTML control characters that should be interpreted by the client's browser.
noSelectionString	What to display if there is no selection. This will be displayed if the selection binding is null, and the selection binding will be set to null if the user selects this text.

To use the WOPopUpButton, add it inside the form using the WOPopUpButton icon. To add a WOPopUpButton that modifies the studio relationship in the Movie entity, you must retrieve all the studios for the WOPopUpButton's list binding. This is most easily done by adding a WODisplayGroup. Make sure that you select the Fetches on Load button in the display group options dialog. You must also add a key for the item binding, so go ahead and add one called studio of type Studio. Finally, the selection is bound to the relationship that you want to modify. Table 7.3 lists the WOPopupButton bindings to modify the studio relationship.

Table 7.3

WOPopUpButton *Bindings for Modifying the Studio Relationship*

Attribute	Value
list	studioDisplayGroup.allObjects
item	studio
displayString	studio.name
selection	movie.studio

After you build and run this, you will find that it works well, but the reason why might be a bit confusing. The key to why this works is that the pop-up's list always contains the selection. This is because the selection is a Studio, and the list is of all studios. When the pop-up is displayed, the studio that is selected is determined by the studio relationship in the movie object. When the pop-up is submitted back to the server, the studio relationship is set based on what the user selected.

Many-to-Many Relationships

Most databases have at least one many-to-many relationship. Due to the limitations of how relational databases work, this usually involves a third "join" table to connect the two tables. For example, in the Movies database there is a many-to-many relationship between the Movie and Talent tables through the Director table. In this database, a Talent can direct many movies and a movie can have many directors. Notice that the Director table contains just the primary keys for the two other tables.

In code, it would be nice to access the directors directly through one relationship rather than having to go through the Director entity. This can be accomplished by flattening the talent relationship from the Director entity to the Movie entity. The opposite is also true: The movie relationship can also be flattened from the Director entity to the Talent entity.

This is done in EOModeler using the Flatten Selected Property icon, or by selecting the "Property, Flatten Property" menu item. The way it works is that you start by selecting the entity where you want the final relationship, for example, Movie. We will eventually call the relationship directors, so if there is a relationship called directors, rename it toDirectors or something else. From the Movie entity, select the to-many relationship to the Director entity, and then select the to-one relationship to the Talent entity. With this relationship selected, click on the Flatten Selected Property icon. The resulting relationship appears in bold letters in the Movie entity. The name of the relationship is the name of the two relationships that were selected connected with an underscore. Double-click on this relationship and change the name to directors, as shown in Figure 7.14

To avoid confusion, it is also appropriate at this time to uncheck the class attribute diamond for the relationship that was flattened. If you are using a custom class, you can regenerate the class file now, using FileMerge to save any code you have written.

You now have a to-many relationship from the Movie entity to the Talent entity. As you add objects to this relationship, the appropriate records in the join table will be created, and as you remove objects, the appropriate records will be removed.

WOBrowser
A list could be used to administer a to-many relationship. All the potential records could be displayed, with the highlighted records representing the contents of the

relationship. The WOBrowser dynamic element is used to display such a list. You can add a WOBrowser to a component in WebObjects Builder by selecting the "Forms, WOBrowser" menu item.

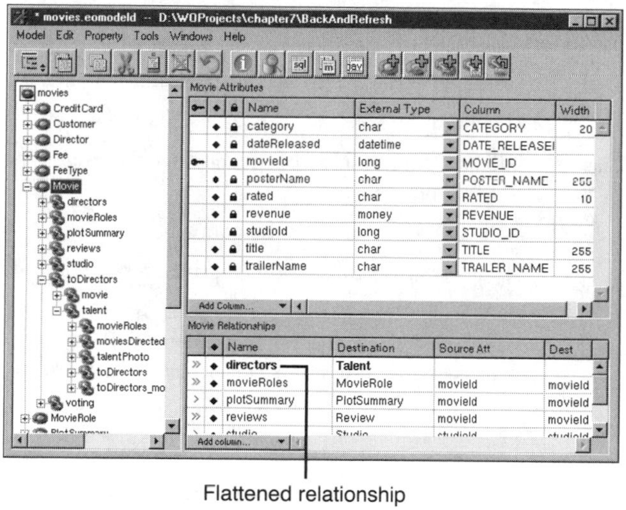

Flattened relationship

Figure 7.14

directors *is a flattened to-many relationship between Movie and Talent.*

The WOBrowser is extremely similar to the WOPopUpButton. The list is bound to an NSArray that contains all the items to display, and the item attribute is used as the temporary storage for looping through the list. The big difference is that the WOBrowser allows for multiple selections if the multiple attribute is set to true or YES. In this case, selections is bound to an NSArray that represents the selected objects. A complete list of WOBrowser attributes is given in Table 7.4.

Table 7.4

WOBrowser *Attributes*

Attribute	Description
list	Bound to an NSArray; the objects that are to be displayed in the WOBrowser.
item	Bound to an object of the same type as the objects in the NSArray bound to list.
displayString	What should be displayed, normally an attribute of the object bound to item.

Table 7.4

Continued

Attribute	Description
value	Can be used as a unique identifier for each object in the NSArray bound to list. This is useful if two displayStrings are equal.
escapeHTML	If this resolves to true or YES, the HTML control codes in the displayString are escaped; otherwise, they are interpreted.
selections	Bound to an NSArray that represents the selections that the user made.
selectedValues	Bound to an NSArray of Strings that represents the selections that the user made.
name	The HTML name for the control.
disabled	If this resolves to true or YES, the control is not displayed; otherwise, it is.
multiple	If this is true or YES, the WOBrowser allows multiple selections; otherwise, it allows only one selection to be made.
size	The number of rows to be displayed at one time.

This control can be used to modify a to-many relationship, for small resultsets. The list of potential objects for the to-many relationship is placed in the WOBrowser, with the objects in the to-many relationship highlighted. In the MovieEditPage created earlier, this could be used to modify the set of directors for a movie as shown in Figure 7.15.

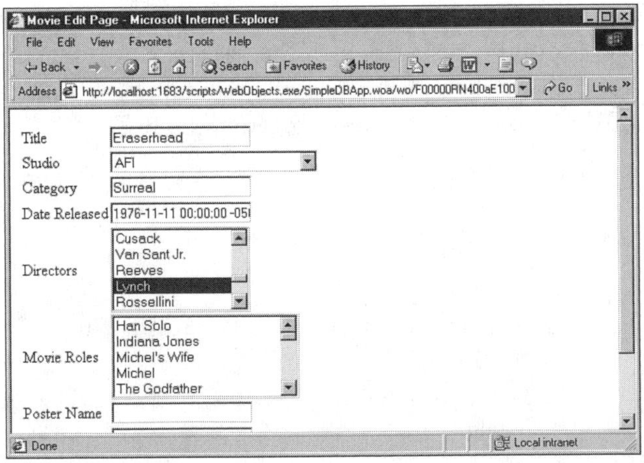

Figure 7.15
The movie edit page, with a WOBrowser for modifying the directors.

Remember, directors is a flattened relationship with the destination entity being Talent. Because this is the case, we need to display all the Talent objects in the WOBrowser, so add a Talent display group to the component. The display group's allObjects key will be bound to the list of the WOBrowser. Also required is a Talent key that will be bound to the item attribute, and displayString can be bound to the item's lastName attribute.

So far, this is similar to the way we used the WOPopUpButton. The difference is that with this WOBrowser, you are allowing the user to have multiple selections. To enable this, bind multiple to YES. Then bind selections to the to-many relationship you are modifying. Table 7.5 lists the WOBrowser bindings for this example.

Table 7.5

WOBrowser *Bindings for Editing the Directors Relationship*

Attribute	Value
list	talentDisplayGroup.allObjects
item	talent
displayString	talent.lastName
multiple	YES
selections	movie.directors

Using this approach, the setDirectors() method is called, with the new NSArray of Talent objects passed in. This does a wholesale replacement of the directors array, which will leave some incorrect references from the Talent objects back to the Movie object. All the Talent objects have NSArrays that reference Movie objects for the moviesDirected relationship. If the Movie code is left untouched, none of the Talent references will be updated.

The solution is to implement the setDirectors() method in the Movie class. Change the implementation to remove all the talent objects from the array one by one, and then add all the new ones. If the relationship management methods are used, the inverse relationships will also be set. The code for this method is given in Listing 7.13.

Listing 7.13

The setDirectors() *Method in the Movie.java File*

```
public void setDirectors(NSMutableArray value)
{
    int index;
```

Listing 7.13

Continued

```
    this.willChange();

    for ( index=0; index<this.directors().count(); index++ )
    {
        Talent talent = (Talent)this.directors().objectAtIndex(index);
        this.removeObjectFromBothSidesOfRelationshipWithKey(
            talent,"directors" );
    }
    for ( index=0; index<value.count(); index++ )
    {
        Talent talent = (Talent)value.objectAtIndex(index);
        this.addObjectToBothSidesOfRelationshipWithKey( talent, "directors");
    }
}
```

The relationship management methods,
`addObjectToBothSidesOfRelationshipWithKey()` and
`removeObjectFromBothSidesOfRelatoinshipWithKey()`, will both update the
relationships in the destination objects. It is dependent on the
`inverseForRelationshipKey()` method, and it assumes that this method will return the
inverse relationship. Because directors is a flattened relationship, this method is not
able to return the correct value, so it also needs to be implemented. The
`inverseForRelationshipKey()` method is given in Listing 7.14.

Listing 7.14

Example of the `inverseRelationshipForKey()` *Method for the Movie Class*

```
public String inverseForRelationshipKey( String key )
{
    if ( key.equals("directors") )
    {
        return "moviesDirected";
    }
    return super.inverseForRelationshipKey( key );
}
```

This might seem like a lot of work, and to a certain extent, it is. However, the only
time these methods must be implemented is when the set method is used to set the
entire NSArray for a to-many relationship.

Modifying the Database

After running the sample program we have been building in this chapter, you have probably noticed that the changes you make do not persist when you stop the application. This is because the changes are not being saved in the database. Using the EOEditingContext, saving changes to the database will be simple.

The EOEditingContext keeps track of all the changes that you make to an enterprise object, and then saves all the changes to the database when the saveChanges() method is called. The editing context finds out about changes when the willChange() method is called in the EOEnterpriseObject. Notice that this method was called in Listing 7.13. Also, notice that the method is not called in all the set methods; this is because it is invoked in the takeStoredValueForKey() method.

So, if you modify the action method in the MovieEditPage to call saveChanges() in the EOEditingContext, all the changes will be saved to the database. Every session has a default editing context, which can be retrieved with the defaultEditingContext() method. An example of the action method is given in Listing 7.15.

Listing 7.15

An Action Method for the MovieEditPage Component Modified to Save the Changes to the Database

```
public WOComponent submitChanges()
{
    Session session = (Session)this.session();
    EOEditingContext editingContext = session.defaultEditingContext();
    editingContext.saveChanges();

    return this.backComponent();
}
```

You will probably also need to bind the action for the Submit button to submitChanges.

Inserting and removing objects are also similarly easy, using the EOEditingContext's insertObject() and removeObject() methods. Using these methods, you can insert and remove objects at will; when you call saveChanges(), the appropriate records are inserted and removed from the database.

Deleting Objects

Deleting objects in the database sometimes causes some problems, mainly due to the maintenance of referential integrity. There are a number of options to choose when deleting a record that contains relationships to other records in the database. Should the other records be removed, or should the delete be cancelled? These rules are all specified as part of the relationship definition in EOModeler, and more information about this was detailed in Chapter 2, "Creating a Model."

For an example of removing records, consider the Fee objects that were created in the first example in this chapter. Let's say, for example, that a late fee was generated erroneously and the customer wants that fee to be removed. We need some way to delete Fee objects. The first place to start is a FeeListPage, as shown in Figure 7.16.

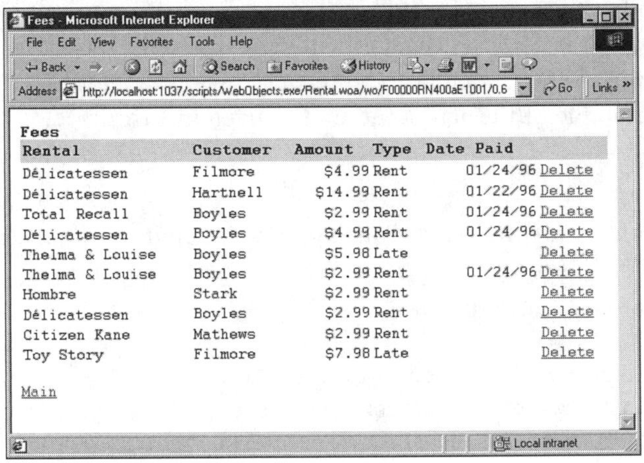

Figure 7.16
The Fees page.

The FeeListPage displays fees using a display group, and contains a hyperlink, called delete, for each record. When the user selects that hyperlink, the fee should be removed. The FeeListPage is shown in WebObjects Builder in Figure 7.17.

The action for the hyperlink is bound to `deleteFee`, and the code for this method is given in Listing 7.16.

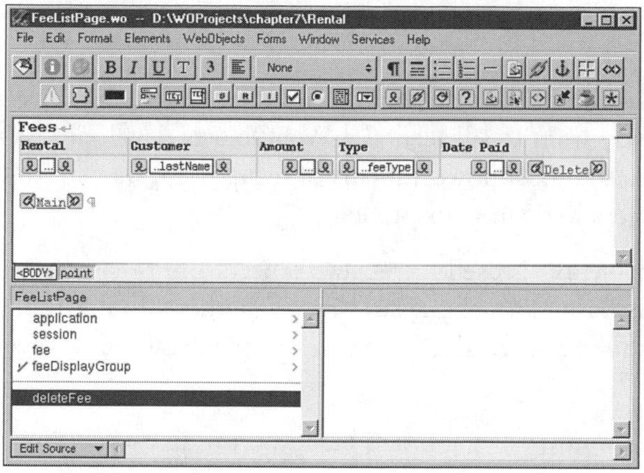

Figure 7.17
The FeeListPage in WebObjects Builder.

Listing 7.16

The Action Method to Delete a Fee, Located in the FeeListPage Class

```
public WOComponent deleteFee()
{
    feeDisplayGroup.setSelectedObject( fee );
    feeDisplayGroup.delete();
    feeDisplayGroup.dataSource().editingContext().saveChanges();

    return null;
}
```

This method uses the display group methods to delete a fee. The display group's `delete()` method will cause the fee to be removed from the `displayedObjects` and `allObjects` arrays, and tell the editing context to delete the object. Similar to `insertObject()`, the editing context has a method called `deleteObject()` that removes an object from the editing context. Also similar to the `insertObject()` method, for this operation to be reflected in the database, `saveChanges()` must be called. In this case, the editing context is retrieved from the display group's data source.

If a display group were not used, the session's default editing context would be used by calling `session().defaultEditingContext()`. The object could then be deleted by calling the editing context's `deleteObject()`, and then `saveChanges()`.

Summary

If you don't know anything else about WebObjects, you should know the contents of this chapter if you want to succeed as a WebObjects developer. Writing enterprise objects classes is the most powerful part of using the framework. This allows you to keep your business logic in your model.

The EOEditingContext is used to retrieve objects and track changes that need to be made to the database. This class uses various methods to insert and remove objects, along with methods to save all the changes to the database or revert to the previous changes.

At this point, you know all the basics behind creating a WebObjects application. If you understand all the concepts that have been presented in this book so far, you should be able to create small, working WebObjects applications and even contribute to a team of developers on a larger project. The next step is to take your application to the next level with some advanced features.

C H A P T E R 8

USING INHERITANCE WITH EOF

There are a few things that make an object-oriented language object-oriented. The ability to specify classes, instance and class methods, instance variables, polymorphism, and inheritance are important in an OO language. Even though in the past few years, a number of designers have opted to go with relatively flat inheritance trees in favor of using more object and class composition techniques, inheritance is still extremely important in any object-oriented design. So far, we have shown using enterprise objects doing everything but inheritance.

The reason that inheritance has been conveniently left off is because inheritance is tricky. It's not tricky in Java, it's just tricky to specify inheritance in a relational database. The parts of the framework that have been discussed so far have easily matched the concepts found in a relational database: fetching, updating, deleting, inserting, and relationships between tables. Inheritance is not something that is natural for a relational database, and because of this, there are three ways to implement inheritance for enterprise objects. Each has advantages and disadvantages that will be discussed in this chapter.

Using Inheritance with Relational Databases

Inheritance, being a relationship between classes, enables you to extend or change the functionality of a class. It also enables you to add instance variables to a class, and this is where it becomes tricky from a relational database point of view. How will the additional instance variables be represented? When selecting all the objects for a class that contains subclasses, should the objects from the subclasses also be retrieved? These are all things to consider when writing an OO framework that uses inheritance. There are three methods used by EOF to answer these questions: single-table mapping, vertical mapping, and horizontal mapping. The method you choose depends on a number of factors: the size of your data, the number of changes you intend to make to the design, and the most common way that you would want to access the data.

Single-Table Mapping

Single-table mapping places all the attributes for a class and all subclasses in the same table. The advantage is that it is fast; all the data for the entire inheritance hierarchy is located in one table, as shown in Figure 8.1.

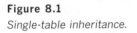

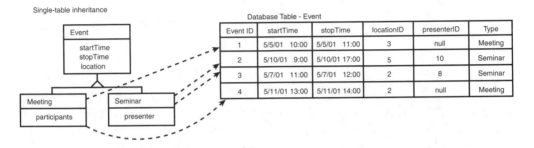

Figure 8.1
Single-table inheritance.

There is a column, called Type in the table, which associates a row for a specific entity. The values in this column correspond with values specified in the entity in EOModeler.

The Scheduler Application

A new example will be used to describe how to implement single-table inheritance. In this example, a rudimentary scheduling application will be implemented. There will be an abstract class called Event, with subclasses called Meeting and Seminar. The difference between a Meeting and a Seminar is that a Meeting has participants and a Seminar has a presenter. It's assumed that the people attending the seminar do not need to be tracked. The class diagram for this model is given in Figure 8.2.

You will be responsible for setting up the project and the necessary components on your own. This chapter focuses on the details of configuring the entity inheritance. It's also up to you to determine the types for the attributes described in the class diagram given in Figure 8.2, along with the appropriate database types and table names. In general, use number types for primary keys.

Scheduler application

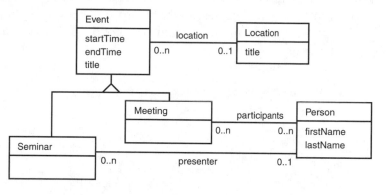

Figure 8.2
The class diagram for the scheduling application.

Modeling in EOModeler

To model this in EOModeler, first create the Location and Person entities, and then create the Event entity. You will need to add an attribute to Event called type, which is a character type with a width of 10. This will be used by the subclasses to indicate which class each row goes with. The Event entity in EOModeler is shown in Figure 8.3.

Figure 8.3
The Event entity.

Because this is an abstract class, it should be denoted as such in EOModeler. To do this, open the inspector and select the Advanced inspector button (see Figure 8.4). There is a check box, labeled Abstract, at the bottom of the inspector. Click this check box and close the inspector.

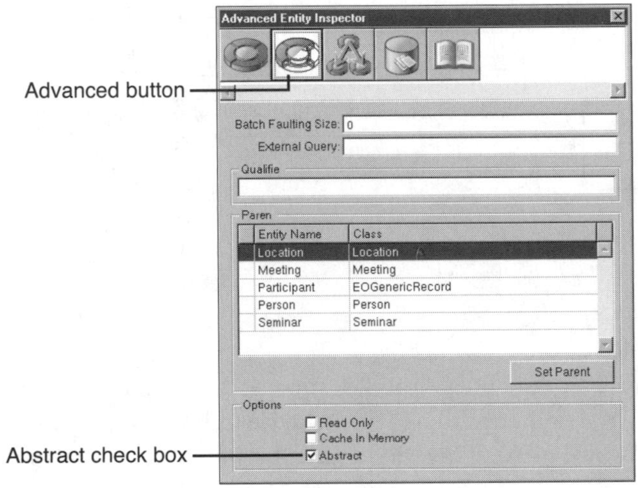

Figure 8.4
The advanced entity inspector.

Now you are ready to create the two concrete subclasses: Meeting and Seminar. To do this, leave the Event entity selected and choose the Property, Create Subclass menu item. This creates an entity called Entity with the table EVENT, and the class named Entity. The first entity we will create is the Seminar. Change the entity name to Seminar and the class to Seminar, but leave the table name as EVENT.

If you take a look at the attributes in Seminar, you'll notice that they are all italicized. This indicates that the attribute or relationship is inherited. You can now add attributes to the entity. The attribute to add is the personID, which is a foreign key into the person table. This will represent the presenter for the seminar. Also add a to-one relationship, called presenter, to Person, joining on the personID. This entity in EOModeler is displayed in Figure 8.5.

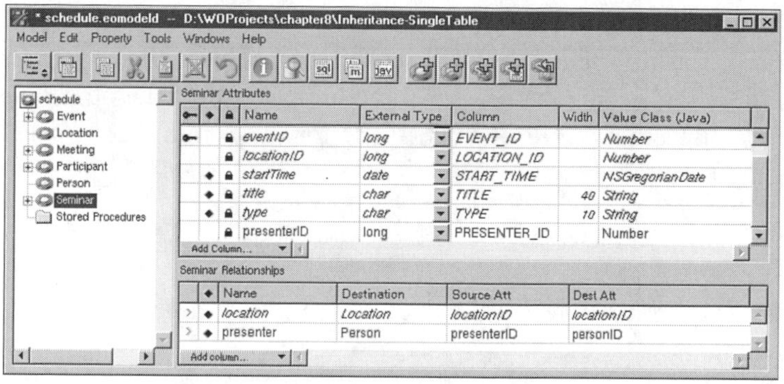

Figure 8.5
The Seminar entity.

To find out how the Seminar's superclass was set, take a look at the advanced entity inspector. The superclass is specified in the Parent list box. The parent is the class with the circle beside it, Event.

Remember the type attribute that was added to the Event class? Well, this is what we will use in the Qualifier field to determine which rows are associated with the Seminar entity. Type the expression **(type='Seminar')** into the Qualifier field as shown in Figure 8.6. This will make it so that only rows in which the type column is equal to Seminar will be returned as Seminar objects. For this to work, the Seminar class file must be modified.

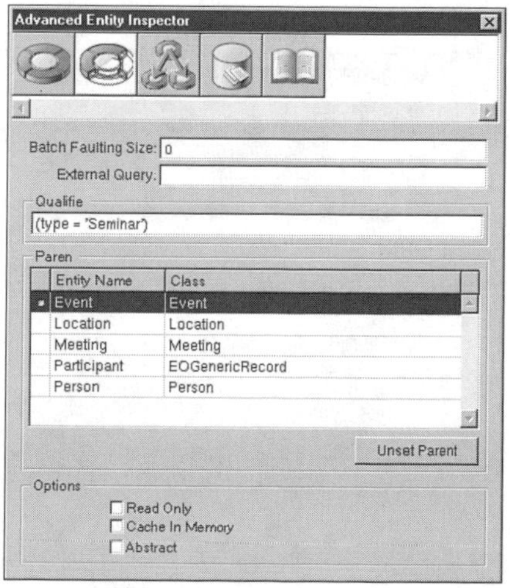

Figure 8.6
The advanced entity inspector for the Seminar entity. You must set the qualifier to denote this entity.

Modifying the Seminar Class

A constructor must be added that will set the type. This is the only place where the type should be set; setting the type to something else after the object has been created will produce unpredictable results. The code for the Seminar constructor is given in Listing 8.1.

Listing 8.1

The Constructor for the Seminar Class

```
public Seminar()
{
    super();
    this.setType( "Seminar" );
}
```

At this point, you can create and insert Seminar objects.

The Meeting Entity

The process is similar for the Meeting entity, but there is a to-many relationship between Meeting and Person. (A meeting can have many people; a person can attend many meetings.) This requires another table to perform the many-to-many join in the database. In this example, add an entity called Participant that contains an eventID and a personID; both are primary keys. Figure 8.7 shows the new entity in EOModeler. Also add a to-one relationship to the Person entity, joined on the personID.

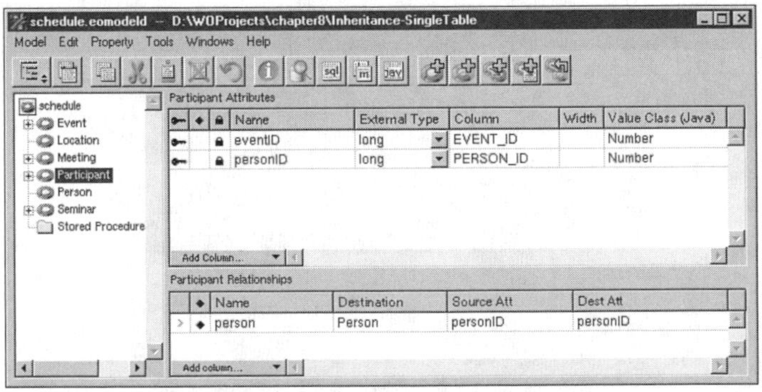

Figure 8.7

The Participant entity is required for the many-to-many relationship between Meeting and Person.

Now you can create the Meeting entity by selecting the Event entity and choosing the Property, Create Subclass menu item. Again, change the entity name and class name, but not the table. Also, change the qualifier in the advanced entity inspector as shown in Figure 8.8.

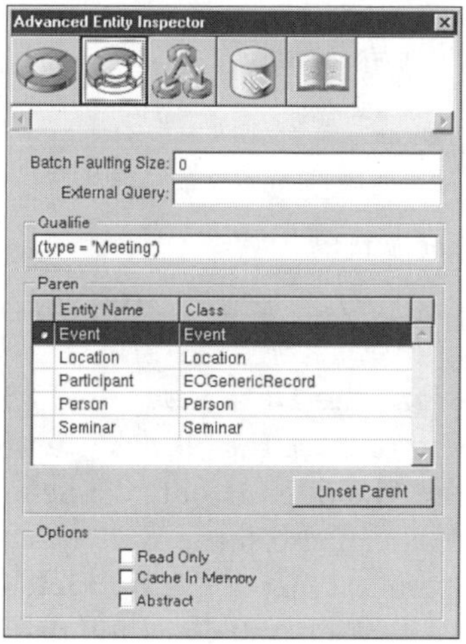

Figure 8.8
The advanced entity inspector for the Meeting entity.

At this point, you can add a to-many relationship to the Participant entity, and flatten the relationship to the Person entity. For information on flattening relationships, refer to Chapter 7, "Writing Enterprise Objects Classes." The entity is shown in Figure 8.9.

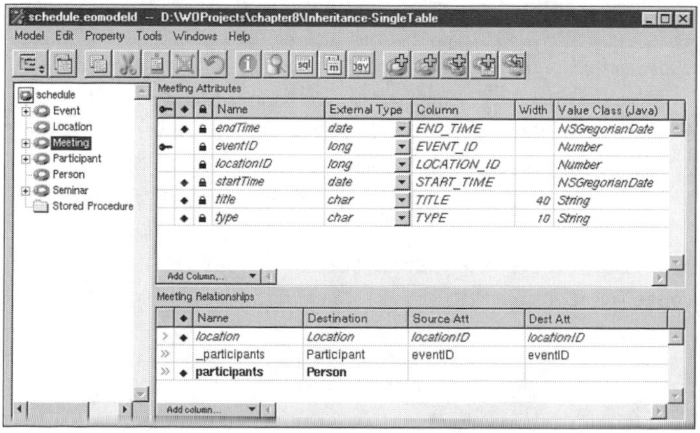

Figure 8.9
The Meeting entity in EOModeler.

You will also need to modify the Meeting constructor as you did with the Seminar constructor. This example is given in Listing 8.2.

Listing 8.2

The Constructor for the Meeting Class

```
public Meeting()
{
    super();
    this.setType( "Meeting" );
}
```

Retrieving the Objects from the Database

At this point, you're ready to retrieve the objects from the database. You have the option of retrieving only the Meetings or only the Seminars by creating fetch specifications for those entities. You can also retrieve an NSArray of heterogeneous objects, containing Meeting and Seminar objects. Create a fetch specification against the Event entity to do this. Listing 8.3 lists an awake method that will create a fetch specification that returns all Event objects.

Listing 8.3

This Method Will Return All the Event Objects; the Events Array Will Contain Both Meeting and Seminar Objects

```
public void awake()
{
    if ( events == null )
    {
        EOSortOrdering ordering = EOSortOrdering.sortOrderingWithKey(
            "startTime", EOSortOrdering.CompareAscending);
        NSArray orderings = new NSArray( new Object [] { ordering } );
        EOFetchSpecification fetchSpec =
            new EOFetchSpecification( "Event", null, orderings );

        EOEditingContext ec = this.session().defaultEditingContext();
        events = ec.objectsWithFetchSpecification( fetchSpec );
    }
}
```

Displaying the Objects

The cool part about this is that you get an NSArray that contains different objects of different classes. Figure 8.10 shows a potential way in which this could be displayed.

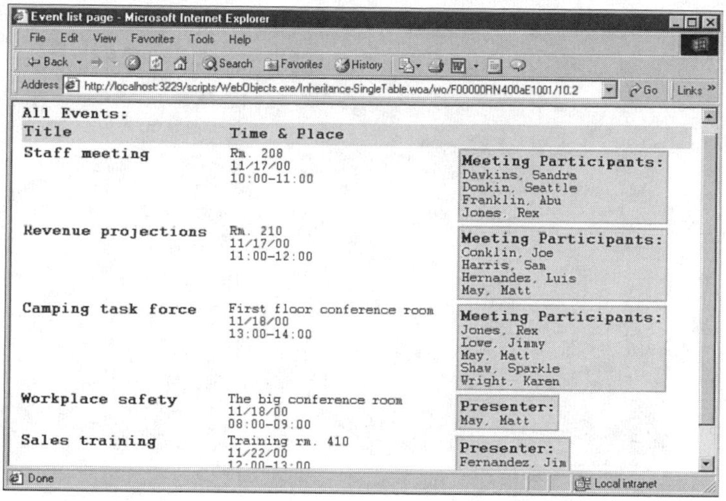

Figure 8.10
Displaying all the events. Notice that if the event is a Meeting, the participants are shown; if it is a Seminar, the presenter is displayed.

This is easily done with a set of WOConditionals and a couple methods in the component class. If the current event is a Meeting, display the participants; if it is a Seminar, display the presenter. Determining the type of an object can be done with the Java instanceof operator. Using this, methods can be written that determine what type of object the current event is. Listing 8.4 gives the two methods.

Listing 8.4

Methods That Help Identify the Type of the Current Object

```
public boolean isMeeting()
{
    return (event instanceof Meeting);
}


public boolean isSeminar()
{
    return (event instanceof Seminar);
}
```

At this point, a pair of conditionals can be placed in the table, with the condition bindings set to the method names as indicated in Figure 8.11.

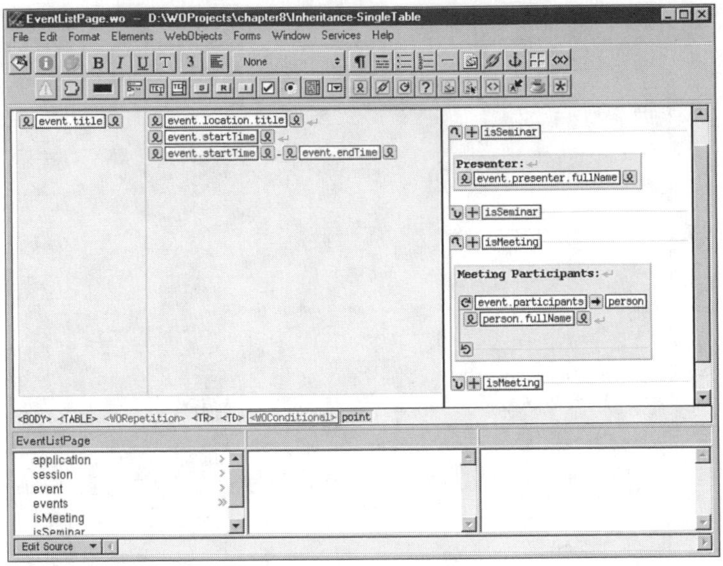

Figure 8.11
The WOConditionals *used to display the Meeting- or Seminar-specific attributes.*

Disadvantages

The example given is a good one for when to use single-table mapping because there is not much wasted space. Only one column is required for a subclass of Event, minimizing the number of columns that aren't used by the three entities. However, there are cases when you do not want to use single-table mapping.

This type of mapping is a classic example of the "speed for storage" tradeoff. Because all attributes for all subclasses are in the same class, there are a number of columns that aren't used by a number of rows. If you have a particularly deep inheritance hierarchy, this could waste a lot of space. Another disadvantage is that a change to any entity in the inheritance hierarchy requires a change to the database table. But, if you have a relatively flat inheritance hierarchy with a small number of attributes in the subclasses, this might be the way to go for you.

Vertical Mapping

Vertical mapping maps every entity to a separate table. When objects are retrieved from one of the subclass entities, the data from the superclass tables is also returned. This requires that the relationships between the tables are represented in EOModeler. Vertical mapping allows the most flexibility at design time; however, it is also the most expensive at runtime. A diagram of Vertical mapping is given in Figure 8.12.

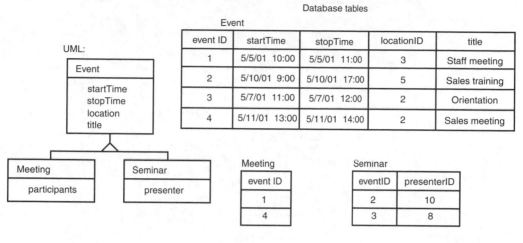

Figure 8.12
Vertical mapping.

Vertical Inheritance in EOModeler

In this example, the model created earlier in the chapter will be converted to use vertical inheritance. When using vertical mapping, each class maps to a different table and the superclass attributes are flattened into each of the subclasses.

The first step is to set the table name for the Meeting and Seminar entities to MEETING and SEMINAR, respectively. You will have to remove most of the attributes and relationships from these entities. Leave the primary keys for these entities as eventID.

Now create a to-one relationship from the Meeting entity to the Event, mapping the eventIDs. This relationship is used only for flattening the Event attributes into the Meeting entity, so you can "unclick" the class attribute diamond.

At this point, flatten all the attributes and relationships from Event to Meeting using the relationship you have created. Initially, the attributes and relationships will be named as shown in Figure 8.13, but go ahead and rename them according to the names in the superclass (Figure 8.14). Make sure to keep the class attribute properties the same as those in the superclass.

You can go ahead and flatten the Event attributes into Seminar as well.

The last step is to remove all references to the type attribute. Now that the data is stored in separate tables, this isn't needed. Remove the type attributes from Event, Meeting, and Seminar, and remove the code to set the type in the constructors for Meeting and Seminar. If this is the only code that you added to Meeting and Seminar, it might be a good idea to regenerate the class files and overwrite the files you have.

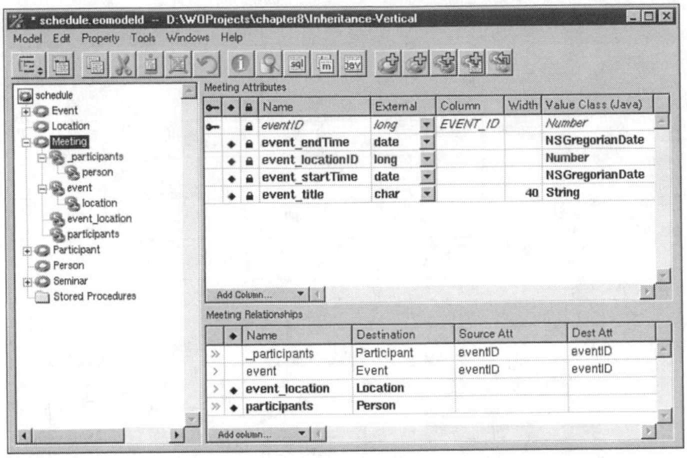

Figure 8.13
The flattened attributes and relationships in the Meeting entity need to be renamed from their initial, flattened names.

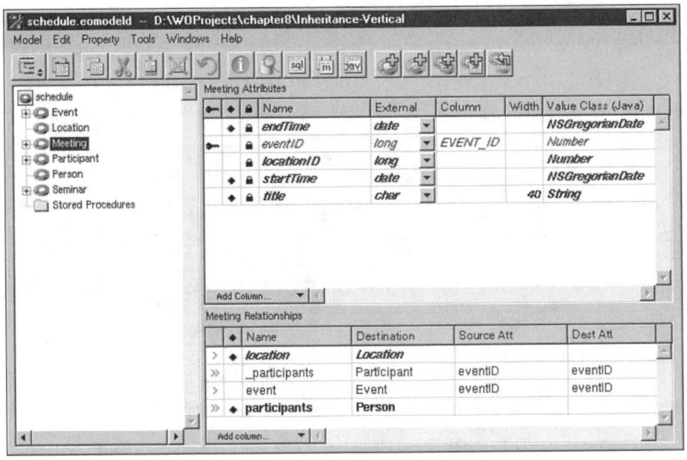

Figure 8.14
As the flattened attributes and relationships are given the names of the superclass attributes and relationships, they are italicized.

At this point, your application should work the same as it did before, it's just that you're using vertical mapping instead of horizontal.

Disadvantages

The advantages of vertical mapping are that it is the most efficient from a storage perspective and it is also the most flexible from a design perspective. There are no "unused" columns as are present in single-table mapping, reducing the amount of wasted space. Also, because every entity is mapped to a separate table, a change to any entity will require a change to only that table.

The cost of this flexibility is the extra time spent retrieving objects. Retrieving objects for a class in an inheritance hierarchy requires a join to all the ancestor tables in the hierarchy. This might not be a big deal if your database is optimized for that type of query by using clustered indexes.

Given this example, vertical mapping is probably not appropriate. The Meeting entity, for example, does not add any additional attributes, and therefore horizontal mapping might make more sense. Access patterns should also be considered when determining which type of inheritance should be used. If it is common to retrieve a number of different types in one query, single-table inheritance is a good choice to reduce the number of joins.

Another solution in this case is to combine inheritance mappings. For example, you could specify `Meeting` as using single-table inheritance and `Seminar` as using vertical inheritance. The `type` attribute would have to be placed back in all three entities, and the `class` attribute turned off in the `Seminar` entity. The constructor for the `Meeting` entity would be changed back to the way it was in Listing 8.2. This technique could be useful for applications with varied access patterns.

Horizontal Mapping

In the examples so far, our focus has been on returning a heterogeneous array of objects; that is, objects of different types that have the same superclass. When given this scenario, single-table mapping probably will be used most often due to its performance advantages. However, consider a scenario in which you do not have to retrieve a heterogeneous set of objects. What if you never have to display Meetings and Seminars on the same page? You still might want to use inheritance to provide some basic functionality in the superclass, but you don't necessarily need to keep all the data together. This is when horizontal mapping is useful.

Horizontal mapping is a mix between vertical and single-table mapping. There's a separate table for every class at the bottom of the inheritance hierarchy (see Figure 8.15). Each table contains all the attributes for all the classes up the inheritance hierarchy to the root class.

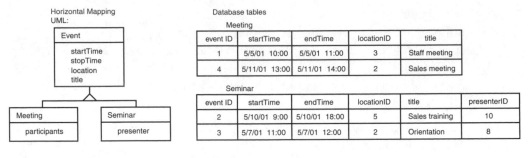

Figure 8.15

Horizontal mapping.

This is optimized for retrieving objects for the leaf classes, and becomes expensive for retrieving objects of one of the classes in the middle of the inheritance hierarchy, depending on the method of retrieval. Also, changes to the superclasses start to become cumbersome because those changes must be made throughout all the subclass tables.

In Horizontal mapping, the table for the superclass entity is not set because all the attributes are stored in subclass tables, as shown in Figure 8.16.

Figure 8.16

Using Horizontal mapping, the table name for the Event class is left blank.

Similar to vertical mapping, the type field is not required, and the parent for the subclass entities is set to the superclass. Also similar to vertical mapping, the subclass entities are stored in separate tables. Unlike vertical mapping, however, there is no relationship from the subclass entities to the superclass, and no flattened attributes. An example of configuring the Meeting entity to use Horizontal mapping is given in Figure 8.17.

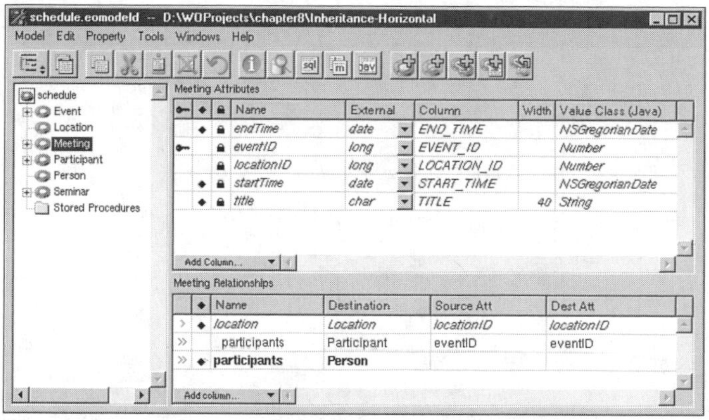

Figure 8.17
The Meeting entity using Horizontal mapping.

Disadvantages
The big disadvantage with horizontal mapping is that modifications to the superclass entity must be reflected in all subclass tables. This can make modifications to the superclass entity quite painful. Another disadvantage is that selecting objects from the superclass entity involves joins between a number of tables. (The number of tables is exactly equal to the number of leaf classes.) So, if your access pattern involves retrieving the objects for a particular superclass and you have a bunch of leaf subclasses, this might not be the choice for you.

Summary

As you can see, there are a few options for implementing an inheritance relationship for your model, and when these options are combined, there are endless possibilities. A lot of power is built in to EOF to handle entity inheritance, but the challenge is determining the proper entity inheritance to choose. That decision depends on the depth of your inheritance tree, the number of attributes added by subclasses, the overhead of NULL values on your database, the number of changes you envision in your superclasses, and finally, the projected access patterns. Each of the inheritance mappings have distinct advantages and disadvantages that will weigh into your decision.

CHAPTER 9

VALIDATING DATA

Updating information potentially opens your application to data-based bugs. This opens the possibility for a user to enter a value that is unacceptable to the system. There are a few ways the information could be corrupt. One is an invalid format, in which the user enters letters for a number field. Another potential error is an invalid range error, in which a number is out of a range or a set of letters is too long. Yet another way an error occurs is when the data that is input causes an object to have an invalid state.

There are a few ways that WebObjects handles this type of validation. It could be handled as part of the user interface using JavaScript, or within the WebObjects framework, or as part of EOF.

This chapter discusses the various ways to validate the data that the user entered, and also discusses a more generic means to handle errors using a validation framework.

Levels of Validation

Validation of user entry can be done at a number of different levels (see Figure 9.1), and each level has its advantages and disadvantages. The area that you choose for validation depends on the user experience you want. In general, you should strive to place most of the validation code with your entity code associated with your model.

UI

The UI validation consists of JavaScript that validates the information before it is submitted to the application along with validation in the WebObjects framework. The advantage of JavaScript validation is that the user gets immediate feedback on the problem without making a round trip to the application server. The feedback comes in the form of a pop-up window that explains the error and does not allow the form submission. Also, the HTML text fields perform basic character length validation, and the WOTextFields will perform character and number validation.

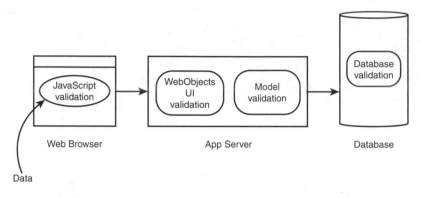

Figure 9.1
Areas for user entry validation.

The disadvantage of this type of validation is that changes in the model also require changes in the user interface. For example, if the maximum allowable value for an attribute changes from 20 to 10, the length of the WOTextField should also change. For that reason, it is not generally an acceptable practice to perform input validation using JavaScript.

Object

Another location where you could provide validation code is within the entity class. This allows simple validation of such things as the maximum length and the format, but also allows object-level state validation. You can validate a value based on how the state is changed in the object. Certain methods in the object are called to validate the object for inserting and saving the object in the database. This is a great place to put most validation logic because it is with the rest of the business logic.

The disadvantage of this type of validation is that a transaction to the WebObjects server is required to perform the validation. This causes extra transactions on your server, and the user has to wait to find out that the data he entered is invalid.

Database

The final place for validation is at the database level. Some basic validation is required here, such as the length of character fields and the types. Most databases also have ways to perform complex validations through triggers and stored procedures. I would advise you not to use this type of validation with EOF unless the database is accessed by other, non-EOF applications. The disadvantage of validating information at this level is that it is problematic to determine the exact error within WebObjects. Also, the logic placed in these procedures is duplicated in the enterprise object code, making changes to the logic more complicated.

UI Validation

In general, you should limit the amount of logic that is performed at the user interface level, for the reasons given earlier. However, you can reduce the number of errors that must be caught in the model layer by verifying that the user has entered data with the correct length and a valid type. Input errors can be avoided with most UI elements such as combo boxes and lists because the user is required to select from a list of items. The places where the user is allowed to mess things up are in the text fields and text areas.

WOTextField

There are a couple of types of validation that you want to perform here. One is setting the maximum number of characters that the user can enter. This is done in the static inspector for the WOTextField in WebObjects Builder.

Use the WOTextField's static inspector to set the maximum number of characters that the user can enter, as shown in Figure 9.2. The Visible Length determines the number of characters that the text field will display, and the Maximum Length determines the number of characters that the text field will allow the user to enter.

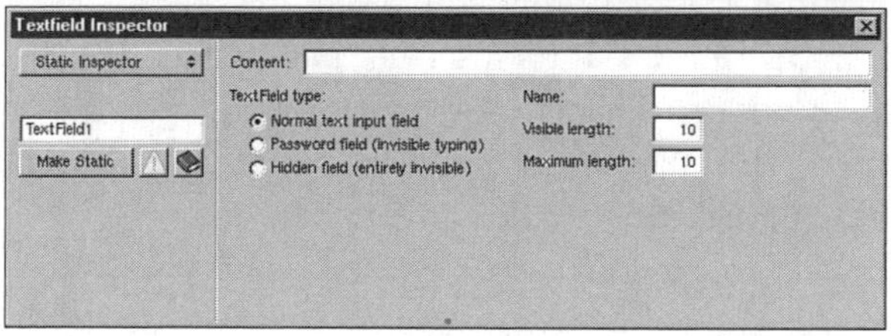

Figure 9.2
The WOTextField's static inspector.

The WOText is more free-form; there is no limit to the amount of text that can be entered, although there is a limit to the amount that is uploaded. The only values that can be set for WOText have to do with the size of the text area (see Figure 9.3). The number of columns specifies how many characters wide the text area will be, and the number of rows specifies how tall the text area will be. As with the values in the WOTextField settings, these values are in characters.

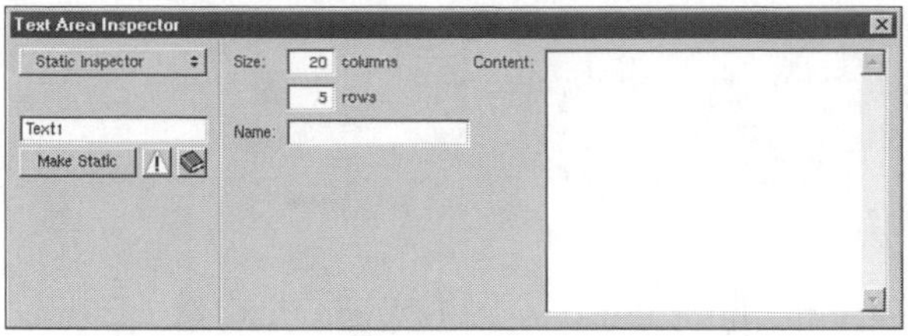

Figure 9.3
Use the WOText*'s static inspector to set the size of the text area.*

> The number of characters for the visible length of a text field or the number of columns for a text area is not precise; it's more of a rounded number. Most text is in a proportional font, meaning that the exact width of each individual character is different. For example, the letter *Z* typically will be wider than the letter *I*. So, how can we specify a number of characters for these widths? It's up to the browser to determine how to display them, but this is typically done by using an average-width letter, such as *m*, for an estimation of the actual width.

Formatting

The next step in user interface validation is determining that the user has entered a set of characters that represent a value of the correct type. WebObjects and the Foundation frameworks provide some basic validation, allowing you to set the formatter for a WOTextField. You can also set the number format or the date format for the text field. After you have done this, WebObjects expects the user to enter the number or date in that format. If the user does not enter the value in the correct format, the value is not set. This is a somewhat "silent" error, in that an exception is not thrown. The result is that nothing is placed in the value bound to the WOTextField's value attribute.

Model Validation

After you have determined that you have the correct object type and length, validation occurs in the enterprise object class. There are two types of validation for the enterprise object class: attribute-level validation and operation-level validation, as shown in Figure 9.4. The methods are part of the EOValidation interface defined in the EOControl layer. The EOGenericRecord class implements these methods. The default implementation performs some basic but necessary validation.

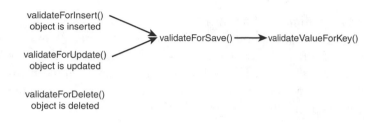

Figure 9.4
The validation methods that are called on an enterprise object.

When an object is about to be inserted, updated, or deleted during a `saveChanges()` operation, a set of validation methods is called. At any point, an `EOValidation.Exception` could be thrown. If one is thrown, the operation is cancelled, including all other pending inserts, updates, and deletes. The primary methods used for validation are `validateForInsert()`, `validateForUpdate()`, and `validateForDelete()`.

Inserts and Updates

When an object is about to be inserted or updated, the `validateForInsert()` or `validateForUpdate()` method is called. The default implementation is for both of these methods to call the `validateForSave()` method, which will validate all the attributes by calling the `validateValueForKey()` method for each attribute. The default implementation enforces the "allows null" settings and the relationship rules. Also, basic conversion is performed at the attribute level. For example, strings are converted to numbers if necessary and possible.

Deletes

When an object is about to be deleted, the `validateForDelete()` method is called. The default implementation enforces any delete rules for relationships.

Attribute-Level Validation

Attribute-level validation is used to make sure that the value being set for the attribute is in a valid range. This is started with a call to the `validateValueForKey()` method:

```
public Object validateValueForKey( Object value, String key )
```

This method attempts to convert the value to an appropriate type if necessary and calls a `validateKey()` method if it exists. This is your opportunity to provide attribute-specific validation.

Attribute-Level Validation Example

Consider the rental application that allowed videos to be checked in and out. There are two dates in the Rental class that could use some validation: the dateOut and the dateReturned. Basically, neither date should be in the future. You can ensure that they aren't by adding the appropriate attribute-level validation methods to the Rental class. An example of such a method is given in Listing 9.1.

Listing 9.1

Validating Appropriate Check-In and Check-Out Dates Can Be Done with a Few Validation Methods in the Rental.java *Class*

```java
public void validateDateReturned( Object value )
    throws EOValidation.Exception
{
    if ( value != null )
    {
        if ( ((NSGregorianDate)value).timeIntervalSinceNow() > 0 )
        {
            NSMutableDictionary userInfo = new NSMutableDictionary();
            userInfo.setObjectForKey( "dateReturned",
                EOValidation.Exception.ValidatedPropertyUserInfoKey );
            userInfo.setObjectForKey( this,
                EOValidation.Exception.ValidatedObjectUserInfoKey );

            throw new EOValidation.Exception(
                "The date returned cannot be in the future",
                userInfo );
        }
    }
}

public void validateDateOut( Object value )
    throws EOValidation.Exception
{
    if ( ((NSGregorianDate)value).timeIntervalSinceNow() > 0 )
    {
        NSMutableDictionary userInfo = new NSMutableDictionary();
        userInfo.setObjectForKey( "dateOut",
            EOValidation.Exception.ValidatedPropertyUserInfoKey );
```

Listing 9.1

Continued

```
        userInfo.setObjectForKey( this,
            EOValidation.Exception.ValidatedObjectUserInfoKey );

        throw new EOValidation.Exception(
            "The date out cannot be in the future",
            userInfo );
    }
}
```

By adding these methods and naming them appropriately (according to the attribute names), they are called automatically from the validateValueForKey() method. Now, if you try to enter a date that is in the future, an exception is thrown and the operation is cancelled.

Both of these methods use the NSDate method timeIntervalSinceNow(), which returns a positive number if the date given is after the current date and time. Because the dateReturned can be null, we do the validation only if a value exists. The dateOut cannot be null, so this validation isn't required. The null validation is performed by the framework in the validateValueForKey() method.

Also, the EOValidation.Exception has a userInfo dictionary that contains additional information about the exception. The EOValidation.Exception defines standard keys that are used in the dictionary, as shown in Table 9.1.

Table 9.1

EOValidation.Exception userInfo *Dictionary Keys*

Key	Description
ValidatedObjectUserInfoKey	The object being validated when the exception was generated.
ValidatedPropertyUserInfoKey	The string key being validated when the exception was generated.
AdditionalExceptionsKey	Any additional exceptions that were generated during the validation. This is an NSArray.

This dictionary is used for the calling method to determine exactly where the validation error occurred.

Operation-Level Validation

Operation-specific validation can be performed by implementing the `validateForInsert()`, `validateForUpdate()`, and `validateForDelete()` methods. Validation specific to inserting, updating, and deleting should be placed in these methods, and the superclass versions of these methods should be called. However, there is another method that is used for validating general saves to the database: `validateForSave()`.

The `validateForSave()` method is called by both `validateForInsert()` and `validateForUpdate()`. The default implementation validates all attributes by repeatedly calling `validateValueForKey()`. When overriding this method, make sure that you call the superclass implementation first.

Operation-Level Validation Example

An example of operation-level validation would be to ensure that the `dateReturned` is after the `dateOut`. This type of inter-attribute dependency is a good example of what should be included in operation-level validation. Because this must be enforced on insert and update, it is implemented in the `validateForSave()` method, as shown in Listing 9.2.

Listing 9.2

The `validateForSave()` *Method Enforces Chronological Order for the* `dateOut` *and* `dateReturned` *Attributes in the Rental class.*

```
public void validateForSave()
    throws EOValidation.Exception
{
    super.validateForSave();

    if ( this.dateOut().timeIntervalSinceDate(this.dateReturned()) > 0 )
    {
        NSMutableDictionary userInfo = new NSMutableDictionary();
        userInfo.setObjectForKey( this,
        EOValidation.Exception.ValidatedObjectUserInfoKey );
        throw new EOValidation.Exception(
            "Date out is later than the returned date", userInfo );
    }
}
```

This code uses the `NSDate`'s `timeIntervalSinceDate()` method, which returns the number of seconds that have elapsed between two dates. A positive number is returned if the date provided is before the object on which the method was invoked, and a negative number if the date provided is after the object on which the method was invoked. For example, the method can be invoked on the dateOut date, and a negative value will be returned if dateReturned is after dateOut. The return value is a double representing the number of seconds.

The userInfo dictionary is created as in the other validation methods, although only the ValidatedObjectUserInfoKey is set.

Handling the Exception

Most of the time, your development efforts are focused toward writing code that does not produce exceptions. In this chapter, we have been writing code that will produce exceptions and acting as if messages like the one in Figure 9.5 were acceptable.

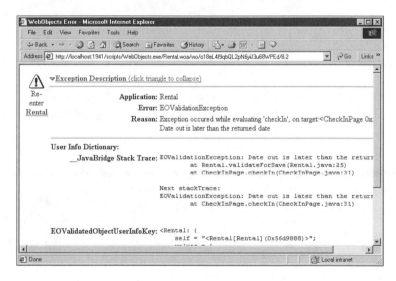

Figure 9.5
The standard exception page; this should probably be changed.

The standard exception page can be avoided by catching and processing the exception in the action method in which the exception was generated. It is better user interface design to present the user with the erroneously entered information along with a chance to correct it. For example, a message could be added to the CheckOutPage that indicates the error, as shown in Figure 9.6.

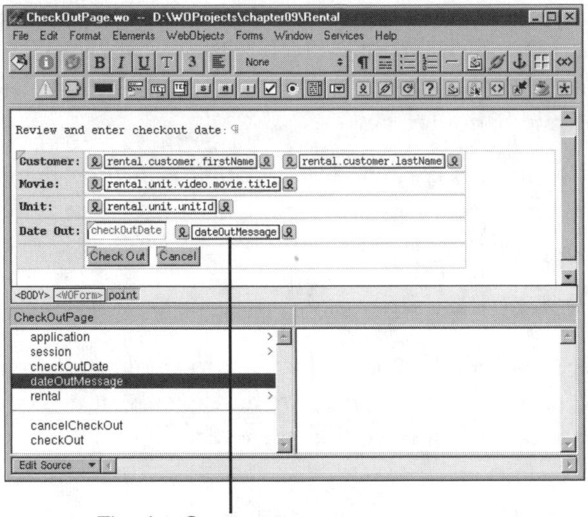

The dateOut error message

Figure 9.6

Adding an error message to the CheckOutPage.

A message attribute is also added. Now on the save() action, catch the EOValidation.Exception that is thrown and set the message appropriately, as shown in Listing 9.3.

Listing 9.3

The checkOut() *Method in the* CheckOutPage.java *Class*

```
public Main checkOut()
{
    Main nextPage = (Main)pageWithName("Main");

    // Initialize your component here
    EOEditingContext ec = this.session().defaultEditingContext();
    ec.insertObject( rental );
    rental.checkOut( checkOutDate );
    try
    {
        ec.saveChanges();
    }
    catch ( EOValidation.Exception e )
    {
        NSDictionary userInfo = (NSDictionary)e.userInfo();
        Object propertyKey = userInfo.objectForKey(
```

Listing 9.3

Continued

```
            EOValidation.Exception.ValidatedPropertyUserInfoKey );

        if ( propertyKey.equals( "dateOut" ) )
        {
            dateOutMessage = e.getMessage();
            return null;
        }
        throw e;
    }
    return nextPage;
}
```

Note that you're catching the exception for the sole purpose of determining whether the validation error occurs on the dateOut attribute. If this is the case, you will want to set the error message appropriately and return null, which causes the same page to display. If the exception is for another attribute, you will need to throw it because we haven't determined what to do with those exceptions yet. After the whole catch block, you can go ahead and return the next page because you only get to that line if an error did not occur.

At this point, the message should appear next to the text field in which the error occurred, as shown in Figure 9.7.

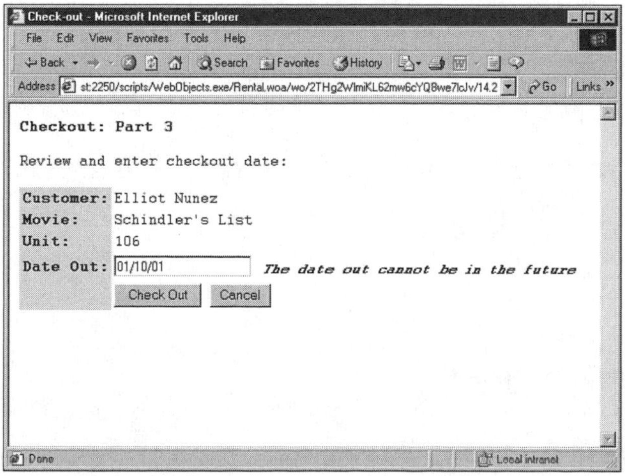

Figure 9.7

The validation error message for the dateOut key.

The userInfo dictionary is retrieved in the catch section of the try-catch block. Remember that the property being validated when the exception is raised is in this dictionary. If it is the key you are interested in, the message is set to the message in the exception. If this approach is taken, you should make sure that the message placed in the exception is suitable for display.

Reusable Validation Components

The code for processing validation exceptions and producing error messages can be reused for other forms if we employ a few reusable components. Consider that the keys for the nonvalidated properties are in the userInfo dictionary in the EOValidation.Exception. A component could be written to conditionally display the exception message when given the key and the exception. Similar to this, the label for the text field could also display the label using normal or bold text if the key for the exception matches the key for the label, as shown in Figure 9.8.

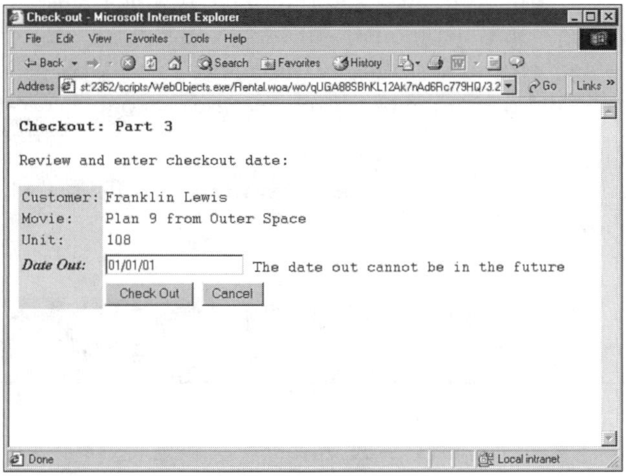

Figure 9.8
Reusable components for form labels and validation messages will make the user interface more consistent.

Creating the Components

The first step is to create two new components: ValidationLabel and ValidationPage, which are both partial documents.

The `ValidationLabel` Component

The purpose of the `ValidationLabel` component is to display the label for a TextField. The label will be displayed differently if the user has entered invalid text. The attributes for the `ValidationLabel` component are given in Table 9.2.

Table 9.2

Attributes for the `ValidationLabel` *Component*

Attribute	Type
exception	EOValidation.Exception
key	String
label	String

In addition, the `ValidationLabel` has a method that returns a `boolean` called `hasException`.

The `ValidationLabel` component displays the label in either normal text or bold, italicized text depending on the value of `hasException`, as shown in Figure 9.9.

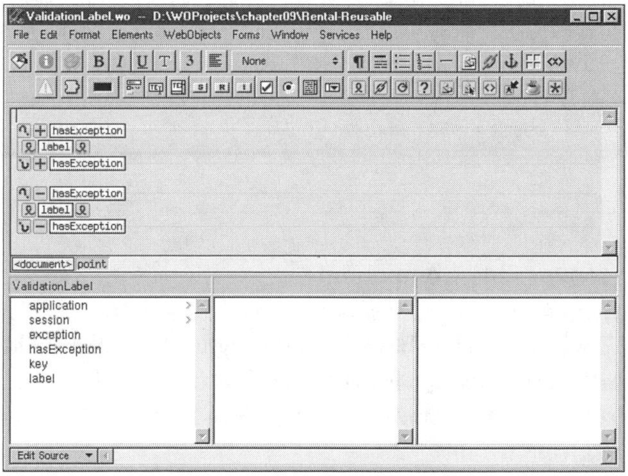

Figure 9.9

The user interface for the `ValidationLabel` *component.*

The `hasException` method returns `true` if there is an exception and the `ValidatedPropertyUserInfoKey` from the exception's `userInfo` dictionary is equal to the `key` in the component. The code for the `ValidationLabel` class is given in Listing 9.4.

Listing 9.4

ValidationLabel.java

```java
import com.apple.yellow.foundation.*;
import com.apple.yellow.webobjects.*;
import com.apple.yellow.eocontrol.*;
import com.apple.yellow.eoaccess.*;

public class ValidationLabel
    extends WOComponent
{
    protected EOValidation.Exception exception;
    protected String label;
    protected String key;

    public boolean hasException()
    {
        if ( exception == null )
        {
            return false;
        }
        NSDictionary userInfo = (NSDictionary)exception.userInfo();
        String exceptionKey = (String)userInfo.objectForKey(
            EOValidation.Exception.ValidatedPropertyUserInfoKey );

        return ( key.equals( exceptionKey ) );
    }
}
```

The ValidationMessage Component

We need another component to display a message associated with a validation error. This message could be placed above or to the right of the TextField with the error. Initially, the ValidationMessage is blank, but it is populated with a message when the user enters erroneous information. The attributes for the ValidationMessage component are given in Table 9.3.

Table 9.3

Attributes for the ValidationMessage *Component*

Attribute	Type
exception	EOValidation.Exception
key	String

The `ValidationMessage` displays the exception message if the key for the exception's `userInfo` dictionary is equal to the key in the component. The user interface for the `ValidationMessage` component is shown in Figure 9.10.

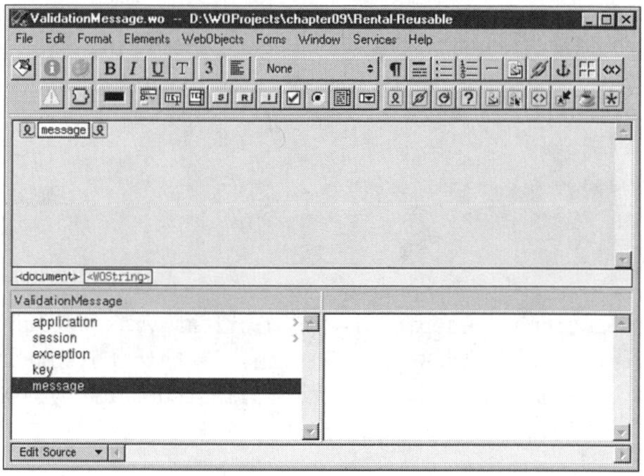

Figure 9.10
The user interface for the `ValidationMessage` *component.*

The trick to the `ValidationMessage` component is to display the exception's message only if the key in the component is the same as the `ValidatedPropertyUserInfoKey`. This is done in `appendToResponse()` in the `ValidationMessage` class, which is given in Listing 9.5.

Listing 9.5

The `ValidationMessage` *Class*

```
import com.apple.yellow.foundation.*;
import com.apple.yellow.webobjects.*;
import com.apple.yellow.eocontrol.*;
import com.apple.yellow.eoaccess.*;

public class ValidationMessage
    extends WOComponent
{
    protected EOValidation.Exception exception;
```

Listing 9.5

Continued

```
    protected String key;
    protected String message;

    public void appendToResponse( WOResponse response, WOContext context )
    {
        if ( exception == null )
        {
            message = null;
        }
        else
        {
            NSDictionary userInfo = (NSDictionary)exception.userInfo();
            String exceptionKey = (String)userInfo.objectForKey(
                EOValidation.Exception.ValidatedPropertyUserInfoKey );
            if ( key.equals( exceptionKey ) )
            {
                message = exception.getMessage();
            }
            else
            {
                message = null;
            }
        }
        super.appendToResponse( response, context );
    }
}
```

The `CheckOutPage`

Both the `ValidationLabel` and the `ValidationMessage` components require that the `exception` attribute be bound to the exception that was thrown. The pages that use these components must catch the exception and store it in an instance variable. This could be done by adding a method called `saveChanges()`, which attempts to call `saveChanges()` on the editing context. If an exception is thrown, it is caught and `null` is returned. This has the effect of redisplaying the same page, with the validation components displaying a new message. The implementation of the `CheckOutPage` is given in Listing 9.6.

Listing 9.6

CheckOutPage.java

```java
import com.apple.yellow.foundation.*;
import com.apple.yellow.webobjects.*;
import com.apple.yellow.eocontrol.*;
import com.apple.yellow.eoaccess.*;

public class CheckOutPage
    extends WOComponent
{

    protected Rental rental;
    protected NSGregorianDate checkOutDate;
    protected Exception exception;

    /** @TypeInfo Rental */
    public Rental rental()
    {
        return rental;
    }

    public void setRental(Rental newRental)
    {
        rental = newRental;
    }

    public WOComponent checkOut()
    {
        Main nextPage = (Main)pageWithName("Main");

        // Initialize your component here
        EOEditingContext ec = this.session().defaultEditingContext();
        ec.insertObject( rental );
        rental.checkOut( checkOutDate );
        return this.saveChanges( ec, nextPage );
    }

    public WOComponent saveChanges(
        EOEditingContext ec,
        WOComponent nextComponent )
    {
```

Listing 9.6

Continued

```
        try
        {
            ec.saveChanges();
            return nextComponent;
        }
        catch ( EOValidation.Exception e )
        {
            exception = e;
            return null;
        }
    }

    public Main cancelCheckOut()
    {
        Main nextPage = (Main)pageWithName("Main");

        // Initialize your component here

        return nextPage;
    }

}
```

The main change is in the addition of the saveChanges() method. This method takes the editing context and the next page as parameters. If the changes are saved successfully, the next page is returned; otherwise, the exception is set and null is returned. Notice that the checkIn() method uses this new method instead of calling the editing context's save changes method directly.

Adding the Components to the CheckOutPage

The last step is to use these components. For example, both the ValidationLabel and ValidationMessage components can be placed in the CheckOutPage, as shown in Figure 9.11.

The bindings for the ValidationLabel and ValidationMessage components for the CheckOutPage are given in Tables 9.4 and 9.5.

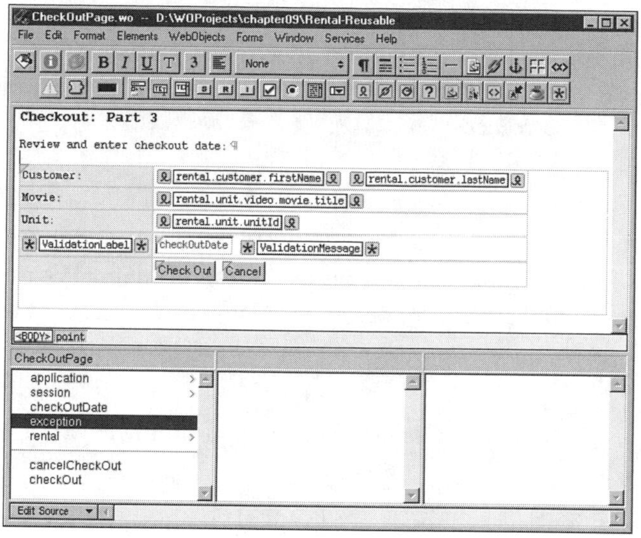

Figure 9.11
Using the ValidationLabel *and* ValidationMessage *components.*

Table 9.4
Bindings for the ValidationLabel *on the* CheckOutPage

Attribute	Value
exception	exception
key	"dateOut"
label	"Date Out:"

Table 9.5
Bindings for the ValidationMessage *on the* CheckOutPage

Attribute	Value
exception	exception
key	"dateOut"

Further Additions

At this point, the single data-entry field will be validated, so the next step is to add the validation components to the CheckInPage. Also, no feedback is given if validateForSave or one of the other operation-level validation methods throws an exception. Another reusable validation component could be created to handle those exceptions. The process for creating the operation-level validation component would be similar to the process for creating attribute-level validation components. This is left as an exercise for the reader.

Summary

The validation of user input can be a bit tricky, especially for Web-based applications. In general, you should attempt to design your application to avoid potential validation problems. Given that, there are a few places in EOF that are used to catch potential validation problems:

- All enterprise objects implement the methods in the EOValidation interface (EOControl).

- The operation-level methods in the EOValidation interface are intended to be extended to provide model-specific validation.

- The attribute-level validation methods will call specific methods with the signature validateKey() to determine key-specific validation rules.

- To determine when a validation error has occurred, catch the EOValidation.Exception that was thrown during the editing context's saveChanges() method.

PART III

ADVANCED TOPICS

CHAPTER 10

ADVANCED UI

As a savvy consumer of software products, I am completely aware that looks count.
Even more than that, the feel counts. The software should know what I want to do
and help me get there. When I want a back button, it should be there, looking good.
Maybe I'm a bit superficial, but software products are a lot like people in this case—
the first impression is really important.

This chapter introduces a number of components that will give you more options in
creating HTML user interfaces. The topics covered are

- Check boxes and radio buttons

- A tabbed view

- An Outline component

- JavaScript

- Frames

Giving the User Some Options

The first part of the chapter is a discussion of providing the user with those staples of
the user interface toolbox, check boxes and radio buttons. Although WebObjects
makes using these user interface objects easier than it would otherwise be, it's not a
walk in the park.

WOCheckBox

The WOCheckBox is used to display an on or off value. It has a binding called checked
that is used to denote whether or not the box should be checked. Table 10.1 lists the
attributes for the WOCheckBox.

Table 10.1

Attributes for the WOCheckBox

Attribute	Description
value	Used in conjunction with the selection binding. If the value and selection bindings are the same, the button is checked.
selection	Used with the value binding. If the button is checked, the selection is set to be the same as the value.
checked	If this resolves to true or YES, the check box will be checked; a false or NO value will result in the check box not being checked. When the form is submitted, the key to which this is bound is set with whatever the user selected (true or false).
name	The HTML name for the check box. If a name is not assigned, WebObjects will assign a name for the check box.
disabled	If this resolves to YES or true, the button will appear but will not be active.

Example

For an example of using the check box, consider the Rental application used in Chapter 7, "Writing Enterprise Objects Classes." In this application, Unit objects were checked out and in, and Fee objects were created. The UnitsInStockPage component listed all the units in stock and allowed the user to select a unit to rent. Let's modify the page to display check boxes beside the unit number, which allows the user to select multiple units to rent at the same time, as shown in Figure 10.1.

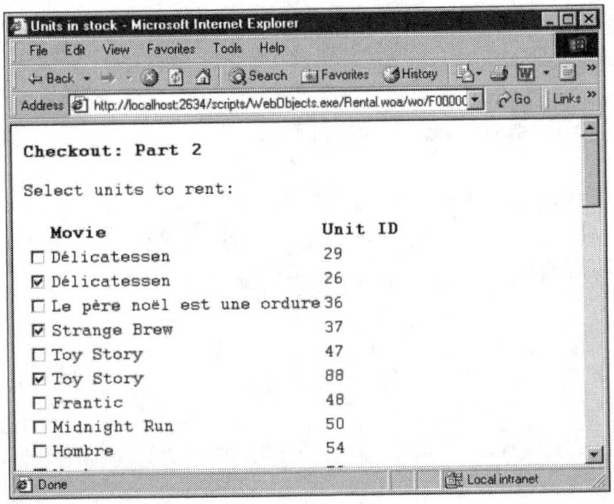

Figure 10.1

The Units in Stock page.

First, let's modify the `UnitsInStockPage`. Add a `WOCheckBox` to the table in a new column to the left of the Movie column as shown in Figure 10.2.

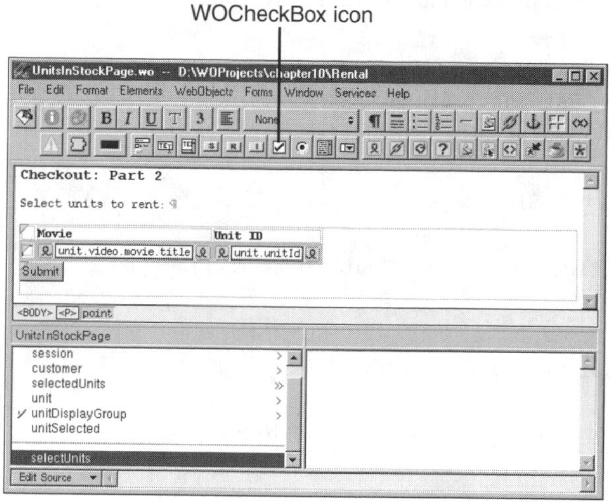

Figure 10.2

Adding the `WOCheckBox` *to the* `UnitsInStockPage`*. When the* `WOCheckBox` *is initially added, the text* `Checkbox` *appears next to it. You can simply delete this text.*

The check box should be placed inside the `WORepetition` so that a separate check box appears on each line. You must also add a form around the table with a submit button at the bottom. You will want to capture all the units that the user selects and place them in an `NSMutableArray`. You will have to determine which `Unit` objects are selected and place them in the `NSMutableArray`. On the `takeValuesFromRequest` method, the `item` of the `WORepetition` contains the current object, as discussed in Chapter 7. This will be used to determine which objects to place in the `NSMutableArray`.

First, bind the `checked` binding for the `WOCheckBox` to `unitSelected`, and create the `setUnitSelected()` and `unitSelected()` methods as outlined in Listing 10.1.

Listing 10.1

The `UnitsInStockPage.java` *File*

```
import com.apple.yellow.foundation.*;
import com.apple.yellow.webobjects.*;
import com.apple.yellow.eocontrol.*;
import com.apple.yellow.eoaccess.*;
```

Listing 10.1

Continued

```java
public class UnitsInStockPage extends WOComponent {
    protected WODisplayGroup unitDisplayGroup;

    protected Unit unit;
    protected Customer customer;
    protected NSMutableArray selectedUnits;

    public UnitsInStockPage()
    {
        selectedUnits = new NSMutableArray();
    }

    public boolean unitSelected()
    {
        return selectedUnits.containsObject( unit );
    }

    public void setUnitSelected( boolean value )
    {
        if ( value )
        {
            selectedUnits.addObject( unit );
        }
    }

    public CheckOutPage selectUnits()
    {
        CheckOutPage nextPage = (CheckOutPage)pageWithName("CheckOutPage");

        // Initialize your component here
        NSMutableArray rentals = new NSMutableArray();

        for ( int index = 0; index<selectedUnits.count(); index++ )
        {
            Unit aUnit = (Unit)selectedUnits.objectAtIndex(index);
            rentals.addObject(
                new Rental( customer, aUnit, new NSGregorianDate() ) );
        }
        nextPage.setRentals( rentals );
```

Listing 10.1

Continued

```
        return nextPage;
    }

    public Customer customer() {
        return customer;
    }
    public void setCustomer(Customer newCustomer) {
        customer = newCustomer;
    }

}
```

The `unitSelected()` method will not be called in any useful way during our application, and it is supplied only because it is required. The `setUnitSelected()` method does all the work for us. If the value that is passed in is true, the current unit is added to the `selectedUnits` array. You will need to add `selectedUnits` as an `NSMutableArray` instance variable, and initialize it on the constructor for the page. In the `takeValuesForRequest` method, the `setUnitSelected` method is called for every unit. In the `appendToResponse` method, the `unitSelected` method is called for all units.

The `selectUnits` method is bound to the `action` for the submit button. This method simply goes through the list of units and creates a Rental object for each one, and then passes them to the next page, which will confirm these units and allow the user to enter another checkout date.

Note that this technique works fine for components that will be visited only once. If this component were visited again, there is a good chance that the `selectedUnits` array would be populated with the same instance multiple times. To fix this, you would add an object only if it did not already exist in the array.

WORadioButton

Radio buttons enable you to display a mutually exclusive group of check box–like buttons. Clicking one of the buttons deselects the rest of the buttons. The attributes and usage of the radio button are similar to those of the check box, but the difference is that you will set the name of all the radio buttons in a group to be the same. Table 10.2 lists the attributes for the radio button.

Table 10.2

Attributes for the WORadioButton

Attribute	Description
value	Used in conjunction with the selection binding. If the value and selection bindings are the same, the button is checked.
selection	Used with the value binding. If the button is checked, the selection is set to be the same as the value.
checked	If this resolves to true or YES, the radio button will be checked; a false or NO value will result in the radio button not being checked.
name	The HTML name for the radio button. To place a set of buttons in a group, give them all the same name.
disabled	If this resolves to YES or true, the button will appear but will not be active.

Example

For an example of using a radio button, consider an Internet-based login page. This page could store two radio buttons for If You Are Already a Member and If You Are a New Member. Figure 10.3 displays the user interface for this page.

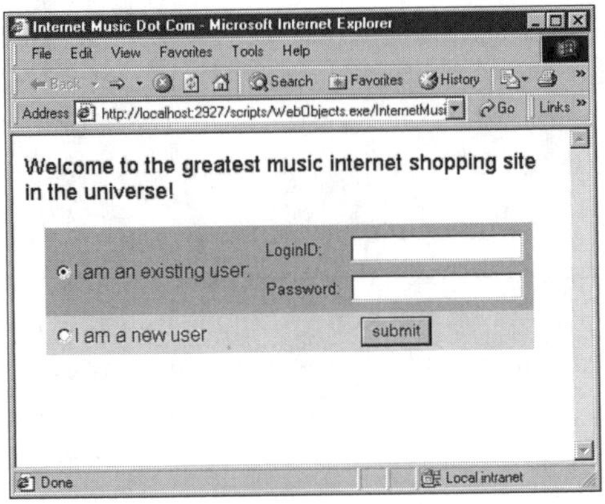

Figure 10.3

Radio buttons are used to present the user with mutually exclusive options.

This is accomplished by first placing the radio buttons on the page using the Radio Button icon as shown in Figure 10.4.

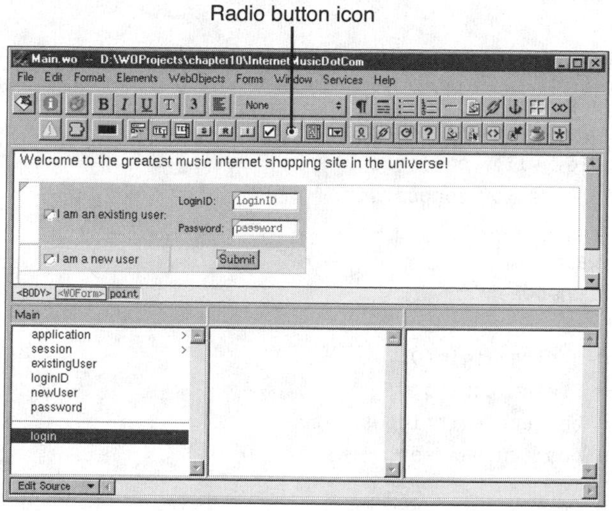

Radio button icon

Figure 10.4

Placing a radio button on a component.

As stated earlier, the attributes for the radio buttons are similar to the attributes for the check boxes. The checked attribute is set to an instance variable in the component, and represents the on/off status of the button. The name for the radio button will also be set in order to place the radio buttons in the same group. Table 10.3 lists the bindings for the two radio buttons on this page.

Table 10.3

Bindings for the Two Radio Buttons on the Sample Page

Control	Attribute	Binding
Radio button 1	checked	existingUser
Radio button 1	name	"userRadioButton"
Radio button 2	checked	newUser
Radio button 3	name	"userRadioButton"

The code for this component is given in Listing 10.2.

Listing 10.2

The Component Java code for the Radio Button Example

```java
import com.apple.yellow.foundation.*;
import com.apple.yellow.webobjects.*;
import com.apple.yellow.eocontrol.*;
import com.apple.yellow.eoaccess.*;

public class Main
    extends WOComponent
{
    protected String loginID;
    protected String password;
    protected boolean existingUser=true;
    protected boolean newUser;


    public WOComponent login()
    {
        if ( existingUser )
        {
            // should probably put some validation in here   :)
            UserStartPage nextPage = (UserStartPage)
                this.pageWithName("UserStartPage");
            nextPage.setLoginID( loginID );
            return nextPage;
        }
        else if ( newUser )
        {
            UserRegistrationPage nextPage = (UserRegistrationPage)
                this.pageWithName("UserRegistrationPage");
            return nextPage;
        }
        return null;
    }

}
```

Notice that the `existingUser` variable is initialized to `true`. This causes the I Am an Existing User radio button to be checked initially. The `login()` method is bound to the submit button's `action`, and will return the appropriate page, depending on which radio button was selected. As with any form control, the radio buttons need to be in the same `WOForm` as the submit button.

"Helper" Dynamic Elements

Also packaged with WebObjects is the WebObjects extensions framework. This framework contains a number of additional dynamic elements that save you time when you are creating your user interface. Four dynamic elements that will help you out are the WOCheckBoxList, WOCheckBoxMatrix, WORadioButtonList, and WORadioButtonMatrix. The reference for these dynamic elements can be found in the WebObjects Info Center under the Reference, WebObjects, WebObjects Extensions Reference.

WOCheckBoxList and WOCheckBoxMatrix

These dynamic elements display a set of check boxes from values contained in an NSArray. These dynamic elements will automatically update another NSArray with the appropriate selected objects, depending on what the user checked. The difference between the two components is that the WOCheckBoxList displays the check boxes as a list of items whereas the WOCheckBoxMatrix displays them as a set of rows and columns.

These dynamic elements are found in two separate locations. The WOCheckBoxList is actually part of the WebObjects framework, but it's not an icon in WebObjects Builder. For this one, you will have to click the Add Custom WebObject icon.

Clicking the Add Custom WebObject will display the Custom WebObject panel. From here, you can select from any of the dynamic elements in the WebObjects and the WebObjects extensions frameworks. The Custom WebObject panel is shown in Figure 10.5.

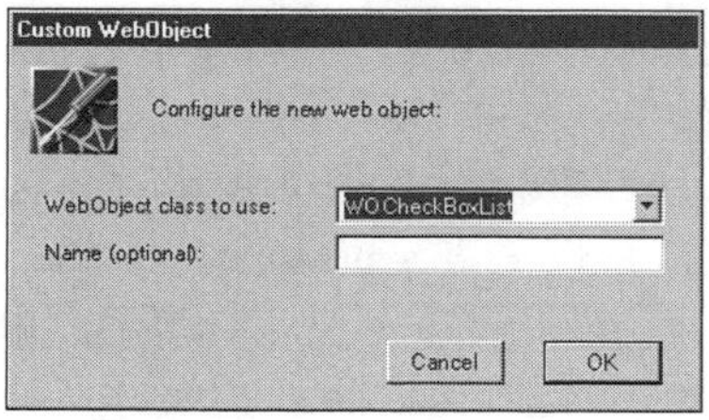

Figure 10.5
The Custom WebObject panel.

The WOCheckBoxMatrix is also available from this panel. Most of the dynamic elements in the extensions framework are also available from the palette. The palette can also be displayed with the Window, Palette menu item. The Extensions palette displays dynamic elements from the WebObjects extensions framework, as shown in Figure 10.6. To use one of these elements, drag it from the palette and drop it in the WebObjects Builder window.

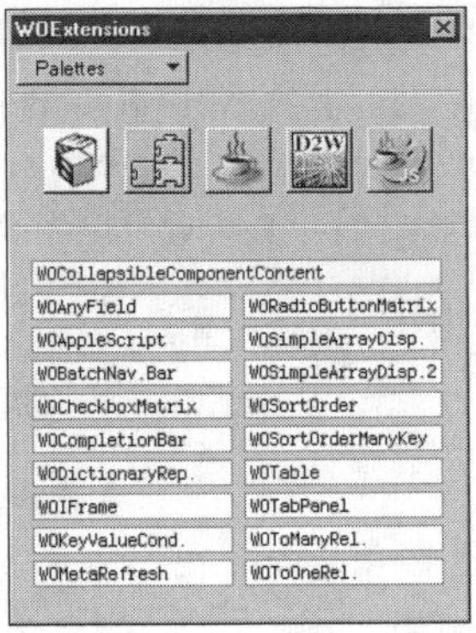

Figure 10.6
The Extensions Palette.

The attributes for the two dynamic elements are similar to the WOBrowser attributes, which were discussed in Chapter 7. The WOCheckBoxList attributes are listed in Table 10.4.

Table 10.4

WOCheckBoxList *Attributes—At a Minimum, You Need to Provide Bindings for* list, item, *and* selections; *the* displayString *and* suffix *Bindings Are Also Useful*

Attribute	Description
list	Bound to an NSArray of objects to be displayed.
item	Similar to the WORepetition, the object used to iterate through the list.
displayString	If the item is bound to a non-String object, the displayString denotes how to display the object.
value	The HTML "value" attribute.
index	The index of the current item in the array bound to list.
prefix	Some HTML that will be inserted before the check box. This is useful for displaying numbers or font tags.
suffix	HTML that will be rendered after the displayString. It is useful to bind this to a line break, " ", in order to display each check box on a separate line.
selections	Bound to an NSArray that will hold the list of objects that the user selected.
name	The HTML name for the element. If you don't supply a name, WebObjects will.

Table 10.4

Continued

Attribute	Description
disabled	Similar to other controls, if this resolves to `true`, the control will be disabled.
escapeHTML	This is bound to a `boolean`. If it resolves to `true`, any HTML in the `displayString` will be "escaped," meaning that it will be displayed in the browser. Set this to `false` if you want the HTML to be rendered.

The `WOCheckBoxMatrix` doesn't give you many options. Its attributes are shown in Table 10.5. The advantage is that you don't have to know a lot to implement it. But the big disadvantage is that if you don't like the way it's displayed, tough luck.

Table 10.5

`WOCheckBoxMatrix` *Attributes; You Will Probably Use All These Attributes*

Attribute	Description
list	Similar to the `WOCheckBoxList`, this is bound to an `NSArray` of objects to be displayed.
item	Also similar to the `WOCheckBoxList`, the object used to iterate through the list.
selections	This is bound to an `NSArray` that will hold the list of objects that the user selected.
maxColumns	Bound to an `int`, this represents the maximum number of columns that the `WOCheckBoxMatrix` will display.

Example

These dynamic elements work really well with objects from the database because they use `NSArrays` for the list of objects displayed and for the list of selected objects. For an example, let's modify the scheduling application written in Chapter 8, "Using Inheritance with EOF," to use check boxes to display the list of potential meeting attendees (see Figure 10.7).

The examples for the `WOCheckBoxList`, `WOCheckBoxMatrix`, `WORadioButtonList`, and `WORadioButtonMatrix` all use the same component, `AddMeetingPage`. The code for this component is presented in Listing 10.3.

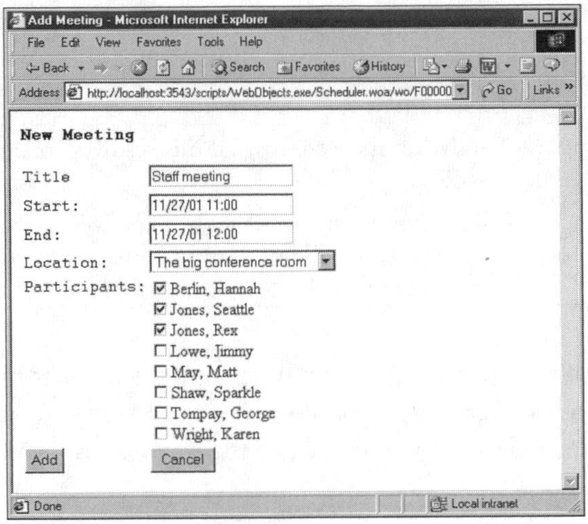

Figure 10.7
The list of potential meeting attendees could be displayed using a `WOCheckBoxList`.

Listing 10.3

`AddMeetingPage.java;` *This Component Is Used for the Next Few Examples*

```java
import com.apple.yellow.foundation.*;
import com.apple.yellow.webobjects.*;
import com.apple.yellow.eocontrol.*;
import com.apple.yellow.eoaccess.*;

public class AddMeetingPage
    extends WOComponent
{
    protected Meeting meeting;
    protected WODisplayGroup locationDisplayGroup;
    protected WODisplayGroup personDisplayGroup;
    protected Person person;
    protected Location location;
    protected WOComponent backComponent;

    public AddMeetingPage()
    {
```

Listing 10.3

Continued

```
        meeting = new Meeting();
    }

    public WOComponent addMeeting()
    {
        EOEditingContext ec = this.session().defaultEditingContext();
        ec.insertObject(meeting);
        ec.saveChanges();
        return this.backComponent();
    }

    public WOComponent cancel()
    {
        return this.backComponent();
    }

    public WOComponent backComponent()
    {
        return backComponent;
    }

    public void setBackComponent(WOComponent newBackComponent)
    {
        backComponent = newBackComponent;
    }

}
```

The first step is to add a WOCheckBoxList to the page used to add a meeting. This can be done using the Add Custom WebObject button as described earlier. This will be represented as a custom WebObject, as shown in Figure 10.8.

A WODisplayGroup is used to retrieve all the Person objects, and a key called person is used to iterate over the array. A key called meeting is used to store the Meeting object being edited by this window. The participants for the meeting are represented by the participants relationship. The bindings for the WOCheckBoxList are listed in Table 10.6.

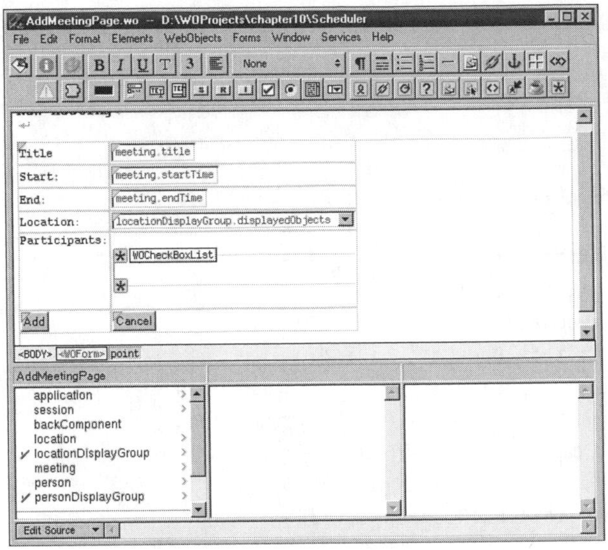

Figure 10.8
The WOCheckBoxList *is displayed as a custom WebObject.*

Table 10.6
The Bindings for the WOCheckBoxList *in the Add Meeting Page*

Attribute	Binding
displayString	person.fullName
item	person
list	personDisplayGroup.displayedObjects
selections	meeting.participants
suffix	" "

Without the suffix binding, all the check boxes would be displayed on the same line.

Using a WOCheckBoxMatrix allows the users to be displayed in columns. Figure 10.9 shows that the order in which the people are displayed is from left to right, and then from top to bottom.

The WOCheckBoxMatrix can be placed in your component using either the palette or the Add Custom WebObject icon. Notice that the WOCheckBoxMatrix does not have displayString, suffix, or prefix bindings as the WOCheckBoxList does. The WOCheckBoxMatrix works in a slightly different way, and requires you to place a

WOString inside it for the display value. Figure 10.10 shows the WOString inside of the WOCheckBoxMatrix.

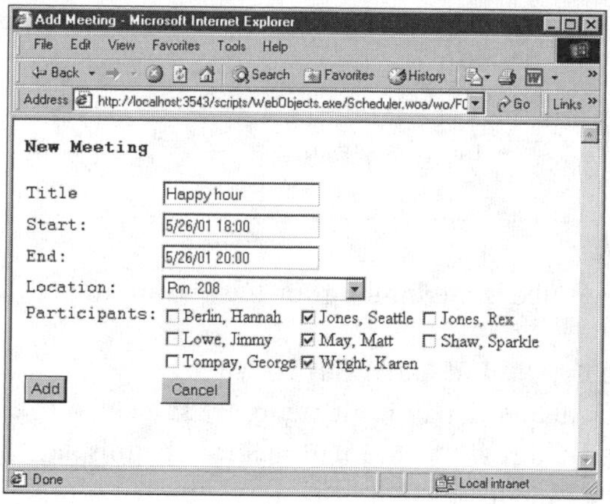

Figure 10.9
The WOCheckBoxMatrix.

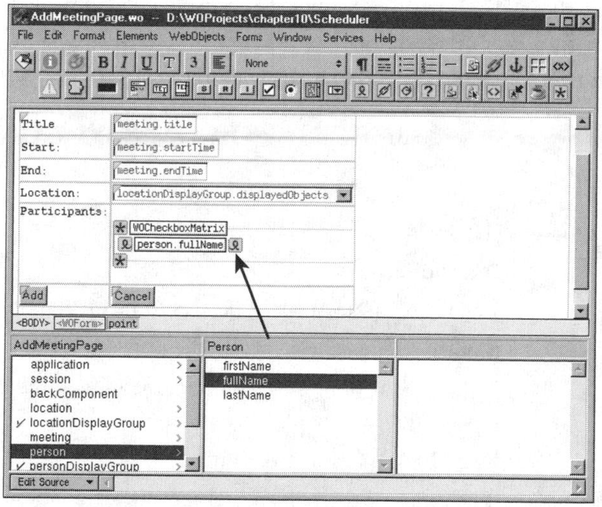

Figure 10.10
You must place a WOString *inside the* WOCheckBoxMatrix *for the appropriate display value.*

The bindings for this WOCheckBoxMatrix are displayed in Table 10.7.

Table 10.7

The Bindings for the WOCheckBoxMatrix *in the Add Meeting Page Are Similar to the* WOCheckBoxList *Bindings*

Attribute	Binding
item	person
list	personDisplayGroup.displayedObjects
selections	meeting.participants
maxColumns	3

The only real difference is the binding for the maximum number of columns.

WORadioButtonList **and** WORadioButtonMatrix

The radio button's helper dynamic elements are similar to the check box's helper dynamic elements. There's a WORadioButtonList that displays a straight list of radio buttons, and a WORadioButtonMatrix that displays the radio buttons as rows and columns. Both dynamic elements can be obtained from the Add Custom WebObject button, and the WORadioButtonMatrix is also on the Extensions palette.

The main difference between these dynamic elements and the check box dynamic elements is that the radio buttons allow only a single selection. For this reason, the selections attribute is replaced with the selection attribute. The attributes for the WORadioButtonList and the WORadioButtonMatrix are displayed in Tables 10.8 and 10.9.

Table 10.8

The WORadioButtonList *Attributes*

Attribute	Description
list	Bound to an NSArray of objects to be displayed.
item	Similar to the WORepetition, the object used to iterate through the list.
displayString	If the item is bound to a non-String object, the displayString denotes how to display the object.
value	The HTML "value" attribute.
index	The index of the current item in the array bound to list.
prefix	Some HTML that will be inserted before the radio button. This is useful for displaying numbers or font tags.
suffix	HTML that will be rendered after the displayString. It is useful to bind this to a line break, " ", to display each radio button on a separate line.

Table 10.8

Continued

Attribute	Description
selection	Bound to an object that will hold the user's selection.
name	The HTML name for the element. If you don't supply a name, WebObjects will.
disabled	Similar to other controls, if this resolves to true, the control will be disabled.
escapeHTML	This is bound to a boolean. If it resolves to true, any HTML in the displayString will be "escaped," meaning that it will be displayed in the browser. Set this to false if you want the HTML to be rendered.

Table 10.9

The WORadioButtonMatrix *Attributes*

Attribute	Description
list	Similar to the WORadioButtonList, this is bound to an NSArray of objects to be displayed.
item	Also similar to the WORadioButtonList, the object used to iterate through the list.
selection	This is bound to an object that will represent the object the user selected.
maxColumns	Bound to an int, this represents the maximum number of columns that the WORadioButtonMatrix will display.

Example

For an example, we can replace the WOPopupButton with a list of radio buttons. On the New Meeting page (see Figure 10.11), a WOPopupButton is used to enable the user to select a location for the meeting.

The list of potential locations is retrieved using a WODisplayGroup, and a key called location is used as temporary storage. The relationship modified by this WOPopupButton is the location relationship on the meeting object. After you've added the WORadioButtonList, the bindings are given in Table 10.10.

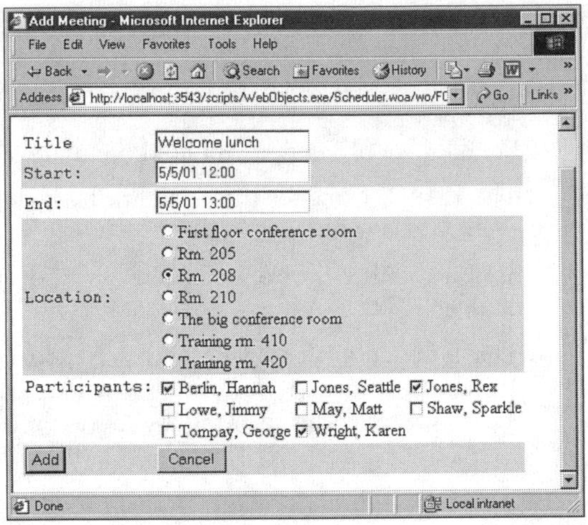

Figure 10.11
The locations can be displayed as a set of radio buttons.

Table 10.10

The `WORadioButtonList` *Bindings for the New Meeting Example*

Attribute	Binding
displayString	location.title
item	location
list	locationDisplayGroup.displayedObjects
selection	meeting.location
suffix	" "

If you were to use a `WORadioButtonMatrix`, you would have to place a `WOString` inside it, similar to the `WOCheckBoxMatrix`. Figure 10.12 shows how to do that.

The bindings for this example are given in Table 10.11.

Table 10.11

The `WORadioButtonMatrix` *Bindings for the New Meeting Example*

Attribute	Binding
list	locationDisplayGroup.displayedObjects
item	location
maxColumns	2
selection	meeting.location

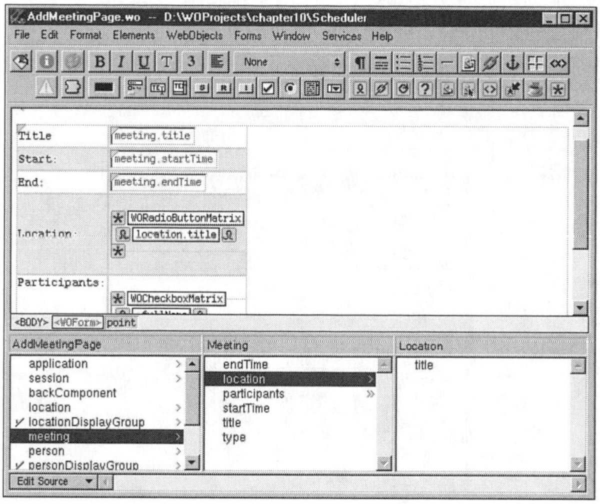

Figure 10.12
Placing a WOString *inside a* WORadioButtonMatrix *is required if you want to display anything.*

The completed example for this section is located on the book's Web site,
www.wowack.com.

Tab View

A useful component in user interface design is the tab view. This display enables you
to organize a lot of information in different panels that are stacked on top of each
other. Tabs stick up from each panel, allowing the user to select a panel. It is really
useful for organizing large amounts of information so that it's more easily digestible.
In the New Meeting example, the display became convoluted with radio buttons and
check boxes. It would be better displayed using a tab view (see Figure 10.13).

Creating a tab view in HTML is no easy feat; it involves organizing images and tables
to get the appropriate look. This has already been done for us in the WOTabPanel
dynamic element, which is located in the WebObjects extensions framework.

WOTabPanel

The WOTabPanel automatically displays a set of tabs and allows the user to move
between them. This component manages only the display of the tabs; managing the
display of the content is up to you. The WOTabPanel uses an NSArray bound to the tabs
attribute for the list of tabs. Another attribute, called selectedTab, represents the

currently selected tab. You can use the currently selected tab to determine what to display. It is common to use a WOKeyValueConditional dynamic element for this. The attributes for the WOTabPanel are listed in Table 10.12.

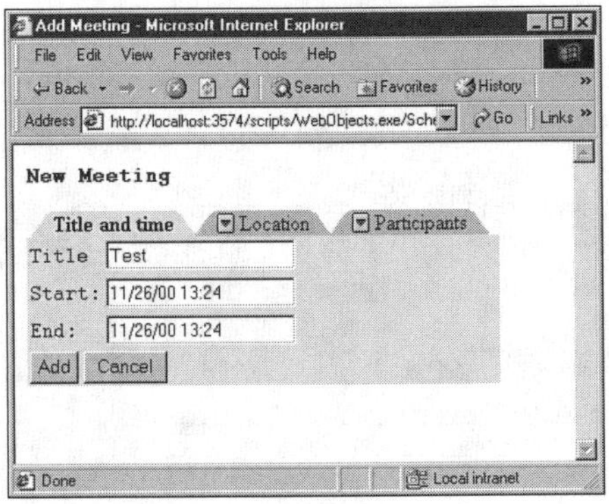

Figure 10.13
Reorganization of the New Meeting page.

Table 10.12

The Attributes for the WOTabPanel

Attribute	Description
tabs	Bound to an NSArray that represents the tabs.
selectedTab	Bound to an object that represents the currently selected tab.
tabNameKey	If the items in the NSArray are non-String objects, the name of the key that will be used to display the tab.
nonSelectedBgColor	The background color of the non-selected tabs.
bgcolor	The background color of the selected tab.
textColor	The text color for all the tabs.
submitActionName	The name of the action method used when the tabs are switched. Leave this blank if you want your tabs to be hyperlinks.

You can configure the background colors for the selected and non-selected tabs in the WOTabPanel, along with the text color. However, the overall background color cannot be configured, which means that the WOTabPanel can be placed only on a page with a white background.

Also, the tab panel can be configured to use either hyperlinks or submit buttons by setting the submitActionName. If this is set, the tab panel will use submit buttons that act when switching tabs; if `submitActionName` is not set, the tab panel will use hyperlinks to switch tabs. If the `submitActionName` is set to the name of an action, the tab panel must be inside a form with `multipleSubmit` set to YES. If you have form controls inside the tab panel, you should set a value for the `submitActionName`.

After the bindings are set, it's up to you to determine the content that is displayed inside the tab panel. The `WOKeyValueConditional` dynamic element is good for this.

WOKeyValueConditional

This dynamic element compares a key in the parent component (the one you write) to a specific value. If the comparison is equal, the contents are displayed; if the values are not equal, the contents are not displayed. The attributes are listed in Table 10.13.

Table 10.13

Attributes for `WOKeyValueConditional`

Attribute	Description
key	Bound to a string that is the name of the key to compare. This is not bound to the key that you want to compare; it is bound to the *name* of the key you want to compare.
value	The value to compare with the key's value. If this is equal to the value for the key binding, the contents are displayed.

Example

For an example of using the `WOTabPanel` and `WOKeyValueConditional` together, let's split the controls on the New Meeting page into three tabs: Title and time, Location, and Participants. The first step is to create an instance variable called `tabs` that is an `NSArray` of `Strings` that represent the three tabs. This can be done in the constructor, as shown in Listing 10.4.

Listing 10.4

The Constructor for the `AddMeetingPage`, *Modified to Initialize the* `NSArray` *of Tabs*

```
public AddMeetingPage()
{
    String [] tabsStrings = new String []
        { "Title and time", "Location", "Participants"};
    tabs = new NSArray(tabsStrings);

    meeting = new Meeting();
}
```

You will also need to add a `String` instance variable to store the currently selected tab, called `currentTabSelection`. Finally, add an action method called `tabSelected` that returns `null`.

After the tab view has been added to the page in WebObjects Builder, set the bindings as described in Table 10.14.

Table 10.14

Bindings for the `WOTabPanel` *Used in the New Meeting Page*

Attribute	Binding
selectedTab	currentTabSelection
submitActionName	"tabSelected"
tabs	tabs

Now you have to display different sets of components depending on the tab that is selected. This can be done easily by adding three `WOKeyValueConditional` dynamic elements. This is a good place to set the names of the conditionals to better identify them. The name for the dynamic element can be set in the inspector as shown in Figure 10.14. Name the three conditionals `titleAndTimeConditional`, `locationConditional`, and `participantsConditional`.

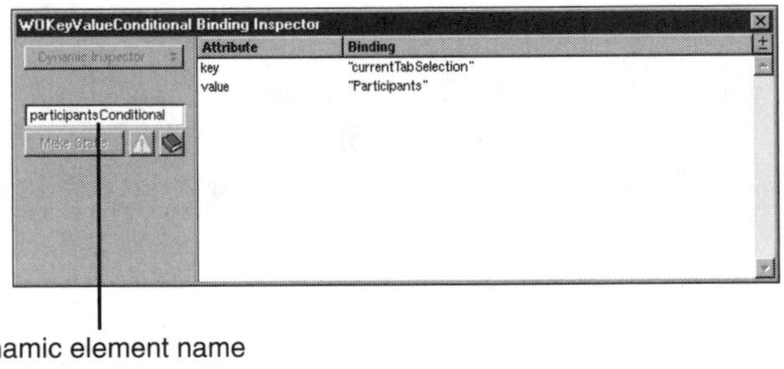

Dynamic element name

Figure 10.14
The name for a dynamic element can be set in the inspector.

The bindings for these three conditionals are displayed in Table 10.15.

Table 10.15

Bindings for the WOTabPanel *Used in the New Meeting Page*

Conditional	Attribute	Binding
titleAndTimeConditional	key	"currentTabSelection"
titleAndTimeConditional	value	"Title and time"
locationConditional	key	"currentTabSelection"
locationConditional	value	"Location"
participantsConditional	key	"currentTabSelection"
participantsConditional	value	"Participants"

The key bindings for these three conditionals should all be the same because they are used to determine which tab is to be displayed. Also, the value for each of these conditionals should match with a String that was placed in the tabs array in Listing 10.4. Finally, notice that the key is placed in double quotation marks because this dynamic element expects this binding to be to the *name* of the key, not the key itself.

At this point, you can place the appropriate controls inside each conditional, and the Add and Cancel buttons should be at the bottom of the tab view, but not in a conditional. These items should be arranged as shown in Figure 10.15.

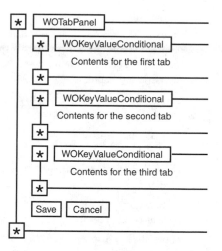

Figure 10.15

Arranging the WOTabPanel, WOKeyValueConditionals, *and the submit buttons.*

It might take some time to become familiar with this component, but mastering it adds an important tool to your user interface toolbox.

Outline Component

Another advanced type user interface object that is useful in certain situations is the Outline component. This component will display some text with a control beside it. When the user clicks on the control, items will be displayed below that control. This is useful for displaying hierarchical information such as file systems.

This type of component is used in the old-style Mac File Manager to display directories and their contents. It is also used in the WOInfoCenter for the main navigation.

WOCollapsibleComponentContent

The dynamic element used to display an outline-like component is the WOCollapsibleComponentContent. Using this component, you simply place all the content you want to be collapsible inside the dynamic element, and it will be displayed when the user selects it. The attributes for this dynamic element are displayed in Table 10.16. The most commonly used attributes are the openedLabel and closedLabel, which set the label for the dynamic element when it is opened and closed.

Table 10.16

The Attributes for the WOCollapsibleComponentContent

Attribute	Description
condition	This binding is set to YES or NO and determines whether the content is initially collapsed or displayed. Set the value to YES to initially display the content; set the value to NO to initially collapse the content.
visibility	This binding is used to identify whether the dynamic element is currently collapsed or open.
openedImageFileName	The filename for the image to be displayed when the content is displayed.
closedImageFileName	The filename for the image to be displayed when the content is collapsed.
framework	The framework for the openedImageFileName and closedImageFileName.
openedLabel	The label to display when the content is displayed.
closedLabel	The label to display when the content is collapsed.
submitActionName	Similar to the WOTabPanel, the action to be called if this dynamic element is in a form.

If you want to use custom images for the controls, you can specify the image filenames using `openedImageFileName` and `closedImageFileName`. This assumes that the images are in your Web Server Resources directory. If the images are part of a WebObjects framework, bind the framework name to the `framework` binding. If you don't set these images, the standard, pale blue Mac triangle icons will be used.

Example

For an example of using this dynamic element, let's change the display of events in the scheduling application that we started in Chapter 8. The display was a little convoluted before, with everything about the event being displayed on a single line in the table. It would be nice to use the `WOCollapsibleComponentContent` to create a better user interface, as shown in Figure 10.16.

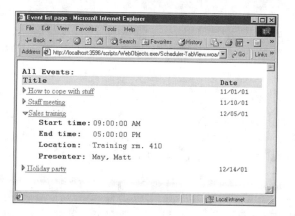

Figure 10.16
Changing the `EventListPage` *to use a* `WOCollapsibleComponentContent`.

The `EventListPage` retrieves the Event objects from the database on the `awake()` method and stores them in an `NSArray` called `events`. A key called `event` is used as temporary storage for the `WORepetition`.

The amazing thing about modifying the existing application to use this component is that no code is required! In WebObjects Builder, add a `WOCollapsibleComponentContent` inside the `WORepetition` that displays all the events. Inside the `WOCollapsibleComponentContent`, place all the information that you want displayed when the user clicks on the item. Figure 10.17 shows this modification in WebObjects Builder.

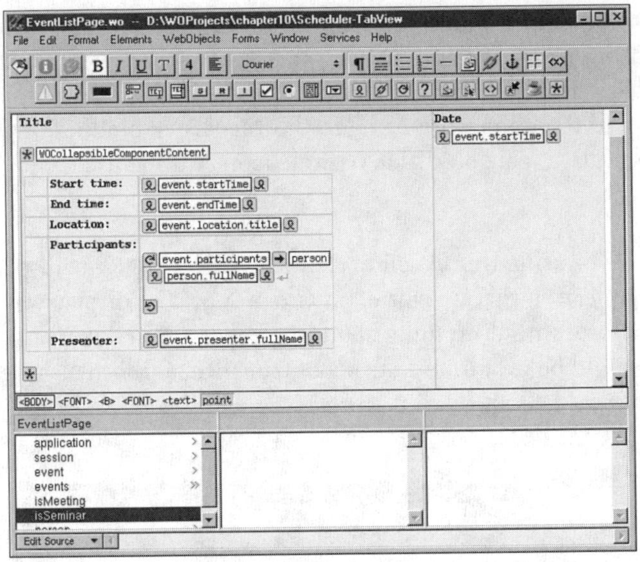

Figure 10.17
Using the WOCollapsibleComponentContent *inside a* WORepetition.

The bindings for this component are fairly simple if you want to use the standard display for the control. The only bindings you really need to be concerned with are the label bindings. Those bindings are listed in Table 10.17.

Table 10.17
The Bindings for Adding a WOCollapsibleComponentContent *to the* EventListPage

Attribute	Binding
closedLabel	event.title
openedLabel	event.title

At this point, your page of events should have the new functionality. As always, the complete project for this example can be found at www.wowack.com.

JavaScript

Netscape originally developed JavaScript as a scripting language that is embedded in HTML and has a Java-like syntax. JavaScript is a function-based scripting language. All the functions in JavaScript are event-based, meaning that they are called when a certain event occurs. An event could be the HTML page loading, or the user typing in a text field or clicking on a submit button. To learn how to use JavaScript, take a look at Sams Publishing's *Sams Teach Yourself JavaScript in 24 Hours, Second Edition*, by Michael Moncur.

JavaScript functions are either embedded within a pair of `<script>` tags within the `<head>` tag, or loaded from an external file. The standard extension for these files is `js`. You can find plenty of free JavaScript files on the Web, but before you employ one of those scripts, make sure that it fits your purpose.

In general, JavaScript should be used to enhance your site; it should not be used to implement required functionality. There are a number of browsers still out there that do not support JavaScript. Make sure that the users with those browsers can still use your site.

WOJavaScript

The `WOJavaScript` dynamic element is useful for embedding a complete JavaScript file in your component. Using `WOJavaScript`, you can specify the filename for the script file, or the actual JavaScript itself. This opens possibilities for dynamic creation of JavaScript from your Java code. You can add the JavaScript file in your Web Server Resources directory, and reference it using the `scriptFile` attribute. Table 10.18 lists the attributes for the `WOJavaScript` dynamic element.

Table 10.18

The Attributes for the WOJavaScript *Dynamic Element*

Attribute	Description
scriptFile	The filename for the script file. This should match a file in your Web Server Resources suitcase.
scriptString	A String that represents the script.
scriptSource	The URL for the script.
hideInComment	It is typical to "hide" JavaScript in an HTML comment, so browsers that do not support JavaScript can still display the page. You should set this to YES.

Premade JavaScript Dynamic Elements

`WOJavaScript` is useful if you have existing JavaScript functions or if you want to write your own, but sometimes you just want to use a cool JavaScript feature without writing a lot of code. Also, you might find it difficult to integrate custom JavaScript code within a WebObjects-generated page due to the dynamic naming of HTML elements.

There are some dynamic elements provided in the WebObjects `extensions` framework that are useful for resolving this difficulty.

`JSAlertPanel` and `JSConfirmPanel`

If the user clicks a hyperlink that either could possibly do some damage or could result in an unexpected state, it's a good idea to let the user know that. There are two dynamic elements for this: the `JSAlertPanel` and the `JSConfirmPanel`. Use these dynamic elements in place of hyperlinks, and a JavaScript panel will be displayed when the hyperlink is clicked.

The `JSAlertPanel` displays a panel with a message. The user can simply click on the OK button that is provided; there are no other options. When the user clicks the button, the action bound to the `JSAlertPanel` is then executed, as shown in Figure 10.18.

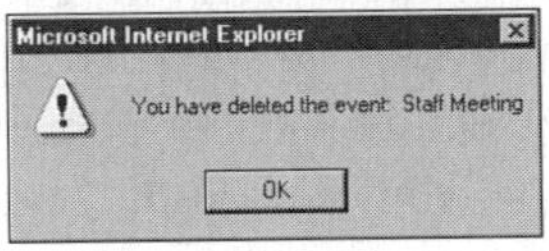

Figure 10.18
A JavaScript alert panel.

Because there is nothing that the user can do except select the OK button, there is not much use for this panel. In general, you don't want to display a window that the user has to click to get rid of if there is not a decision in the process.

The `JSConfirmPanel` works the same as the `JSAlertPanel`, except the user has the option of canceling the action (see Figure 10.19). The `JSConfirmPanel` contains OK and Cancel buttons. If the user selects the OK button in the JavaScript panel, the action method bound to the dynamic element is called. If Cancel is selected, nothing is submitted back to the server.

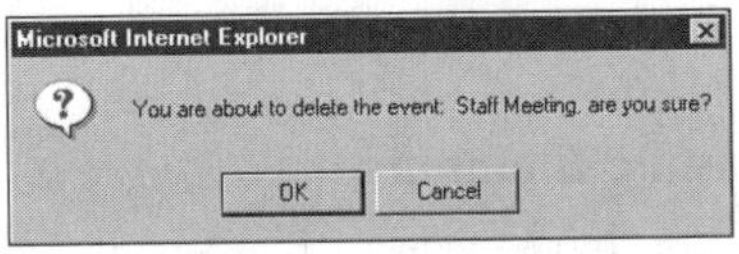

Figure 10.19
The `JSConfirmPanel` is more useful than the `JSAlertPanel` because it allows the user to cancel an action.

The attributes for the `JSConfirmPanel` are given in Table 10.19.

Table 10.19

The Bindings for the JSConfirmPanel

Attribute	Description
action	The action that is called if the user clicks the OK button in the JavaScript panel.
javaScriptFunction	The name of a JavaScript function that is called if the user clicks the OK button in the JavaScript panel.
pageName	The name of a WebObjects component that will be loaded if the user clicks the OK button in the JavaScript panel.
confirmMessage	The message to be displayed in the JavaScript panel.
altTag	If filename is set to an image filename, the text to display if the file can't be loaded.
filename	If supplied, the filename for an image to be displayed instead of a text hyperlink. This is a filename of a file in the Web Server Resources suitcase.
targetWindow	When using frames, the target into which the results of the action should go.
string	Text to be displayed in the hyperlink that opens the confirm panel.

The confirmMessage binding is required, and is the text in the window. You must also supply one of the action, pageName, or javaScriptFunction attributes.

The attributes for the JSAlertPanel are identical, except that the alertMessage attribute replaces the confirmMessage attribute.

Example

For an example of using the JSConfirmPanel, let's add a Delete This Event hyperlink to the EventListPage. Instead of a hyperlink, however, it can be a JSConfirmPanel.

In WebObjects Builder, add the JSConfirmPanel inside the WORepetition that displays all the events, as shown in Figure 10.20.

You must also add an action method that deletes an event and another method that returns a String for the confirm message. Those methods are given in Listing 10.5.

Listing 10.5

Methods Added to the EventListPage

```
public WOComponent deleteEvent()
{
    this.session().defaultEditingContext().deleteObject(event);
```

Listing 10.5

Continued

```
    this.session().defaultEditingContext().saveChanges();
    this.loadEvents();

    return null;
}

public String confirmMessage()
{
    return "You are about to delete the event:   "+
        event.title()+", are you sure?";
}
```

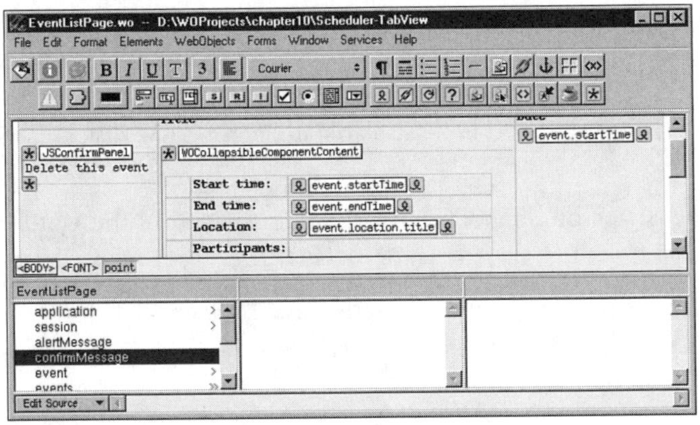

Figure 10.20
Adding the JSConfirmPanel *to the* EventListPage.

At this point, you're ready to set the bindings for the JSConfirmPanel. Those bindings are given in Table 10.20.

Table 10.20

Bindings for the JSConfirmPanel *in the Delete Event Example*

Attribute	Binding
action	deleteEvent
confirmMessage	confirmMessage

At this point, your application will display the confirmation panel every time you try to delete an event.

Other JavaScript dynamic elements, such as the JSImageFlyover and the JSTextFlyover, enhance the appearance of your Web site; the JSModalWindow displays the results of an action in a modal window. For more information about these dynamic elements, consult the documentation found in the WebObjects Info Center.

Frames

HTML frames are another HTML design tool. Frames allow more than one HTML document to appear in the browser simultaneously. Each document has its own scrollbars and can be scrolled separately. Also, each document can be loaded separately, which might reduce the overall load time.

Each frame has a name, and when a navigation element such as a hyperlink, active image, or submit button is selected, the results from the server are placed in the frame that was designated as the target for the navigation item. The WOHyperlink has a target binding, as does the WOActiveImage, but the target for a submit button is placed in the WOForm associated with the button.

For the frames in WebObjects, at least three components are involved: the frameset component, and a component for each of the frames. If you consider that there are at least two frames, that's three components. But you cannot create a frameset component the same way we have created them in WebObjects Builder.

Creating Frames in WOBuilder

To create a new frameset component, select the File, New Frameset menu item in WebObjects Builder. This will change the appearance of WebObjects Builder, as shown in Figure 10.21.

At this point, you can split the frameset horizontally or vertically using the icons in the toolbar or the Format, Frame, Split Horizontally and the Format, Frame, Split Vertically menu choices, respectively.

Frameset Example

Let's create a frameset for movies and their contents, placing all the movie titles in the left frame. When a movie is clicked, all the movie information will display in the right frame. The resulting application is shown in Figure 10.22.

Split vertically ——— ┌— Split horizontally

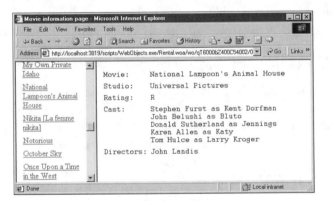

Figure 10.21

A new frameset in WebObjects Builder.

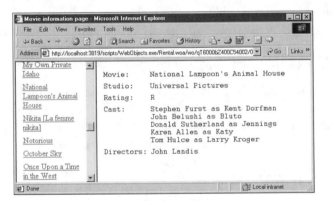

Figure 10.22

The movie information frameset.

The first step is to save the frameset in your project directory by selecting File, Save As in WebObjects Builder. Make sure that you are saving the frameset in your project directory, and call it `MovieFrameset`. You will be prompted for the type of script, so select the Java option button and click Create, as shown in Figure 10.23.

Now go ahead and create two more components from WebObjects Builder. Call one component `MovieListPage` and the other one `MovieDetailPage`.

The `MovieListPage` simply lists all the movie titles, with each surrounded by a hyperlink. The `action` for the hyperlink should be bound to an action method called `movieSelected`, which returns a `MovieDetailPage`.

Figure 10.23

When creating a frameset, you must specify the type of component being created.

The MovieDetailPage should have a key called movie, which is a Movie. This page should display the cast, director, rating, and studio information. Figure 10.24 shows the MovieDetailPage in WebObjects Builder.

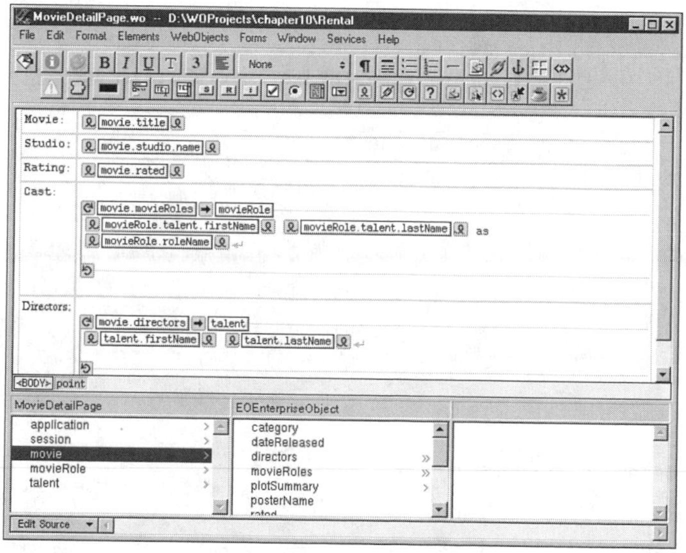

Figure 10.24

The MovieDetailPage.

The movieSelected() method in the MovieListPage should set the movie on the MovieDetailPage appropriately before returning it. The code for these two classes is given in Listings 10.6 and 10.7.

Listing 10.6

The MovieListPage *Class*

```
import com.apple.yellow.foundation.*;
import com.apple.yellow.webobjects.*;
import com.apple.yellow.eocontrol.*;
import com.apple.yellow.eoaccess.*;

public class MovieListPage
    extends WOComponent
{
    protected WODisplayGroup movieDisplayGroup;

    /** @TypeInfo Movie */
    protected EOEnterpriseObject movie;


    public MovieDetailPage movieSelected()
    {
        MovieDetailPage nextPage =
            (MovieDetailPage)pageWithName("MovieDetailPage");

        // Initialize your component here
        nextPage.setMovie( movie );

        return nextPage;
    }

}
```

Listing 10.7

The MovieDetailPage *Class*

```
import com.apple.yellow.foundation.*;
import com.apple.yellow.webobjects.*;
import com.apple.yellow.eocontrol.*;
import com.apple.yellow.eoaccess.*;

public class MovieDetailPage
    extends WOComponent
{
```

Listing 10.7

Continued

```
/** @TypeInfo MovieRole */
protected EOEnterpriseObject movieRole;

/** @TypeInfo Talent */
protected EOEnterpriseObject talent;

/** @TypeInfo Movie */
protected EOEnterpriseObject movie;

/** @TypeInfo Movie */
public EOEnterpriseObject movie()
{
    return movie;
}

public void setMovie(EOEnterpriseObject newMovie)
{
    movie = newMovie;
}
}
```

Placing the Components in the Frames

Now, the trick to this is to keep the MovieListPage component in the left frame and the MovieDetailPage component in the right frame. This involves setting the frame name appropriately and changing the target for the hyperlink to be the same as the name of the frame.

Open the MovieFrameset in WebObjects Builder. The first step is to make each of the frames dynamic by inspecting each one and clicking the Make Dynamic button in the inspector. The color of the frame in WebObjects Builder should turn to a pale blue.

The next step is to set the pageName binding for each frame. In the inspector for the left frame, set the pageName to "MovieListPage". Then inspect the right frame and set the pageName to "MovieDetailPage".

Finally, you need to give each of the frames a name. Initially, the name of the frame is not in the bindings, so you will need to add it. You can add a binding using the ± button in the upper-right corner of the inspector (see Figure 10.25).

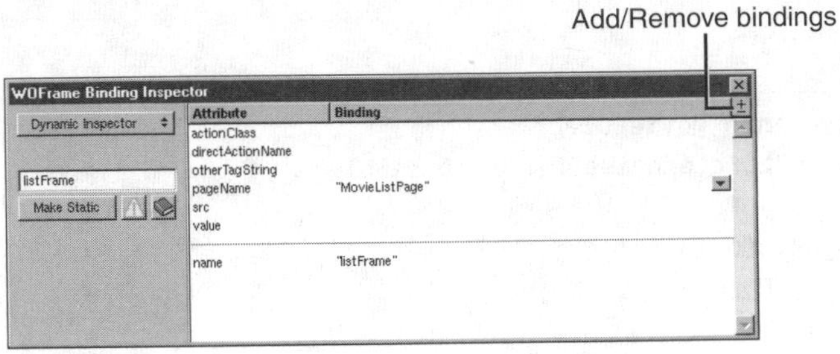

Add/Remove bindings

Figure 10.25
Adding the name binding.

After the binding is added, change the name of the binding to name; the value is
"listFrame" for the left frame and "contentFrame" for the right frame. Be sure to set
the names of both frames, although you will be using only the right frame's name.

Finally, go back and change the WOHyperlink in the MovieListPage. Bind the target of
the hyperlink to "contentFrame". Now when you click these hyperlinks, the content
returned will be placed in the frame with the name "contentFrame". At this point your
frames should work.

What Have We Done?

If you've gotten this far and followed the frame tutorial, you officially "know enough
to be dangerous." You can now skip the next chapter. (Just kidding!)

The error message in Figure 10.26 can be displayed in your application simply by
clicking more than 30 movies and then hitting the refresh button. So what's going on
here? Well, as the error message points out, you have backtracked too far. Every
WOSession caches up to 30 components and then tosses them.

The default for the WOApplication page cache size is 30. This can be changed by
calling the WOApplication's setPageCacheSize method with a different value. Realize
that this will create additional overhead for your application because every session will
now store more copies of the components. It also doesn't solve our problem; it just
delays it a little.

Notice in the WebObjects URL that there are a bunch of numbers. One number is
the session ID, something like F00000RN400aE1001. This keeps track of which session
on the server is yours. In addition to the session ID, another number in the URL is
the context ID.

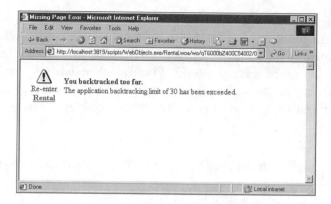

Figure 10.26
Simply by setting up frames, you have allowed a bug to creep into the application.

Context ID

The context ID isat the end of the URL, something like 5.1.3.5.0.9.19.3.1.0. The context ID keeps track of which object responded to the request that displays the page. The problem with using the back arrow in a WebObjects application is that if you click it enough times, you might backtrack to a point at which the context ID references an object that no longer exists on the server because it was removed from the session's page store. "So," you might be wondering, "what does that have to do with our problem?"

Well, remember that the frameset itself is a component. Also remember that the frameset was created from an action in another component; in this case, it was Main. When the user clicks on the refresh button, WebObjects looks for the component involved when that frameset was originally created, the Main component. So, we need to store this component in a *permanent* page cache somehow.

The Permanent Page Cache

Luckily for us, a permanent page cache is associated with the WOSession. There's a method to add a component to the permanent page cache:

```
public void savePageInPermanentCache( WOComponent aComponent)
```

This method adds the specified component to a page cache associated with the session. The documentation about this provided by Apple is a little ambiguous, but the permanent page cache is associated with the session and is removed when the session is removed. Having said this, you can set the size of the permanent page cache using the WOApplication method, setPermanentPageCacheSize(int aSize).

Using the Permanent Page Cache

So, back to the problem we created with the frameset. The solution is to store the Main component in the permanent page cache. A good place to put the Main component is in your Session.java file. Placing it there enables you to keep track of the components you add to the permanent page cache. The Session.java code is given in Listing 10.8, and the associated Main.java code is in Listing 10.9.

Listing 10.8

The Session.java *Code for Adding the* Main *Component to the Permanent Page Cache*

```java
import com.apple.yellow.foundation.*;
import com.apple.yellow.webobjects.*;
import com.apple.yellow.eocontrol.*;

public class Session
    extends WOSession
{
    Main main;

    public Main main()
    {
        return main;
    }

    public void setMain( Main value )
    {
        if ( main == null )
        {
            main = value;
            this.savePageInPermanentCache( value );
        }
    }

}
```

Listing 10.9

The Main.java *Code Associated with Code Listing 10.8*

```java
import com.apple.yellow.foundation.*;
import com.apple.yellow.webobjects.*;
```

Listing 10.8

Continued

```
import com.apple.yellow.eocontrol.*;
import com.apple.yellow.eoaccess.*;

public class Main
    extends WOComponent
{
    public void awake()
    {
        super.awake();

        Session session = (Session)this.session();
        session.setMain( this );
    }
}
```

Summary

This chapter served as a discussion of a number of user interface components that can be used in WebObjects. Most of these components can be used with little or no code, but the trick is in knowing how to bind the attributes. The following components were discussed in this chapter:

- `WOCheckBox` and `WORadioButton`—Basic components for display of check boxes and radio buttons

- `WORadioButtonList` and `WORadioButtonMatrix`—Components that allow easy display of radio buttons

- `WOCheckBoxList` and `WOCheckBoxMatrix`—Components that allow easy display of check boxes

- `WOTabView` and `WOKeyValueConditional`—Components that are used together to display tabbed content in a component

- `WOCollapsibleContent`—A component that displays a tree view

- `WOJavaScript`, `JSAlertPanel`, and `JSConfirmPanel`—Components used to access JavaScript

Also, the proper use of frames was discussed. As you can see, you will be able to use the skills acquired in this section to create some outrageous looking Web applications.

CHAPTER 11

CREATING REUSABLE COMPONENTS

A component-based software development framework brings many advantages, as we discussed in Chapter 3, "WebObjects Components." One of the main advantages of using this type of framework is the ability to add components that you create to your application. If your component is written to the component specification, it will be available to use with other components.

Even though all components are created in the same manner, there are a few different scenarios in which you would want to create a reusable component. One such scenario is when different pages in your application share something in common. This "shared something" could be your main navigation, a Help button, or a common way to select items. Another use of these components is to create a completely reusable component that transcends a particular project; for example, a reusable date selector or a self-validating form.

These different types of components will be discussed in this chapter, including such topics as

- Nesting components, including using component bindings
- Creating a standard look using the WOComponentContent
- Packaging components into a framework

Nesting Components

So far, this book has discussed using a separate WOComponent per HTML page, but that isn't all that you can do with WOComponents. You can also nest a WOComponent inside another one. This places the nested component in the element tree of the parent component (see Figure 11.1). The methods invoked during the request/response loop, such as awake() and appendToResponse(), are all called in the nested component from the parent component as part of the default implementation.

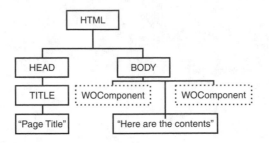

Figure 11.1

Nesting a component in the element tree.

Creating the Reusable Components

The first step in nesting a component is to indicate that the WOComponent is a partial document. For example, let's say that we need a standard header and footer for the MovieBuster project. First, as usual, create the StandardHeader and StandardFooter pages using the File, New in Project menu item in Project Builder. Then open both of the components in WebObjects Builder, and inspect the <BODY> tags. In the inspector, change the Full Document drop-down setting to Partial Document as shown in Figure 11.2.

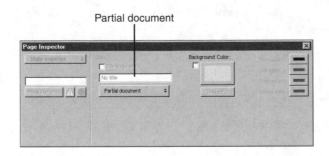

Figure 11.2

Setting the page to be a partial document.

When you select this option from the drop-down, you will get a confirmation panel indicating that you will lose the <HEAD> and <BODY> tags (see Figure 11.3). Click the Continue button to create a partial document.

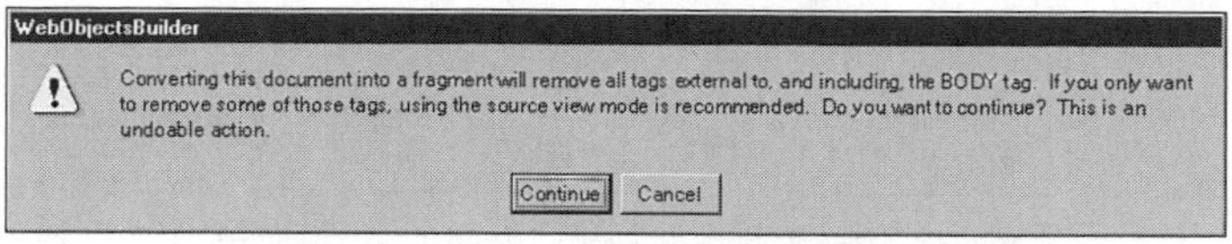

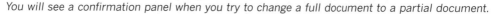

Figure 11.3
You will see a confirmation panel when you try to change a full document to a partial document.

If you've written any custom HTML in the <HEAD> tag or as part of the <BODY> tag, it will be lost. The contents of the <BODY> tag will be kept, however. Partial documents can be edited the same way that full documents can. But you can't change anything inside the <HEAD> tag, such as the title of the document, and you can't change anything that's part of the <BODY> tag, such as the background color. The HTML file for a partial document just becomes HTML that will be placed in another <BODY> tag. The reason that the background for a partial document becomes gray is to indicate that the background color cannot be changed.

In this example, we will place an image in the StandardHeader, as shown in Figure 11.4, and the current date and time in the StandardFooter, as shown in Figure 11.5.

Figure 11.4
The StandardHeader.

The code for the StandardFooter must update the instance variable with the current date and time. The code to do this is given in Listing 11.1.

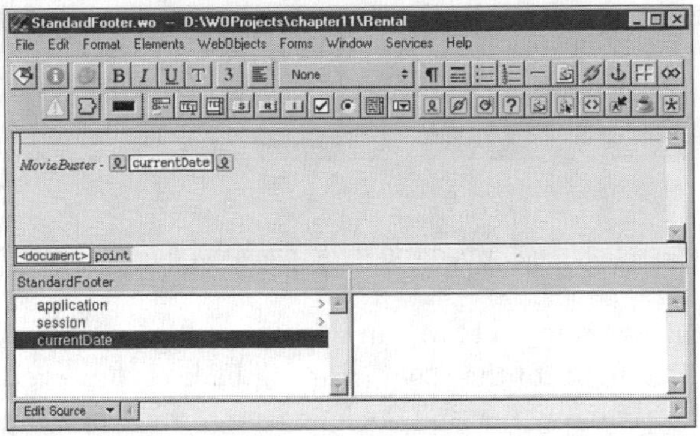

Figure 11.5
The StandardFooter.

Listing 11.1

The Code for the StandardFooter.java *File*

```
import com.apple.yellow.foundation.*;
import com.apple.yellow.webobjects.*;
import com.apple.yellow.eocontrol.*;
import com.apple.yellow.eoaccess.*;

public class StandardFooter
    extends WOComponent
{

    protected NSGregorianDate currentDate;

    public void awake()
    {
        currentDate = new NSGregorianDate();
    }
}
```

Using the Components

At this point, these components can be used in the other components in the application. Simply drag the component icon from Project Builder to the appropriate component in WebObjects Builder. This is similar to dragging an image from the Resources suitcase in Project Builder to WebObjects Builder to add an image to the page, as shown in Figure 11.6.

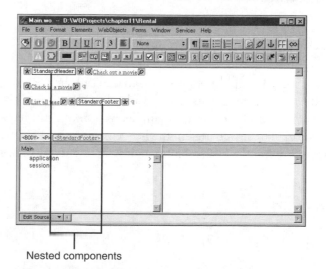

Figure 11.6
Drag the component icon in Project Builder for a nested component to WebObjects Builder.

At this point, the `StandardHeader` and `StandardFooter` components will appear in WebObjects Builder (see Figure 11.7). They look somewhat like custom dynamic elements, but notice that you cannot place other elements inside them. A dynamic element allows the parent component to specify other elements that should be contained within the dynamic element, which is not possible with most components. Dynamic elements and components are both containers, but only dynamic elements allow the parent component to specify children.

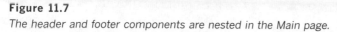

Figure 11.7
The header and footer components are nested in the Main page.

Notice that when you drag the component from Project Builder, it is placed where the cursor is located in WebObjects Builder. You should be able to add these components to all your pages at this point, and changes made to the header and footer components will be reflected throughout the application.

The final application (including the standard header and footer) is shown in Figure 11.8.

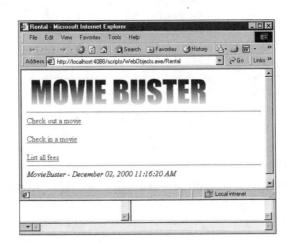

Figure 11.8
The MovieBuster main page.

Creating a Standard Template

Essentially, a standard template has been created for all the pages in the application. It's just that these two components must be added to all the pages in the application. This creates some room for error; for example, what if one of the pages has a different background color? The image used in the header expects that the background will be white. Manually adding the header and footer components to all pages creates room for errors. Figure 11.9 shows the text before the header and the obvious difference between the gray background color and the background color of the image.

A dynamic element, the WOComponentContent, is specifically used to address this issue.

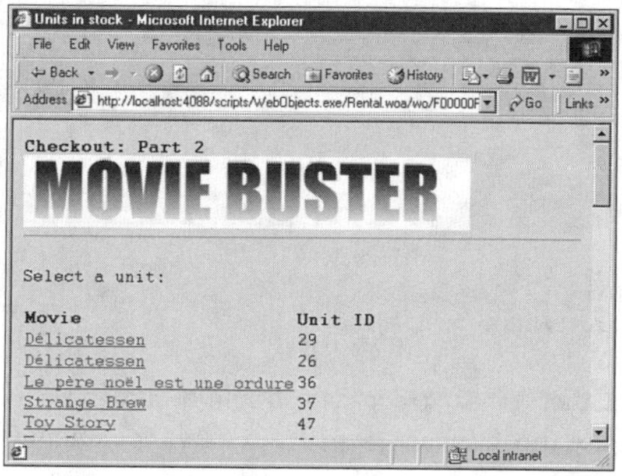

Figure 11.9
Errors created from manually adding the header and footer.

WOComponentContent

WOComponentContent works unlike any other dynamic element in the framework. When it is added to a component, this dynamic element is used to determine where the component's *parent* content should be located. The steps for using this dynamic element are to create a component that will be used as a template, add this dynamic element to that component, and then add your component to other components. It's best demonstrated with an example, so let's put the header and footer in a standard component that uses the WOComponentContent.

The first step is to create a component called StandardTemplate. This will be a full document that contains the StandardHeader and StandardFooter components. In WebObjects Builder, add these components to the StandardTemplate, as shown in Figure 11.10. Also add the WOComponentContent in the middle. This can be done by clicking the icon or selecting the WebObjects, WOComponentContent menu item.

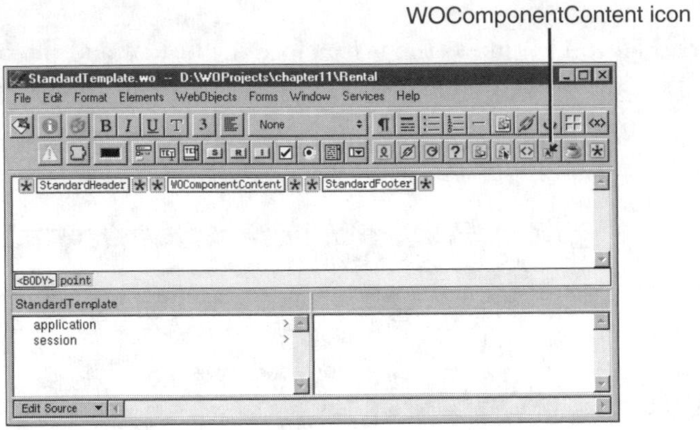

WOComponentContent icon

Figure 11.10
Creating the `StandardTemplate` *component.*

After this is done, the `StandardTemplate` should be added to the pages in your application. Because the `StandardTemplate` is a full document, the rest of your pages will be partial documents. That means the standard template will determine the background color to ensure that all your pages look the same.

Notice that the standard template does not have the same appearance as a nested component. There is room to add content within the standard template. That is a fundamental difference between components that contain a `WOComponentContent` dynamic element and those that do not. All the content for the page should be placed within the `StandardTemplate` component. As shown in Figure 11.11, all the page contents are placed within the `StandardTemplate` component.

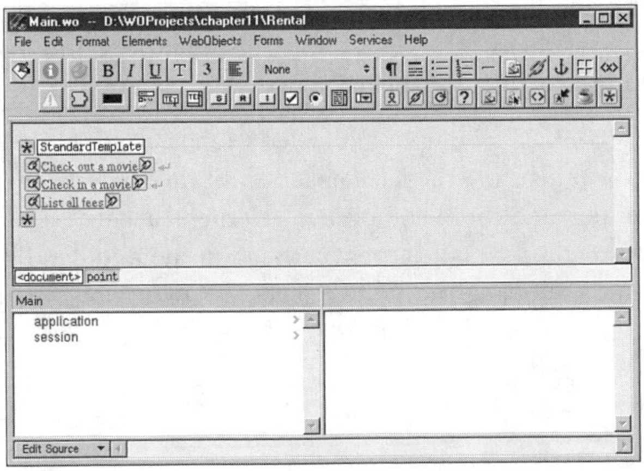

Figure 11.11
Adding the `StandardTemplate` *component to a page.*

At this point, all your components should be partial documents except for the StandardTemplate, and they should all look the same. Now, making changes to the StandardTemplate changes the look of the entire application. In addition to the <BODY> tag, notice that the <HEAD> tag is also in the StandardComponent.

Component Communication

One of the things lost when we converted to using the StandardTemplate component for all the pages was the ability to set the page title for each page. This is something that is now done in the StandardTemplate. So the page title must somehow be set in the StandardTemplate for each page. This is done by creating a key in StandardTemplate and binding it in the parent component.

The first step is to make the title dynamic in the StandardTemplate. Add a string key called pageTitle with the associated methods to return the value and to set the value. Now, make the page title dynamic by inspecting the <BODY> tag and clicking the Title Is Dynamic check box, as shown in Figure 11.12.

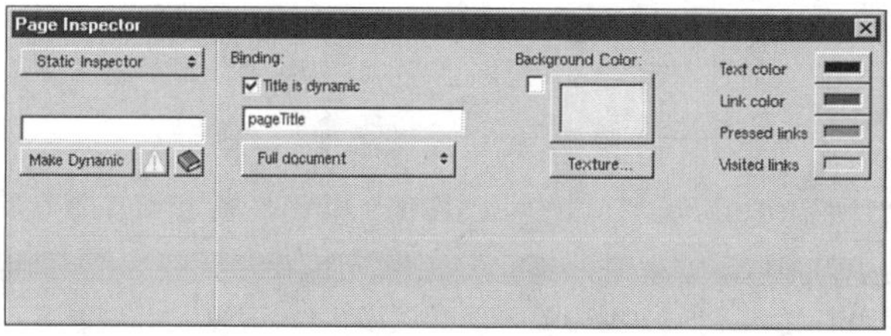

Figure 11.12

You can give the page a dynamic title by inspecting the <BODY> tag and checking the Title Is Dynamic check box.

Now, modify the code to return a predefined page title if one is not already set. A good page title to return would be the name of the application. The code for the StandardTemplate class is given in Listing 11.2.

Listing 11.2

The StandardTemplate *Class*

```
import com.apple.yellow.foundation.*;
import com.apple.yellow.webobjects.*;
import com.apple.yellow.eocontrol.*;
import com.apple.yellow.eoaccess.*;
```

Listing 11.2

Continued

```
public class StandardTemplate
    extends WOComponent
{
    protected String pageTitle;

    public String pageTitle()
    {
        if ( pageTitle == null )
        {
            return this.application().name();
        }
        return pageTitle;
    }

    public void setPageTitle(String newPageTitle)
    {
        pageTitle = newPageTitle;
    }

}
```

In the pageTitle() method, the application's name is returned if the pageTitle has not been set. The parent component will set the pageTitle through a binding in WebObjects Builder. This binding is made in exactly the same way as a binding is made to a dynamic element, as shown in Figure 11.13.

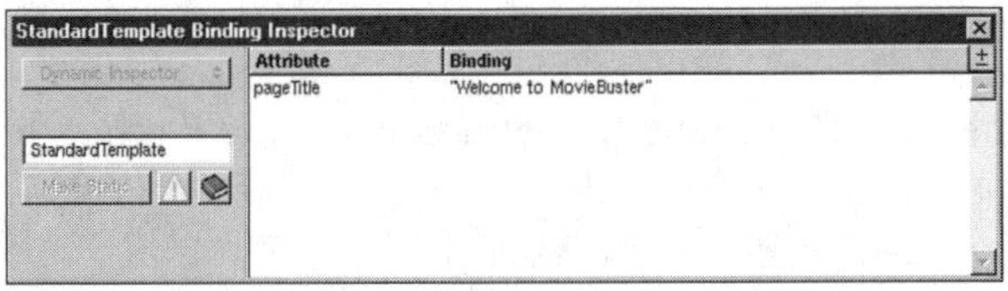

Figure 11.13
The pageTitle *key is available for binding in the dynamic inspector for the* StandardTemplate *component.*

Advertising Keys, the API Editor

For the developer of the parent component to understand what keys are available in a nested component, the keys must be displayed in the dynamic inspector for the component; this is done using the API editor. Using the API editor, you can specify what keys are displayed in the dynamic inspector. The API editor (see Figure 11.14) can be opened from WebObjects Builder by selecting the Window, API menu item. It's also available as an icon in the toolbar. To modify the keys to display for the StandardTemplate, open the API editor with the StandardTemplate opened in WebObjects Builder.

Figure 11.14
The API editor for the StandardTemplate component.

To start, click the Add Keys from Class button. This adds all the keys from the class as bindings. There are other options; for example, you can add and remove individual bindings by using the Add/Delete Bindings button. You have the option of specifying that a binding is required, and whether the binding is a Will Set binding. A Will Set binding actually sets the value in the parent component, similar to the way that a WORepetition sets the item binding. If a binding is not a Will Set binding, it only reads the value from the parent component. Also, you can specify a type of value to be set in the Value Set column if a binding uses common values such as YES/NO, common date formats, or page names.

For the current example, the API editor simply needs the `pageTitle` binding, as displayed in Figure 11.14. At this point, you can bind values to the `pageTitle` for the `StandardTemplate` on each page the same as you would if it were a dynamic element.

A More Reusable Component

The `StandardTemplate` component is an example of a component that is reusable throughout a single application. Another type of reusable component is one that could be reused throughout multiple applications. Such components are generally more difficult to create due to the level of generality built in to the component. One such component displays buttons for modifying a value in a WOTextField, as shown in Figure 11.15.

Figure 11.15
Adding an up/down arrow component to modify a date.

The component that will be created in this section is the `UpDownDateArrows` component. This component is intended for placement beside a text field; clicking on the arrows modifies the value of the text field. This type of component is useful for both dates and numbers, although we will write this one only for dates.

The first step is to create the component in Project Builder and make it a partial document in WebObjects Builder. You can then create the user interface for the component in WebObjects Builder. Because the component is intended for placement in a WOForm, the up and down arrows should be submit buttons. If the arrows are hyperlinks, any data that the user entered before the buttons were clicked will be lost. However, notice in Figure 11.15 that the arrows are represented as images. Use a WOImageButton to obtain images that can be used to submit forms. This dynamic element can be placed on your page either by using the Add WOImageButton icon or by selecting Forms, WOImageButton. The UpDownDateArrows component in WebObjects Builder is shown in Figure 11.16.

The two arrows are JPEGs that can be found on the book's Web site. They're placed in a one-column, two-row table with zero border, spacing, and cell padding.

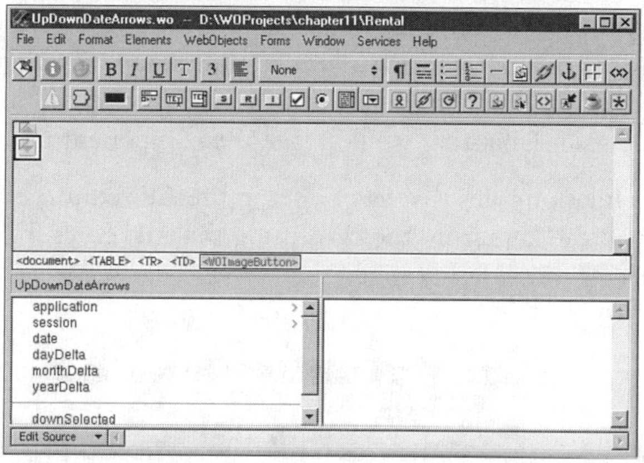

Figure 11.16
The UpDownDateArrows *component.*

You must also add two action methods, called upSelected() and downSelected(), that both return null. These are bound to the appropriate WOImageButton action bindings. These methods will actually change the value of the date. The code for these methods will be discussed later in this chapter.

Table 11.1 lists the attributes that are required for this component. When creating the attributes, you should also create the methods to set and retrieve the values.

Table 11.1

Attributes for the UpDownDateArrows *Component*

Attribute	Type
date	NSGregorianDate
monthDelta	Integer
dayDelta	Integer
yearDelta	Integer

The date attribute holds the date that will be modified by the component. The monthDelta, dayDelta, and yearDelta keys hold the amount that the date is changed when the user clicks on the up and down arrows. The date key is required because the component has nothing to do if it can't set a date. One (and only one) of the monthDelta, dayDelta, and yearDelta keys is required. This component will change only one of the date components at a time. In reality, we could make the arrows change multiple values, but that would make the component more confusing.

These are all validation rules that can be set in the API editor. First, open the API editor and add all the keys from the class using the Add Keys from Class button, as shown in Figure 11.17.

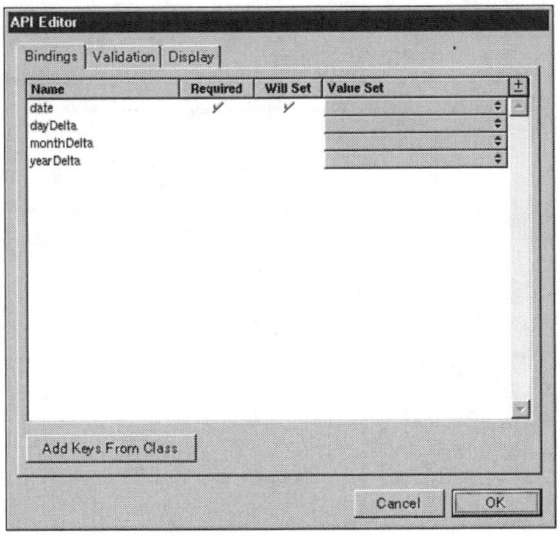

Figure 11.17
Use the Add Keys from Class button to advertise all the keys you created.

Check the Required and Will Set cells for the `date` key. Enabling Will Set indicates that anything bound to this key will be set by the component. In addition to these keys, this component has significant validation logic that can be set in the Validation tab (see Figure 11.18).

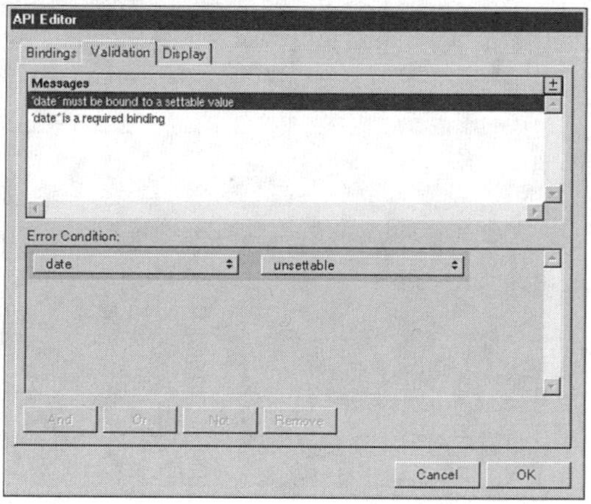

Figure 11.18
This component has a number of validation rules, starting with the `date` rules.

The Validation tab is used to set the binding error conditions. The Error Condition part of the window enables you to specify various conditions, and to provide Boolean operators as part of creating the conditions. The conditions involve selecting a key and whether the key is bound, unbound, settable, or unsettable. The bound and unbound settings indicate whether or not that key is bound to the parent component. A key is settable if the key in the parent component to which this key is bound is settable. This could mean that the parent's key is an instance variable with the appropriate visibility level, or that a method exists to set the value.

The validation rules for the `date` key are already set because of the check marks we set on the Bindings tab. We now need to set the error conditions for the delta bindings, which are as follows:

- `monthDelta`, `dayDelta`, and `yearDelta` are all unbound.

- `monthDelta` is bound and the `dayDelta` key or the `yearDelta` key is bound.

- `dayDelta` is bound and the `monthDelta` key or the `yearDelta` key is bound.

- `yearDelta` is bound and the `dayDelta` key or the `monthDelta` keys is bound.

We must add these rules to the validation logic for this component. To do so, you first add a rule to the logic using the Add/Delete Rules button, as shown in Figure 11.19.

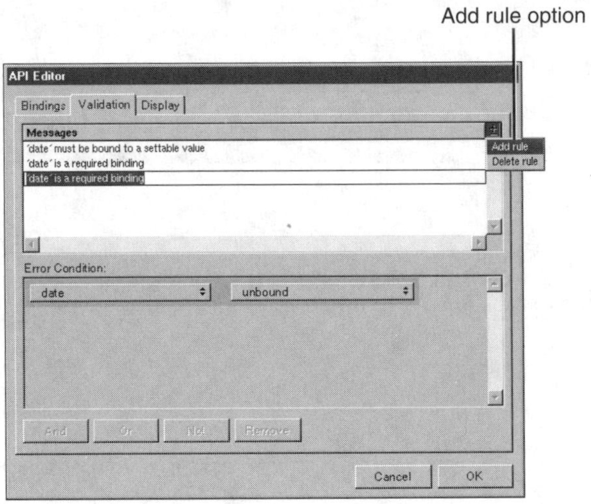

Figure 11.19
Use the Add/Delete Rules button to add a rule to a component's validation rules.

After a rule is added, use the lower portion of the window to modify that rule. The first rule we will add says that one of the delta keys should be bound. First, select the dayDelta key in the Error Condition window, as shown in Figure 11.20.

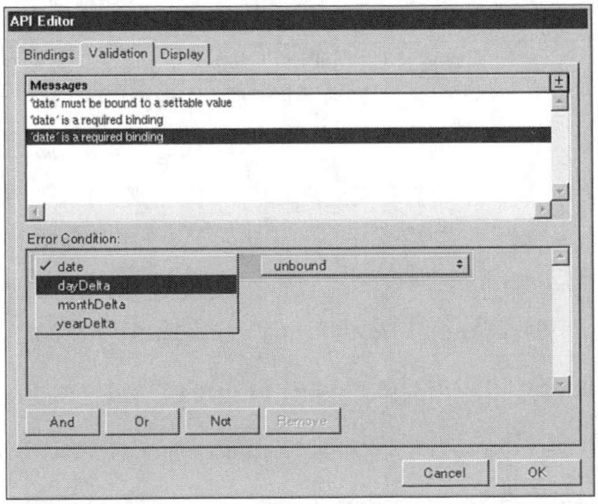

Figure 11.20
Selecting the key that the rule will affect.

After you have specified that the `dayDelta` is unbound, click the And button to specify another key. Next, specify that the `monthDelta` key is unbound. Click on the And button to add the final condition, which is that `yearDelta` is unbound. The API editor should match Figure 11.21.

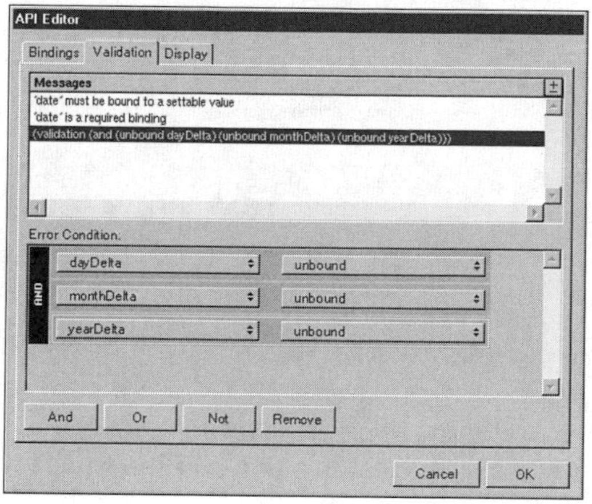

Figure 11.21
The error conditions for the final rule, which ensures that one of the delta keys is bound.

The Mutually Exclusive Rules

The next three rules are used to make sure that the delta keys are mutually exclusive. This works by specifying an And condition with two Or conditions. For example, the `monthDelta` is bound and the `dayDelta` is bound or the `yearDelta` is bound.

First, add a new rule using the Add/Delete Rules button. Set the error condition so that `monthDelta` is bound. Then click on the And button and set the `dayDelta` key to bound. The And button should be selected when the `dayDelta` is being specified. Click on the Or button and set the `yearDelta` key to bound. The final validation window should look like the one displayed in Figure 11.22.

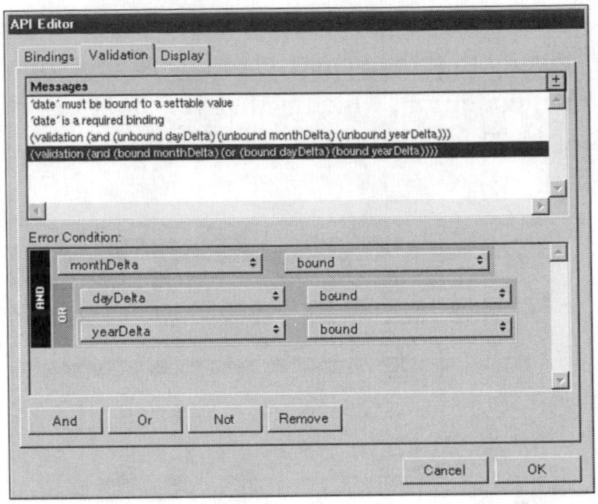

Figure 11.22
One of the three mutually exclusive rules.

After you have set one of these rules correctly, the other two are very similar; just change the names. The final validation window is shown in Figure 11.23.

The Code
The code for this component is given in Listing 11.3.

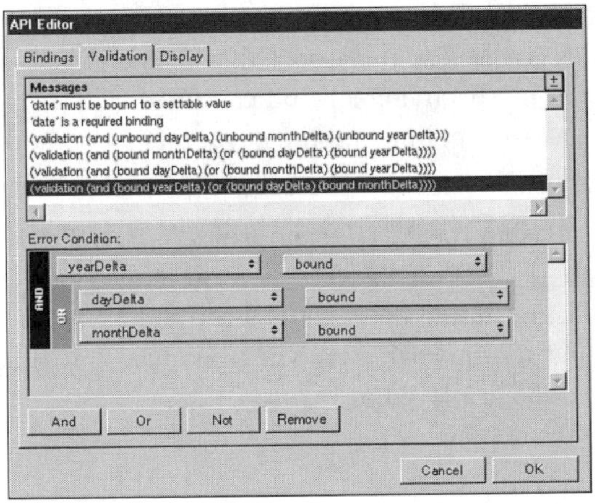

Figure 11.23
The validation window for the UpDownDateArrows *component.*

Listing 11.3

A Partial Listing of the Code for the UpDownDateArrows *Component*

```
protected NSGregorianDate date;
protected Integer monthDelta;
protected Integer dayDelta;
protected Integer yearDelta;

private int intFromInteger( Integer value )
{
    if ( value == null )
    {
        return 0;
    }
    else
    {
        return value.intValue();
    }
}

public WOComponent downSelected()
{
    int intMonthDelta = -1*this.intFromInteger( this.monthDelta() );
    int intDayDelta = -1*this.intFromInteger( this.dayDelta() );
    int intYearDelta = -1*this.intFromInteger( this.yearDelta() );

    this.setDate( this.date().dateByAddingGregorianUnits(
        intYearDelta, intMonthDelta, intDayDelta,
        0, 0, 0 ) );

    return null;
}

public WOComponent upSelected()
{
    int intMonthDelta = this.intFromInteger( this.monthDelta() );
    int intDayDelta = this.intFromInteger( this.dayDelta() );
    int intYearDelta = this.intFromInteger( this.yearDelta() );

    this.setDate( this.date().dateByAddingGregorianUnits(
        intYearDelta, intMonthDelta, intDayDelta,
        0, 0, 0 ) );

    return null;
}
```

The two action methods perform the manipulation on the date instance variable. The new value will be transferred automatically to the key to which the date is bound.

The `intFromInteger()` method is used as a convenience method. It simply returns 0 if the `Integer` given is `null`; otherwise, the conversion is made to a primitive type. This makes the two action methods easier because the `dateByAddingGregorianUnits` method can be passed zeros for values that are not set.

The rest of the class consists of set and retrieve access methods, and those are untouched from what was generated by WebObjects Builder.

Using the `UpDownDateArrows` **Component**

The final step is to use this component in a form. The use of this component is dependent on the form being a "multiple submit" form because the component itself contains two submit buttons. Now it's just a matter of dropping the component in a `WOForm` and binding the values. Open a page in your application that allows for date entry in a `WOTextField`, and place the `UpDownDateArrows` component immediately next to the `WOTextField`. A good component to use for this example is the `CheckInPage` or `CheckOutPage` component. It's a good idea to place the `WOTextField` and the `UpDownDateArrows` component in a one-row, two-column table with `WOTextField` in the left column and `UpDownDateArrows` in the right column, as shown in Figure 11.24.

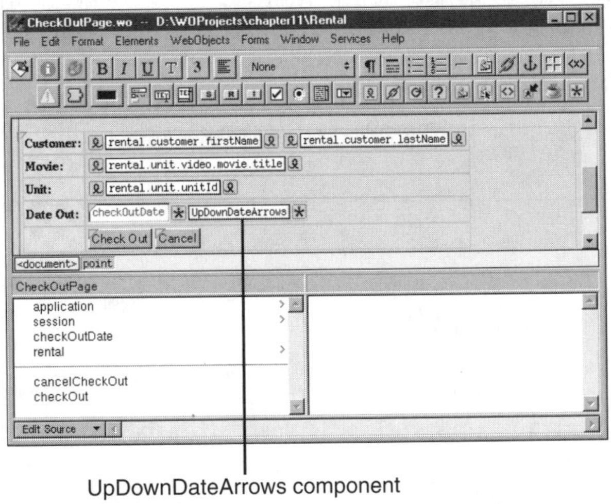

UpDownDateArrows component

Figure 11.24
Using the `UpDownDateArrows` *component in the* `CheckOutPage`.

Now you simply need to set the bindings for the UpDownDateArrows component. The date binding should be the same as the value binding for the WOTextField. We will use these arrows to modify the day of the date, so bind the dayDelta to 1. This will cause the day to change by one day at a time when the arrows are used. The binding inspector for the component is shown in Figure 11.25.

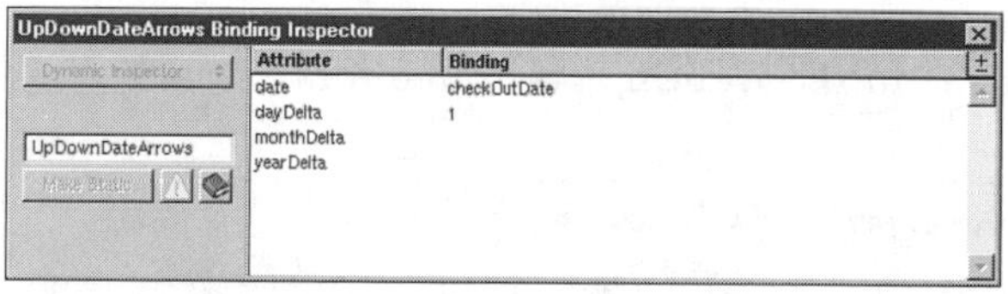

Figure 11.25
The binding inspector for the UpDownDateArrows *component in the* CheckOutPage.

At this point, you can test your application. Clicking the up and down arrows should change the value in the WOTextField.

Frameworks

After you have created this component and others like it, it would be useful to share the component with other applications. WebObjects uses frameworks for this purpose. There are two types of frameworks in WebObjects: frameworks and WebObjects frameworks. A framework contains code, resources, and documentation for server-side objects. Frameworks are typically used to encapsulate EOModels with the associated code.

A WebObjects framework is similar to a framework, but also contains images and resources that can be delivered to the client. A WebObjects framework is used to store reusable components such as the one we created. Because this component is so cool, we will want to place it in a WebObjects framework.

Creating a WebObjects Framework

The first step is to create a WebObjects framework project. Select the Project, New menu item in Project Builder. Select WebObjects Framework as the type of project, and call the project ReusableComponents. This will look like a standard project, but it's actually quite different. You will be able to build the project, but you will not be able to run it.

Now transfer all parts of the UpDownDateArrows from the previous project to the ReusableComponents framework. Table 11.2 lists the files to copy from the previous project and the suitcase to transfer them to. To transfer these files, double-click the appropriate suitcase in the Project Builder window for ReusableComponents and use the File Open dialog to find the files in the previous project.

Table 11.2

The Files to Transfer to the WebObjects Framework Project

File	Suitcase
UpDownDateArrows.java	Classes
UpDownDateArrows.wo	Web Components
UpDownDateArrows.api	Resources
upbutton.jpg	Web Server Resources
downbutton.jpg	Web Server Resources

When you're finished, make sure that all files have been transferred by examining the contents of the appropriate suitcases. You will have to make some changes to the component now that it is in a framework. Modify the component in WebObjects Builder. You should notice that the images are not correctly displayed initially. That is because it is expected that the images are stored in the application, not in a framework. Just inspect the WOImageButtons and set the framework binding to ReusableComponents, as shown in Figure 11.26.

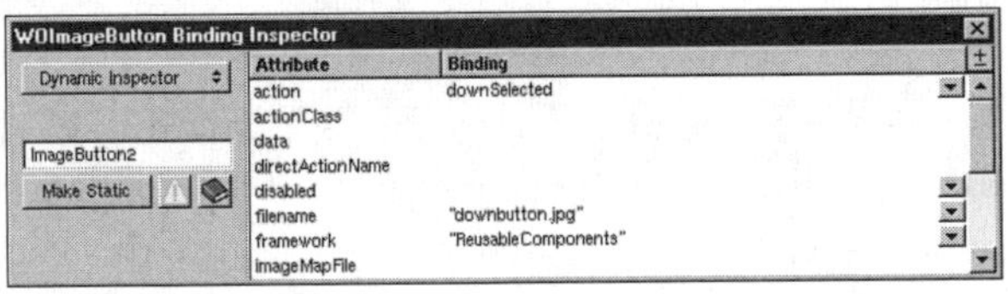

Figure 11.26

The framework binding for the WOImageButtons must be set appropriately.

After this is done, you are ready to create the framework. You must build an install version of this framework. The type of target you are building is set in the Build panel. Bring up the Build panel and click the button with the check mark on it to see the Build Options panel, as shown in Figure 11.27.

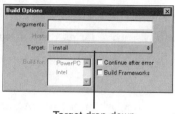

Target drop-down

Figure 11.27
Use the Build Options panel to set the Target drop-down to install.

Set Target to install by using the drop-down list in the Build Options panel. Then close the Build Options panel and build the project. This will now not only build the project, but also install it in the project install directory. The default is to store the framework in the `\Apple\Local\Library\Frameworks` directory on Windows and in the `~/Frameworks` directory on OS X. To change this directory, open the project inspector by clicking the Inspector icon on the main window in Project Builder. Make sure that you are looking at the Build Attributes inspector as denoted by the drop-down list at the top of the window (see Figure 11.28).

Figure 11.28
The Build Attributes inspector.

The install location is set in the Install In text field.

After you build this framework with a Target drop-down setting of install, the framework should appear in the appropriate directory.

Using the Framework

The final step is to use the framework in one of your applications. If you want to use it in the application from which you removed it, be sure to first remove all the files that you moved to the framework, as listed in Table 11.2. To remove a file from a project, select the file and the Project, Remove Files menu item.

To use the framework, you must add it to the framework search order for your project. The easiest way to do this is to double-click the Frameworks suitcase and find the installed framework called ReusableComponents.framework in the Add Frameworks panel (see Figure 11.29).

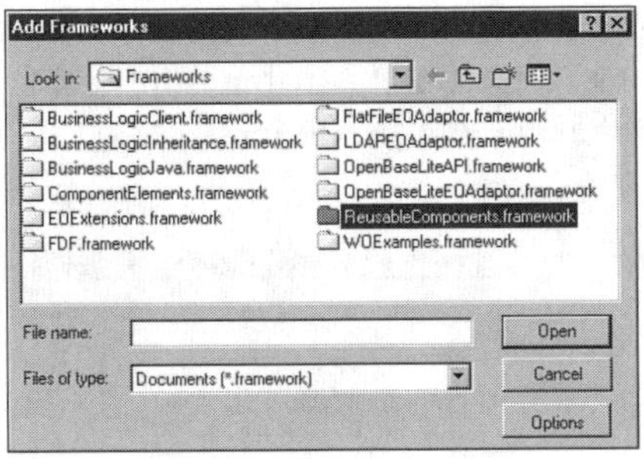

Figure 11.29
The Add Frameworks panel.

You will be asked whether you want to add the framework to the search order. Click the Yes button to continue.

The Final Touches

The last thing to do to make our component complete is to set the image and documentation for the component. The image will be displayed in WebObjects Builder instead of the standard generic WOComponent image, and the documentation will be available when the developer clicks on the Book icon in the inspector for the component. This is set in the Display tab of the API editor for the component, as shown in Figure 11.30.

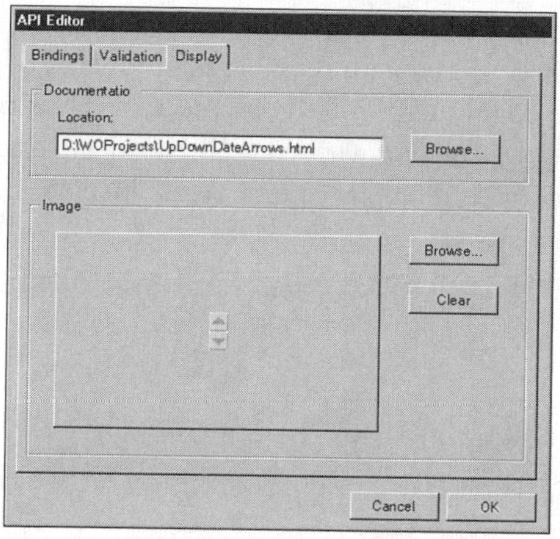

Figure 11.30
The Display tab enables you to set the image to be displayed in WebObjects Builder, along with the developer documentation for the component.

Both the documentation and the image will be placed in the component directory. The image will be converted to a tiff file and placed in the directory as `Image.tiff`. This image should depict what the final version looks like as closely as possible. The documentation should be formatted like the Apple documentation, and should contain an overview of the component, the required bindings, a description of any validation rules, and a list of the bindings and their descriptions.

Summary

In this chapter, we explored all aspects of reusable components in WebObjects. The basic type of reusable component is one that is used across a particular application, such as a header or footer. Certain applications frequently use a wizard in different areas to lead the user through decisions, and a wizard bar could be implemented as a reusable component.

The `WOComponentContent` is used to specify a template for your application, and is also used in conjunction with all the other pages in your application.

Finally, and more complicated to create, are those components that are used across applications. These are generic components that typically provide some sort of user interface nicety, such as the example given in this chapter.

Considering that the entire framework is component-based, you will find that a large part of your application will contain reusable components of some type. It is a good idea to segregate the components into "reusable across this project" and "reusable across all projects" types, starting with your first project. The "reusable across all projects" components should be placed in a WebObjects framework that you can update and add to as necessary.

CHAPTER 12

USING STATELESS TRANSACTIONS

So far, the WebObjects applications created in this book have relied on the persistent state to be stored on the server. That is, the variables we have set are maintained across transactions. This requires a bit of overhead and management, which are contained in the WebObjects framework. WebObjects makes it so simple for us to use these sessions that it is easy to forget that our application is using a stateless protocol to transfer information between the client presentation layer and the server code we are writing. The advantages of using session are numerous, and for a number of sites, sessions are required for normal operation.

However, sessions are not required in every situation, and they add a good deal of overhead to the application. For parts of the application that have simple searching and listing capability, sessions are not required. In those parts of the application, not only are sessions not required, they are probably not desired. Such functions are best implemented using pages that are created using direct actions.

This chapter explores direct actions, including the following topics:

- Writing and using direct action methods
- Using forms and direct actions
- Embedding information in hyperlinks for direct actions

Drawbacks to Sessions

As useful and as powerful the session management features are in WebObjects, sessions should be used only when required. In addition to scalability concerns that will be discussed in Chapter 14, "Deploying Your Application," sessions cannot be bookmarked, require additional overhead, and suffer from timeouts.

Bookmarks

A typical session stores the session ID in the URL. After this is done, a page in your application cannot be bookmarked because the session ID would also be bookmarked. This can be changed with the WOSession method:

```
public void setStoresIDsInURLs(boolean flag)
```

The following method can be used to store the session ID in cookies:

```
public void setStoresIDsInCookies( boolean flag )
```

A session constructor to store the session ID in cookies is given in Listing 12.1.

Listing 12.1

A Session Constructor That Uses Cookies to Store the Session ID

```
public Session()
{
    this.setStoresIDsInURLs( false );
    this.setStoresIDsInCookies( true );
}
```

Even if you store the session ID in cookies, the user will not be able to bookmark pages unless they are direct actions.

Overhead

Sessions also create added overhead that should be avoided if possible. Every session will retain a number of WOComponents, placed in the session's page cache. The default is 30, and it can be changed using the setPageCacheSize() method in the WOApplication. Also stored with these components are the enterprise objects and additional objects depending on the complexity of the component. If your site has a large amount of traffic that does not require sessions, creating sessions for that traffic will increase the memory footprint of your application.

Timeouts

To remedy the overhead problems, each session is given a timeout value. If there is no activity in a session for a predefined length of time, the session is terminated. This helps clean up unused sessions, but can be considered a disadvantage. Assume that a user is surfing a consumer Web site and has found the item that he wants to purchase, but before the purchase is made, an external distraction causes him to be away from the computer for an hour or so. When the user returns, the session has timed out, and he is forced to start over again.

So, for those parts of an application that do not require a session, it is best to use direct actions.

Using Direct Actions

Direct action methods are similar to regular action methods because they return a WOComponent that is responsible for responding to the request. Direct action methods are not implemented in a WOComponent, however; they are implemented in a subclass of WODirectAction. The standard WODirectAction class that is created for your application is the DirectAction class. This is where you can start placing your direct actions.

The actual return value required by a direct action is WOActionResults. This is an interface that is implemented by the WOComponent and WOResponse classes. The reason for this abstraction is simply a matter of convenience. It allows developers either to return a WOComponent or to generate a WOResponse and return that.

The steps for using direct actions are

- Set up your application to use the direct action request handler
- Create a direct action that returns a WOComponent
- Create a hyperlink that uses the direct action method

Avoiding Sessions

One of the most deceptive parts of using direct actions is making sure that a session is *not* created unless desired. Accessing any data in the Session class implicitly creates a session. Also, using any dynamic element that requires state to be stored on the server will create a session. The following dynamic elements will create a session if placed on a page:

- WODisplayGroup
- WOHyperlink when the action attribute is bound
- Any dynamic form element; for example, WOTextField, WOSubmitButton, WOBrowser, WOCheckBox, WORadioButton, and so on
- WOCollapsibleComponentContent
- WOTabPanel

These are the most common elements used by developers that accidentally create a session, but this list is not complete by any means.

The Example

To demonstrate the steps for using direct actions, we will create a separate application to display Movie information that's stored in the Movies database. If the software previously created would be used by the rental store employees to track rentals, this software would be for a kiosk in the store that the customers use to browse movie information. This is a perfect application for direct actions because we do not require the customer to log in. This application simply responds to customer queries with the appropriate data.

So, the first step is to create a new WebObjects application called "Kiosk" and drop the existing model into that application. There is no need for custom business logic, so you can set the class for every entity to EOGenericRecord.

Request Handlers

The first step is to change the default request handler to the direct action request handler. A *request handler* is a concrete subclass of WORequestHandler, and specifies how a particular request will be handled. Three types of request handlers are used in WebObjects:

- The component request handler, WOComponentRequestHandler
- The resource request handler, WOResourceRequestHandler
- The direct action request handler, WODirectActionRequestHandler

The request handler used is dependent on the string immediately following the application name in the URL. A sample URL for a main page is

```
http://localhost:2201/scripts/WebObjects.exe/Kiosk
```

where /scripts/WebObjects.exe is the adapter and /Kiosk is the name of the application. The URL for another component in the application is

```
http://localhost:2201/scripts/WebObjects.exe/Kiosk.woa/wo/F00000RN400aE1001/0.2
```

In this URL, the /wo/ immediately following the application name is the request handler key. The key for the WOComponentRequestHandler is wo, so this URL is using that request handler. This URL also has a session ID, which is the jumbled-up number following the request handler key. The URL to a resource in the application is

```
/scripts/WebObjects.exe/
  Kiosk.woa/wr?wodata=D%3A%5CWOProjects%5Cchapter12%5CKiosk%5Cmoviebuster.jpg
```

Notice the wr immediately following the application name. That is the request handler key for the WOResourceRequestHandler.

These request handler keys are registered with the application, using the registerRequestHandler method in WOApplication. You have the ability to create a concrete subclass of WORequestHandler and to register your object for an unused request handler key, if you choose to do so.

Finally, here is a direct action URL:

```
http://localhost:2213/scripts/WebObjects.exe/Kiosk.woa/wa/talentList
```

The WODirectActionRequestHandler key is wa, as shown in this URL. The talentList text at the end of the URL indicates the direct action name.

Using the WODirectActionRequestHandler

So, the default request handler is the WOComponentRequestHandler; you need to change this to the WODirectActionRequestHandler. The code for this is given in Listing 12.2.

Listing 12.2

Setting the Default Request Handler to the WODirectActionRequestHandler *in Application's Constructor*

```
public Application()
{
    super();
    System.out.println("Welcome to " + this.name() + " !");
    /* ** put your initialization code in here ** */

    String directActionRequestHandlerKey =
        WOApplication.directActionRequestHandlerKey();

    WORequestHandler directActionRequestHandler =
        this.requestHandlerForKey( directActionRequestHandlerKey );

    this.setDefaultRequestHandler( directActionRequestHandler );
}
```

This method first retrieves the direct action request handler key using the directActionRequestHandlerKey() method. This key should always be wa, but this should not be hard-coded into your application. The next step is to get the direct action request handler with the `requestHandlerForKey` method, using the key that you just retrieved. Finally, set the default request handler using `setDefaultRequestHandler`.

Creating the Direct Action

The next step is to create a direct action that returns a component. First, add a component called `TalentListPage` to your application. You might have a component with this name from a previous application, but go ahead and create a new one; it will be different enough to create from scratch. Add a method called `talentListAction()` to `DirectAction.java`. This method will create and return the `TalentListPage` component, and is given in Listing 12.3.

Listing 12.3

The Direct Action That Returns the `TalentListPage`, *in* `DirectAction.java`

```
public WOComponent talentListAction()
{
    return pageWithName("TalentListPage");
}
```

Using a Direct Action in a `WOHyperlink`

After the direct action method is created, you need to use this method in a `WOHyperlink`. On the main page, create a `WOHyperlink` in WebObjects Builder. Bind the `directActionName` attribute to `"talentList"`. Be sure to include the double quotation marks. If you choose the `"talentList"` action from the drop-down list, the `actionClass` attribute is automatically bound to `"DirectAction"`. If this attribute is not bound, the default class will be `DirectAction`.

Notice that the name of the method is `talentListAction` and the `directActionName` attribute is `"talentList"`. This is the way that direct actions work; `"Action"` is automatically appended to whatever is bound to the `directActionName` attribute.

At this point, you can build and run your application. You should be able to navigate to the second page. Add a hyperlink on the second page that returns the first page through the `"default"` direct action. Now navigate back and forth and make sure that a session ID does not appear in the URL.

Accessing the Database Using Direct Actions

When using direct actions, you will mostly display database data and will not need to update the data. For that reason, most of those pages could be displayed using "raw"

SQL rows. You will not be able to use the Session's default editing context, so to use an EOEditingContext, you could create one using the default constructor:

```
EOEditingContext ec = new EOEditingContext();
```

After this has been created, you can use the editing context as normal. An example of retrieving the talent data in the TalentListPage is given in Listing 12.4.

Listing 12.4

Retrieving the Talent Objects Within a Direct Action Application Requires Creating a New Fetch Specification

```
import com.apple.yellow.foundation.*;
import com.apple.yellow.webobjects.*;
import com.apple.yellow.eocontrol.*;
import com.apple.yellow.eoaccess.*;

public class TalentListPage
    extends WOComponent
{
    public NSArray talents;

    /** @TypeInfo Talent */
    EOEnterpriseObject talent;

    public void awake()
    {
        if ( talents == null )
        {
            EOEditingContext ec = new EOEditingContext();

            EOSortOrdering lastName =
                EOSortOrdering.sortOrderingWithKey(
                    "lastName", EOSortOrdering.CompareAscending);
            EOSortOrdering firstName =
                EOSortOrdering.sortOrderingWithKey(
                    "firstName", EOSortOrdering.CompareAscending);
            NSArray orderings = new NSArray(
                new Object [] { lastName, firstName } );

            EOFetchSpecification fetchSpec =
                new EOFetchSpecification( "Talent", null, orderings );
            fetchSpec.setFetchesRawRows( true );
```

Listing 12.4

Continued

```
                talents = ec.objectsWithFetchSpecification( fetchSpec );
        }


    }


}
```

Using the EOFetchSpecification's setFetchesRawRows() method will return the rows as an NSArray of dictionaries. This also could be done in a model-based fetch specification in the Raw Rows tab.

Forms and Direct Actions

As mentioned before, you cannot use dynamic form elements with direct actions. That is because you have to assume that the object that responded to the last request is no longer available to accept the next request. For that reason, you have to use static elements for form controls. To retrieve the data entered, you use the WORequest object stored in the WODirectAction class. The values will be placed in the request as form values.

Text Fields

The text fields used must be static text fields, as must the submit button also. The direct action is then bound to the WOForm containing the submit button and text field. To determine the values that the user has entered, use the formValueForKey() method on the WORequest.

To demonstrate this, a text field that allows the user to enter the first few letters of the talent to search for will be placed on the main page as shown in Figure 12.1.

This involves adding a WOForm with static elements to the Main component and a direct action to the DirectAction class, along with modifying the talent list class to search for particular talents. This can be done in any order because it all has to be completed fieldsin order to work.

Searching for Talents

To retrieve a fieldssubset of talents requires adding a variable to use as the search string for the last name to the TalentListPage. The code for the TalentListPage is given in Listing 12.5.

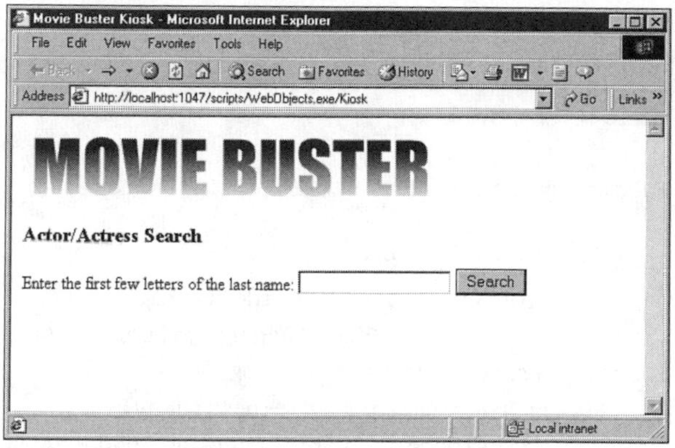

Figure 12.1
The Talent Search Application.

Listing 12.5

Retrieving Talents by Last Name

```
import com.apple.yellow.foundation.*;
import com.apple.yellow.webobjects.*;
import com.apple.yellow.eocontrol.*;
import com.apple.yellow.eoaccess.*;

public class TalentListPage
    extends WOComponent
{
    protected NSArray talents;
    protected String lastNameQueryString;

    /** @TypeInfo Talent */
    EOEnterpriseObject talent;
    public void setLastNameQueryString( String value )
    {
        talents=null;
        lastNameQueryString = value;
    }

    public void appendToResponse( WOResponse response, WOContext context )
    {
```

Listing 12.5

Continued

```
            if ( talents == null )
            {
                EOEditingContext ec = new EOEditingContext();

                EOSortOrdering lastName =
                    EOSortOrdering.sortOrderingWithKey(
                        "lastName", EOSortOrdering.CompareAscending);
                EOSortOrdering firstName =
                    EOSortOrdering.sortOrderingWithKey(
                        "firstName", EOSortOrdering.CompareAscending);
                NSArray orderings = new NSArray(
                        new Object [] { lastName, firstName } );

                EOQualifier qualifier=null;
                if ( lastNameQueryString != null )
                {
                    NSArray qualifierBindings =
                            new NSArray(
                                new String [] { lastNameQueryString+"*" } );
                    qualifier = EOQualifier.qualifierWithQualifierFormat(
                        "lastName like %@", qualifierBindings );
                }
                EOFetchSpecification fetchSpec =
                    new EOFetchSpecification( "Talent", qualifier, orderings );
                fetchSpec.setFetchesRawRows( true );

                talents = ec.objectsWithFetchSpecification( fetchSpec );
            }

            super.appendToResponse( response, context );
        }

    }
```

One of the main differences between this version of the `TalentListPage` class and the original one is that this one retrieves the records in the `appendToResponse()` method.

The awake() method cannot be used because awake will be called before the lastNameQueryString variable is set. Because we are writing the appendToResponse() method, the superclass method must also be called if the default processing is to be used. If the superclass method is not called, you must render the HTML.

Also, fieldsnotice that an asterisk (*) is appended to the lastNameQueryString when the qualifier is created. This is done for you automatically when using the WODisplayGroup, but is required when using a fetch specification.

Creating the Direct Action

The direct action used will create the TalentListPage and set the last name query string. The query string will be determined by the form values used, and can be retrieved using the WORequest method formValueForKey(). The key for the form value will be determined by the HTML name for the form control, which is set in WebObjects Builder. For this example, the control's name will be set to lastNameTextField. This direct action is given in Listing 12.6.

Listing 12.6

The Direct Action That Will Open the TalentListPage *with an Appropriate Query String Value; This Method Is in* DirectAction.java

```
public WOComponent talentListAction()
{
    String lastNameString =
        (String)this.request().formValueForKey( "lastNameTextField" );
    TalentListPage nextPage = (TalentListPage)pageWithName("TalentListPage");
    nextPage.setLastNameQueryString( lastNameString );
    return nextPage;
}
```

As you can see, the request is retrieved using the WODirectAction's request() method.

Creating the Form Controls

The final step is to create the user interface in WebObjects Builder. Create a WOForm, and place some text, a WOTextField, and a WOSubmitButton in it as shown in Figure 12.2.

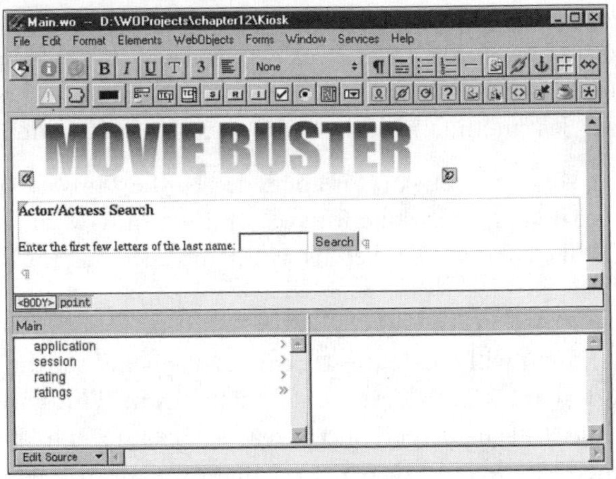

Figure 12.2
The User Interface For the Main *component.*

Bind the WOForm's directActionName attribute "talentList", similar to the way the WOHyperlink was bound in the previous example. Now make the WOSubmitButton a static submit button. This is done by inspecting the submit button and clicking the Make Static button, as shown in Figure 12.3.

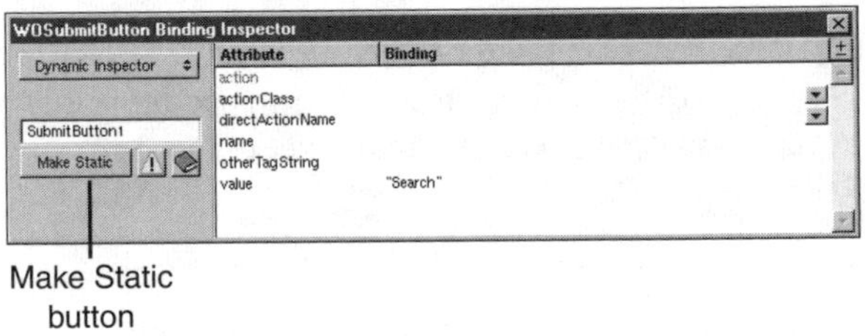

Make Static
button

Figure 12.3
Making the submit button static.

After you have made the submit button static, the Label text field stores the text that appears on the button. The WOTextField should also be static, so follow the same procedure. The WOTextField also needs an HTML name that will be used in the direct action to receive the value. This is set in the static inspector for the button, as shown in Figure 12.4.

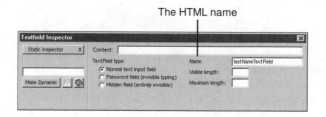

Figure 12.4
The name for the static text field is set in the static Inspector.

At this point, you should be able to build and run the application.

Combo Boxes and Lists

There's a little fieldsextra work in setting up these two controls because the WOPopupButton and the WOBrowser handle a lot for you, and you cannot use these controls without creating a session. An understanding of the underlying HTML is required because you will be using the WOGenericContainer dynamic element.

HTML Selection Lists

Selection lists (both combo boxes and list boxes) are created by using the <SELECT> tag in your HTML. The <OPTION> tag is used to define each option. The code for a drop-down of movie ratings is given in Listing 12.7.

Listing 12.7
The HTML for a Drop-down That Contains Movie Ratings

```
<SELECT NAME="movieRatings">
    <OPTION>G</OPTION>
    <OPTION>PG</OPTION>
    <OPTION>PG-13</OPTION>
    <OPTION>R</OPTION>
</SELECT>
```

In the <SELECT> tag, the SIZE attribute is used to determine the number of options that are visible. Setting the SIZE attribute to a value greater than one will display a list instead of a combo box. Also, specifying the MULTIPLE attribute will create a multiple-selection list box. The code for a list box is given in Listing 12.8.

Listing 12.8

The Code for an HTML List Box

```
<SELECT NAME="movieRatings" SIZE=4>
    <OPTION>G</OPTION>
    <OPTION>PG</OPTION>
    <OPTION>PG-13</OPTION>
    <OPTION>R</OPTION>
</SELECT>
```

The combo boxes in Listings 12.7 and 12.8 are both for static options, but it will be desirable to provide dynamic options. This can be done using the WOGenericContainer.

WOGenericContainer

The WOGenericContainer represents any HTML tag dynamically. This greatly opens the possibilities for the types of dynamic elements that you can create in your HTML. The most important attribute is elementName, which specifies the HTML tag to be used in the container. There are other attributes, and the complete listing is given in Table 12.1.

Table 12.1

Attributes for the WOGenericContainer

Attribute	Description
elementName	Bound to a String, this is the HTML tag name. The contents of the WOGenericContainer will be placed in between HTML tags with this name.
omitTags	Bound to a boolean, this specifies whether the tags should appear.
elementID	The elementID for the element, as determined by the WOComponent when the tag is created. This is a read-only value, and is used only with sessions.
otherTagString	Allows you to place another string within the tag. For example, a multiple-selection list is represented by the <SELECT MULTIPLE> HTML. In this case, the elementName is "SELECT" and the otherTagString is "MULTIPLE".
formValue	When used with a session, this sets the variable bound to this attribute to the value of the element. This is used in input-style elements. This is used only with sessions.
formValues	Similar to the formValue attribute, this attribute is bound to an NSArray variable. The variable will then contain the array of values that the user selected.
invokeAction	For an action-styled element such as a hyperlink, this attribute designates the action method to call. This is used only with sessions.

The WOGenericContainer is used in WebObjects Builder by selecting the WOGenericContainer icon, or by selecting the WebObjects, WOGenericContainer menu item.

Movies by Category

To demonstrate the use of the WOGenericContainer in a direct action form, a Movie Category drop-down list will be added to the main page (see Figure 12.5). When the user selects a category, the MovieListPage will be created with all the movies for that category.

Figure 12.5
Adding a Movie Category drop-down list to the application.

The first step is to create a MovieListPage component and write the code that will display all the movies for a particular category in this component. This code is given in Listing 12.9. This could also be done by using a model-based fetch specification.

Listing 12.9

MovieListPage.java, *Displaying Movies for a Particular Category*

```
import com.apple.yellow.foundation.*;
import com.apple.yellow.webobjects.*;
import com.apple.yellow.eocontrol.*;
import com.apple.yellow.eoaccess.*;
```

Listing 12.9

Continued

```java
public class MovieListPage
    extends WOComponent
{

    protected String categoryQueryString;

    NSArray movies;
    NSDictionary movie;

    public void setCategoryQueryString( String value )
    {
        movies=null;
        categoryQueryString = value;
    }

    public void appendToResponse( WOResponse response, WOContext context )
    {
        if ( movies == null )
        {
            EOEditingContext ec = new EOEditingContext();

            EOSortOrdering title =
                EOSortOrdering.sortOrderingWithKey(
                    "title", EOSortOrdering.CompareAscending);
            NSArray orderings = new NSArray( new Object [] { title } );

            EOQualifier qualifier=null;
            if ( categoryQueryString != null )
            {
                NSArray qualifierBindings = new NSArray(
                    new String [] { categoryQueryString } );
                qualifier = EOQualifier.qualifierWithQualifierFormat(
                    "category = %@", qualifierBindings );
            }
            EOFetchSpecification fetchSpec =
                new EOFetchSpecification( "Movie", qualifier, orderings );
            fetchSpec.setFetchesRawRows( true );
            NSArray keyPaths = new NSArray(
                new String [] { "movieId", "title", "studio.name" } );
            fetchSpec.setRawRowKeyPaths( keyPaths );
```

Listing 12.9

Continued

```
        movies = ec.objectsWithFetchSpecification( fetchSpec );
    }
    super.appendToResponse( response, context );
}


}
```

This code is fairly similar to the `TalentListPage` code. When the `rawRowKeyPaths` for a raw row fetch specification contains a relationship, a logical join is created in the SQL that is generated. Also notice that `movieId` is one of the attributes being retrieved; this will be used in a later example.

> Not all the movies will be displayed using this technique because some of the movies do not have a studio, and selecting those as raw rows will automatically perform a logical SQL join. The solution is to make the `studio` relationship in the `Movie` entity a left-outer join. Unfortunately, that will not work for OpenBase Lite because outer joins are not supported. Another option is to fetch enterprise objects rather than raw rows.

The next step is to write the code to return distinct categories in the `Main` component. This is done in the `awake` method. The code for the `Main` component is given in Listing 12.10.

Listing 12.10

The `Main` Component Now Retrieves the Distinct Categories for the Combo Box in the `awake` Method

```java
import com.apple.yellow.foundation.*;
import com.apple.yellow.webobjects.*;
import com.apple.yellow.eocontrol.*;
import com.apple.yellow.eoaccess.*;

public class Main
    extends WOComponent
{

    /** @TypeInfo com.apple.yellow.foundation.NSDictionary */
    protected NSArray categories;
    protected NSDictionary category;
```

Listing 12.10

Continued

```
public void awake()
{
    if ( categories == null )
    {
        EOEditingContext ec = new EOEditingContext();

        EOSortOrdering categoryOrder =
            EOSortOrdering.sortOrderingWithKey(
                "category", EOSortOrdering.CompareAscending);
        NSArray orderings = new NSArray( new Object [] { categoryOrder }
);

        EOFetchSpecification fetchSpec =
            new EOFetchSpecification( "Movie", null, orderings );
        fetchSpec.setFetchesRawRows( true );
        fetchSpec.setUsesDistinct( true );
        NSArray keyPaths = new NSArray( new String [] { "category" } );
        fetchSpec.setRawRowKeyPaths( keyPaths );

        categories = ec.objectsWithFetchSpecification( fetchSpec );
    }
}
}
```

Finally, add a direct action that will retrieve the option that the user selected and send the value to the MovieListPage (see Listing 12.11).

Listing 12.11

The moviesByCategory *Direct Action in the* DirectAction.java *Class*

```
public WOComponent moviesByCategoryAction()
{
    MovieListPage nextPage = (MovieListPage)pageWithName( "MovieListPage" );

    String category =
        (String)this.request().formValueForKey( "categoryOptionList" );
    nextPage.setCategoryQueryString( category );

    return nextPage;
}
```

This method assumes that the control placed in the component will be called `categoryOptionList`.

So, now we have the component that will display the movies, the code to retrieve the distinct categories, and the action method to pull everything together. The last step is to place a form on the main component that displays a combo box. We will use the `WOGenericContainer` for both the `SELECT` and `OPTION` tags. This involves adding a `WOGenericContainer` for the `SELECT` tag, adding a `WORepetition` inside the container, and then adding a `WOGenericContainer` for the `OPTION` tag, with a `WOString` inside for each option.

First, add a `WOForm` and the text `"Select a genre:"`. Bind the `directActionName` for the `WOForm` to `"moviesByCategory"`. Add a static submit button called Search. The `WOGenericContainer` goes between the text and the submit button.

Then add a `WOGenericContainer` and bind the `elementName` attribute to `"SELECT"` (see Figure 12.6). Also add a binding called name, and bind it to `"categoryOptionList"`. This is the name that is used in Listing 12.11. A binding can be added by clicking on the small ± button in the upper right corner of the inspector.

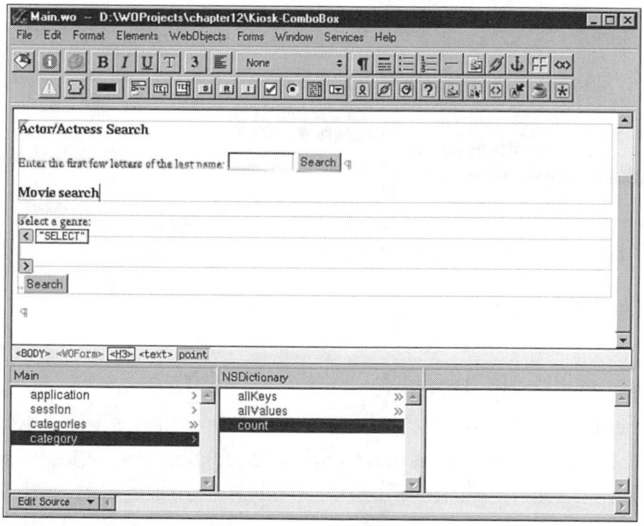

Figure 12.6
The `WOGenericContainer` *for the* `SELECT` *tag.*

Then, add a `WORepetition` inside the `SELECT` generic container. The `list` for the repetition should be bound to the `categories` array and the `item` is bound to the `category` dictionary.

Now, add a `WOGenericContainer` inside the repetition, and bind the `elementName` to `"OPTION"`.

Finally, add a `WOString` inside the `WOGenericContainer`. Bind the `value` of the `WOString` to `category.category`, where the first category is the name of the `NSDictionary` instance variable and the second category is the key that will be returned from the database query. Your `WOGenericContainer` should look like the one displayed in Figure 12.7.

If you build and run the application, it should work at this point.

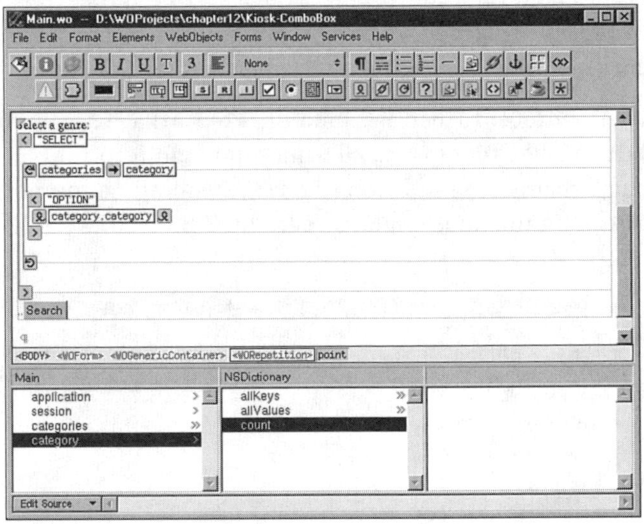

Figure 12.7
The final `WOGenericContainer`.

Check Boxes and Radio Buttons

These controls work similar to the option list. You will need to understand the underlying HTML, but you can start with `WOCheckBox` and `WORadioButton` dynamic elements and make them static. The `INPUT` tag is used for both check boxes and radio buttons; the difference is the `TYPE` attribute. For example, check boxes would be denoted by the following HTML:

```
<INPUT TYPE="CHECKBOX" NAME="useLastName"> Use the last name in the query
<INPUT TYPE="CHECKBOX" NAME="useFirstName"> Use the first name in the query
```

Key-value pairs for only the selected check boxes are sent to the server. The check box status can be retrieved using the `formValueForKey()` method. If a value is returned for one of the check box names, it means that check box was selected. If the check boxes have the same name, the `formValuesForKey()` method can be used. You must then set the value for each check box to something unique to determine what the user selected.

Radio Buttons

Radio buttons are used similarly to check boxes. To make a set of radio buttons mutually exclusive, simply give them all the same HMTL name. The only difference is that radio buttons will never return more than one value for a group. Radio buttons are denoted by the following HTML:

```
<INPUT TYPE="RADIO" NAME="sameName" VALUE="all"> Return all records
<INPUT TYPE="RADIO" NAME="sameName" VALUE="matching"> Return matching records
```

Check Box Example

To demonstrate how to use check boxes, let's add a check box to the talent query form on the main component (see Figure 12.8). If the box is checked, return all `Talent` objects; otherwise perform the query as normal.

Figure 12.8
Adding a check box to the main page.

The first step is to add a `WOCheckBox` to the existing form in WebObjects Builder as shown in Figure 12.9.

Inspect the check box and make it static. Set the name for the control to `"displayAllTalentsCheckbox"` in the static inspector as shown in Figure 12.10.

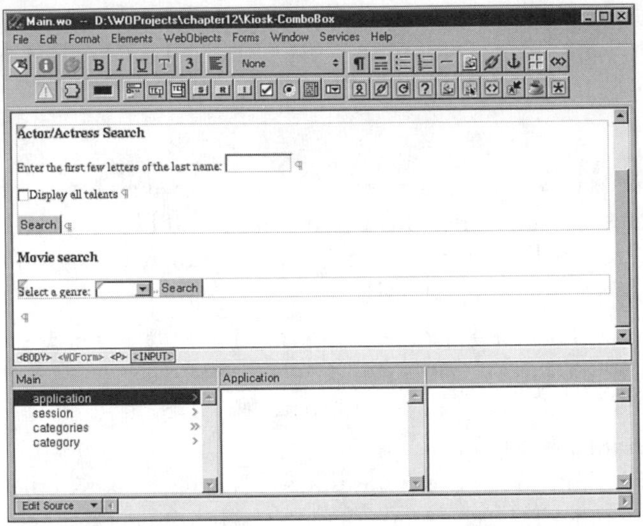

Figure 12.9
Adding a WOCheckbox *to the talent query form.*

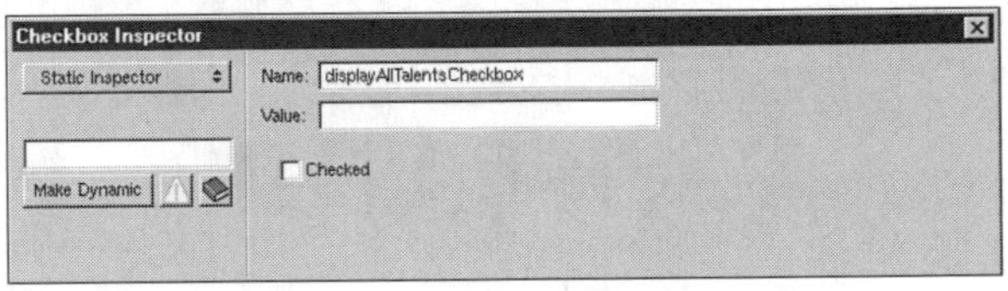

Figure 12.10
The static inspector for a static check box.

Now you must write the code to determine whether the check box has been selected. The check box has been selected if a form value is available for the key of the check box. This can be determined using the WORequest's formValueForKey() method, as shown in Listing 12.12.

Listing 12.12

The Revised talentList *Direct Action, in the* DirectAction.java *Class*

```
public WOComponent talentListAction()
{
    String lastNameString =
        (String)this.request().formValueForKey( "lastNameTextField" );
    TalentListPage nextPage = (TalentListPage)pageWithName("TalentListPage");
    if (this.request().formValueForKey( "displayAllTalentsCheckbox" ) == null)
    {
```

Listing 12.12

Continued

```
        // checkbox is not checked
        nextPage.setLastNameQueryString( lastNameString );
    }
    else
    {
        // checkbox is checked
        nextPage.setLastNameQueryString( null );
    }
    return nextPage;
}
```

In the `talentListAction()` method, if the check box is not checked, the query string is passed to the next component. If the check box is checked, the query string in the next component is set to `null`.

Repeating Check Boxes

Check boxes are commonly used as a selection mechanism in HTML-based applications. In this scenario, each row in a result set will have a check box. The user can then select a set of rows and perform an action such as delete (see Figure 12.11).

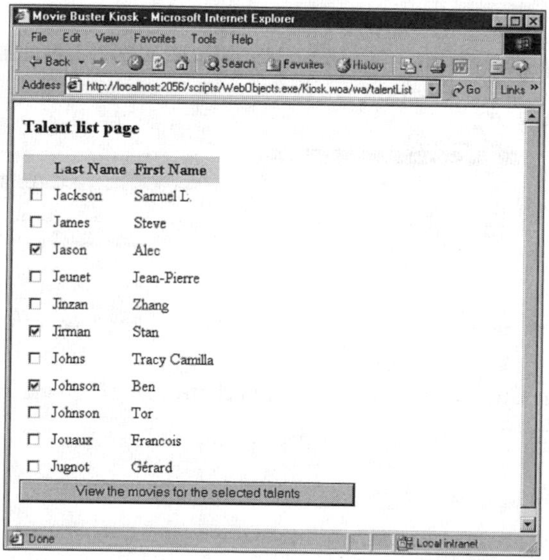

Figure 12.11

Check boxes can be used to mark multiple rows for deletion.

In this example, a check box will be added to each row in the talent list table. If the user clicks on the check boxes and then clicks the View Movies button, all the movies starring those talents will be displayed on the next page. This involves adding a WOGenericContainer and a WOForm to the TalentListPage, and writing the logic to retrieve the movies for a set of talents as one NSArray.

Add a WOForm around the entire table in the TalentListPage component. Set the directActionName for the form to "moviesForSelectedTalents", a method that we will create later.

Now add a WOGenericContainer to the WORepetition on the TalentListPage, as shown in Figure 12.12. We need to have some way to uniquely identify a particular row when the check box is selected, so the VALUE attribute of the check box will be used. Because this is dynamic, the static check box cannot be used; we have to use a WOGenericContainer.

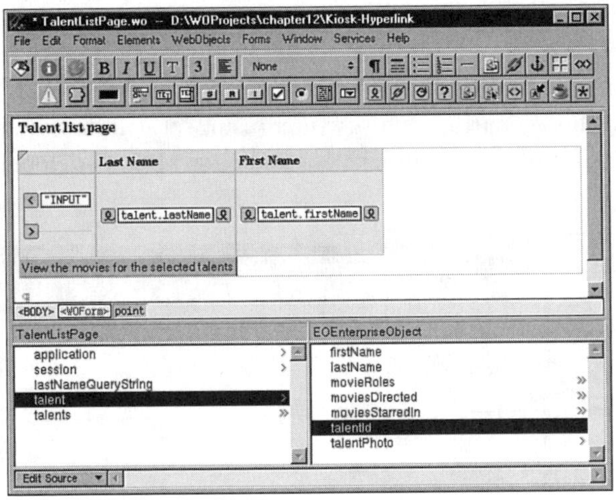

Figure 12.12
The WOGenericContainer is placed in the WORepetition for the table in the TalentListPage.

The bindings for the WOGenericContainer attributes are given in Table 12.2.

Table 12.2

Bindings for the WOGenericContainer *Used in the* TalentListPage

Attribute	Binding
elementName	"INPUT"
NAME	"talentSelectionCheckbox"
TYPE	"CHECKBOX"
VALUE	talent.talentId

By setting the VALUE to the talent.talentId, each check box will have the value of the primary key for the Talent objects, making each value unique. This will also help us in retrieving the Talent objects in the next transaction.

To retrieve the talentIds that the user selected, use the formValuesForKey() method. This will return an NSArray of Strings. Eventually these Strings must be converted to Numbers, but for now, the Strings will do. This will all be done in the moviesForSelectedTalentsAction() method in DirectAction.java. The code for this method is given in Listing 12.13.

Listing 12.13

The moviesForSelectedTalent *Action in the* DirectAction.java *Class*

```
public WOComponent moviesForSelectedTalentsAction()
{
    NSArray talentIds =
        this.request().formValuesForKey( "talentSelectionCheckbox" );
    // pass the talent IDs to the movieListPage
    MovieListPage nextPage = (MovieListPage)pageWithName( "MovieListPage" );
    nextPage.setTalentIds( talentIds );
    return nextPage;
}
```

That's really all there is to retrieving multiple values for a control. The next part is more of an exercise in using EOF than in using direct actions, but it will be covered for completeness.

The final step is to modify the MovieListPage component to retrieve all the movies for an NSArray of talentIds. An NSArray called talentIds should be added to the MovieListPage.java file, along with a method to set the talentIds, as shown in Listing 12.14.

Listing 12.14

The Array of `talentIds` *Will Be Used to Retrieve the Talents with Those* `talentIds`

```
NSArray talentIds;

public void setTalentIds( NSArray value )
{
    movies = null;
    talentIds = value;
}
```

The code to return the movies by category has been removed from the `appendToResponse()` method and placed in a method called `populateMoviesByCategory()`. The code for retrieving the movies for a set of `talentIds` will be placed in a method called `populateMoviesByTalentIds()`. The `appendToResponse()` method needs to be modified to reflect this change, as shown in Listing 12.15.

Listing 12.15

The Modified `appendToResponse` *in the* `MovieListPage` *Class Uses Other Methods to Retrieve the Movies*

```
public void appendToResponse( WOResponse response, WOContext context )
{
    if ( movies == null )
    {
        if ( categoryQueryString != null )
        {
            this.populateMoviesByCategory();
        }
        if ( talentIds != null )
        {
            this.populateMoviesByTalentIds();
        }
    }
    super.appendToResponse( response, context );
}
```

The most difficult part is retrieving the movie objects for a set of `talentIds`. This involves first retrieving the `Talent` objects for the set of `talentIds`. This can be done by converting the `talentIds` into a big OR statement using the `EOOrQualifier`. The `EOOrQualifier` takes an `NSArray` of qualifiers as the parameter for the constructor.

The second part of the method must construct an NSArray of movies from a to-many relationship in the Talent objects. There is a middle table in between the Talent entity and the Movie entity called MovieRoles. This is a useful table because it contains the roleName, but is not necessary for this particular task. To complete this, a flattened relationship in the Talent entity called moviesStarredIn would be useful. This relationship would be flattened from the movieRoles.movie relationship.

To construct an NSArray of movies, you need to loop through all of the Talent objects you retrieved and add the associated objects in the moviesStarredIn array, as shown in Listing 12.16. You also have to keep track of the movies you add to make sure that you do not add a movie twice.

Finally, you can reorder the movies array in memory by using the sortedArrayUsingKeyOrderArray in the EOSortOrdering class.

Listing 12.16

The Mammoth populateMoviesByTalentIds() *Method*

```
public void populateMoviesByTalentIds()
{
    EOEditingContext ec = new EOEditingContext();
    // first get the talent objects
    NSMutableArray qualifiers = new NSMutableArray();
    int index;
    for ( index=0; index<talentIds.count(); index++ )
    {
        EOKeyValueQualifier qualifier =  new EOKeyValueQualifier(
            "talentId",
            EOQualifier.QualifierOperatorEqual,
            new Integer( (String)talentIds.objectAtIndex( index ) ) );

        qualifiers.addObject( qualifier );
    }
    EOOrQualifier orQualifier = new EOOrQualifier( qualifiers );
    EOFetchSpecification fetchSpec =
        new EOFetchSpecification( "Talent", orQualifier, null );
    NSArray talents = ec.objectsWithFetchSpecification( fetchSpec );
    // now retrieve the movies
    NSMutableArray tempMovies = new NSMutableArray();
    for (index=0; index<talents.count(); index++ )
    {
        EOEnterpriseObject talent =
            (EOEnterpriseObject)talents.objectAtIndex(index);
```

Listing 12.16

Continued

```
            NSArray newMovies = (NSArray)talent.valueForKey( "moviesStarredIn" );
            // only add the movies if they do not currently
            // exist in the destination array
            for ( int newMovieIndex=0;
                    newMovieIndex <newMovies.count();
                    newMovieIndex ++ )
            {
                if ( ! tempMovies.containsObject(
                            newMovies.objectAtIndex( newMovieIndex ) ) )
                {
                    tempMovies.addObject(
                        newMovies.objectAtIndex( newMovieIndex ) );
                }
            }
        }
        // finally, order the array
        EOSortOrdering movieTitle =
            EOSortOrdering.sortOrderingWithKey(
                "title", EOSortOrdering.CompareAscending);
        NSArray orderings = new NSArray( new Object [] { movieTitle    } );

        movies = EOSortOrdering.sortedArrayUsingKeyOrderArray(
            tempMovies, orderings );
    }
```

A Small Bug

You might notice that some of the talents listed do not have associated movies. That is because the Talent entity includes directors along with actors and actresses. Because we are dealing with only actors and actresses, it would be useful to display only actors and actresses.

There are a few ways to do that. One approach is to construct a where clause with a nested select statement that retrieves the talent IDs from the MovieRole entity. This can be accomplished by adding an EOSQLQualifier to the qualifier used to retrieve the talents. The EOSQLQualifier does not parse the qualifier format, so you must use specific table names. It should be used only when all other options have been tried, because it might tie your application to a particular database. To add this option, the appendToResponse() method in the TalentListPage must be modified as shown in Listing 12.17.

Listing 12.17

Modifying the appendToResponse() *Method in the* TalentListPage *to Display Only* Talents *That Have* MovieRoles

```
public void appendToResponse( WOResponse response, WOContext context )
{
    if ( talents == null )
    {
        EOEditingContext ec = new EOEditingContext();

        EOSortOrdering lastName =
            EOSortOrdering.sortOrderingWithKey(
                "lastName", EOSortOrdering.CompareAscending);
        EOSortOrdering firstName =
            EOSortOrdering.sortOrderingWithKey(
                "firstName", EOSortOrdering.CompareAscending);
        NSArray orderings =
            new NSArray( new Object [] { lastName, firstName } );

        EOEntity talentEntity = EOUtilities.entityNamed( ec, "Talent" );
        EOSQLQualifier sqlQualifier = new EOSQLQualifier( talentEntity,
            "TALENT_ID IN ( SELECT TALENT_ID FROM MOVIE_ROLE )" );
        EOQualifier qualifier=sqlQualifier;
        if ( lastNameQueryString != null )
        {
            NSArray qualifierBindings =
                new NSArray( new String [] { lastNameQueryString+"*" } );
            qualifier = EOQualifier.qualifierWithQualifierFormat(
                "lastName like %@", qualifierBindings );
            qualifier = new EOAndQualifier(
                new NSArray( new Object [] { qualifier, sqlQualifier } ) );
        }
        EOFetchSpecification fetchSpec =
            new EOFetchSpecification( "Talent", qualifier, orderings );
        fetchSpec.setFetchesRawRows( true );
        talents = ec.objectsWithFetchSpecification( fetchSpec );
    }

    super.appendToResponse( response, context );
}
```

To maintain the same functionality, the new EOSQLQualifier can be combined with the existing qualifier using an EOAndQualifier. With this modification, you should see only actors and actresses.

Using Dynamic Hyperlinks

Hyperlinks can contain additional information that is transferred in key-value pairs similar to form values. This information appears after the hyperlink address, and the key-value pairs are separated by ampersands (&). The form information is separated from the URL by a question mark (?).

This is useful if you want to pass around a primary key for an object. Each method could then retrieve that object from the database. This is used often in many of the online shopping sites. It is common to see a URL that contains an address such as

```
http://www.us.buy.com/retail/toc_feature.asp?loc=13198
```

Even though Active Server Pages are used here, the question mark after the URL indicates that the next part contains key-value pairs.

You can place key-value pairs in WOHyperlinks by adding attributes that begin with question marks. These values can then be retrieved using the WORequest's formValueForKey() method.

Movie Detail Example

A place where hyperlinks could be used is in providing a movie detail hyperlink on the MovieListPage as shown in Figure 12.13.

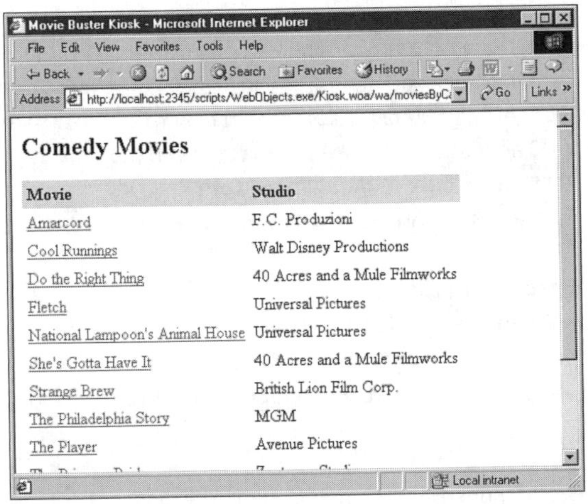

Figure 12.13
Adding a Movie Detail Hyperlink to the application.

First, create a `movieDetail` direct action that returns a `MovieDetailPage` component. You will have to create this component as well. In the `movieDetailAction` method, retrieve the `"movieId"` form value and pass it on to the `MovieDetailPage` that you create.

First add the `WOHyperlink` to the `MovieListPage`, and then bind the `directActionName` to `movieDetail`. You must also create a new binding called `?movieId`, bound to `movie.movieId` as shown in Figure 12.14. For this to work, the `movieId` either is a class property, or the display is a set of raw rows in which the `movieId` was one of the selected attributes.

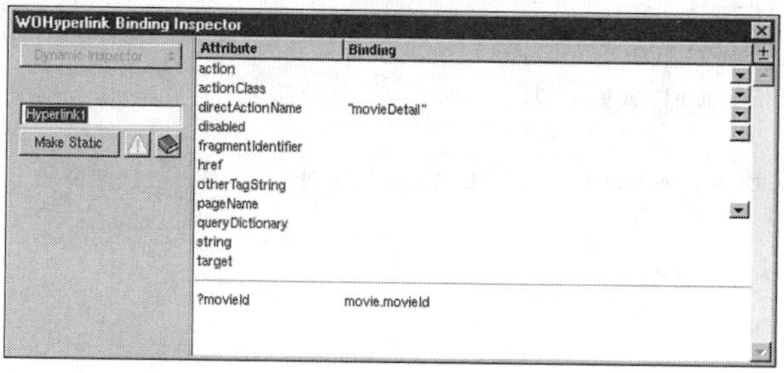

Figure 12.14
The inspector for the `WOHyperlink` *that passes the current* `movieId` *to the next component.*

At this point, you can retrieve the value from the request in the direct action and pass it off to the movie detail component. The code for the direct action is given in Listing 12.18 and the code for the `MovieDetailPage` component is given in Listing 12.19.

Listing 12.18

The `movieDetail` *Direct Action in the* `DirectAction.java` *Class*

```java
public WOActionResults movieDetailAction()
{
    MovieDetailPage nextPage =
        (MovieDetailPage)this.pageWithName( "MovieDetailPage" );
    nextPage.setMovieId( (String)this.request().formValueForKey( "movieId" ) );
    return nextPage;
}
```

Listing 12.19

The Code for the movieDetailPage *Class*

```
import com.apple.yellow.foundation.*;
import com.apple.yellow.webobjects.*;
import com.apple.yellow.eocontrol.*;
import com.apple.yellow.eoaccess.*;

public class MovieDetailPage
    extends WOComponent
{

    /** @TypeInfo Movie */
    protected EOEnterpriseObject movie;
    protected String movieId;

    public void setMovieId( String value )
    {
        movieId = value;
    }

    public void appendToResponse( WOResponse response, WOContext context )
    {
        EOEditingContext ec = new EOEditingContext();

        NSArray bindings =
            new NSArray( new Object [] { new Integer( movieId ) } );
        EOQualifier qualifier = EOQualifier.qualifierWithQualifierFormat(
            "movieId = %@", bindings );

        EOFetchSpecification fetchSpec = new EOFetchSpecification(
            "Movie", qualifier, null );

        NSArray results = ec.objectsWithFetchSpecification( fetchSpec );
        movie = (EOEnterpriseObject)results.objectAtIndex(0);
        super.appendToResponse( response, context );
    }

}
```

Multiple Submit Buttons

Only one submit button has been used for the examples in this chapter, but what if you want to use more than one submit button? In an application that uses sessions, you would simply set the WOForm's multipleSubmit attribute to YES and bind separate actions to each submit button in the form. With direct actions, the action is set for the form, not the individual submit button. However, you can determine the submit button that was selected by looking for the name of the submit button in the form values. If the submit button was pressed, a key-value pair for that button is sent to the server; otherwise, the key is not sent.

A Login Example

Consider a situation in which you want to use a form to log in a user or start the creation of an account. You would first create a user interface similar to the one demonstrated in Figure 12.15.

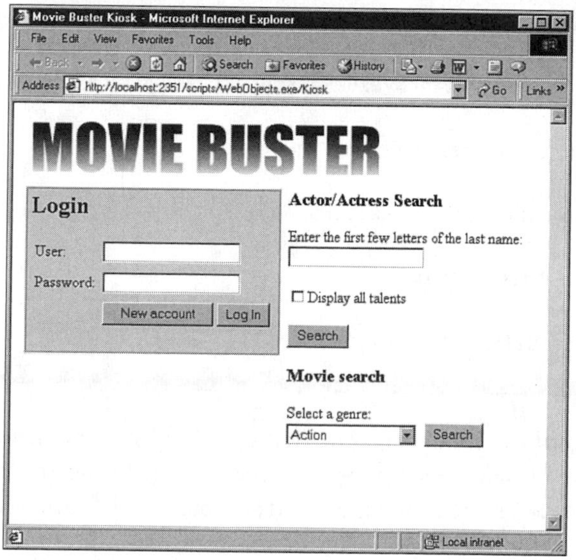

Figure 12.15

Adding a Login Panel to the application.

The directActionName for the form is "login", and the names of the two buttons are "createAccount" and "login", respectively. At this point, you can add the code in Listing 12.20 to your application to determine the button that was pressed.

Listing 12.20

The Direct Action to Determine the Button That Was Pressed in a Multiple-Submit Direct Action Form

```
public WOActionResults createAccount()
{
    return this.pageWithName( "CreateAccountPage" );
}

public WOActionResults login()
{
    return this.defaultAction();
}

public WOActionResults loginAction()
{
    if ( this.request().formValueForKey("createAccount") != null )
    {
        return this.createAccount();
    }
    if ( this.request().formValueForKey("login") != null )
    {
        return this.login();
    }
    return this.defaultAction();
}
```

The loginAction() method is the one that is called from the form; the other two methods are placeholders for future implementation. In the loginAction() method, the form values are searched for the createAccount and login keys. The presence of one of these keys indicates which button was pressed.

Session Management

Eventually, you will probably come to the conclusion that you need a session. To create a session, simply call the session() method in any WOComponent. This is essentially what we have been avoiding all along in this chapter. By calling the session() method, a session is created if one does not exist.

To determine whether a session exists, use the hasSession() method in a component or the existingSession() method in the direct action class. Neither of these methods will create a session, but the hasSession() method returns true if a session exists, false if not. The existingSession() returns the WOSession if a session exists, and null if not.

Finally, to terminate a session, use the WOSession's terminate() method. This method will terminate the session and perform a full garbage collection. You might find it difficult to remove the session ID from the URL after termination. The best way to remove the session ID is to return a page that contains nothing but static hyperlinks or dynamic hyperlinks that use the src attribute bound (not the action attribute). If you want to place a WOHyperlink on your page that starts the application over again, bind the src to application.baseURL. The baseURL() method returns the absolute URL for the start page of your application.

Summary

As you can see, it's a bit more work to write an application that uses direct actions than to write one that uses sessions, simply because a number of the dynamic elements implicitly use sessions. There are a number of things to remember when using direct actions, most importantly the following:

- Place all direct actions in a subclass of WODirectAction.

- The names of all direct action methods must end with Action and return a WOActionResults object.

- When using direct actions, avoid all dynamic elements that implicitly use sessions.

- Use the formValueForKey() method in the WORequest object to determine values that the user entered.

- WOHyperlinks can be used to pass form values by defining attributes that begin with a question mark.

- Methods exist in the WOComponent and the WODirectAction classes to test for the existence of a session.

Well, that's all for this chapter. The next chapter discusses some advanced features and optimizations of EOF.

```
this.session().terminate();
```

CHAPTER 13

OPTIMIZING DATABASE ACCESS

If you've read the book this far, the power of EOF must be apparent. Granted, there is a bit of a learning curve for the class hierarchy and you probably don't know how to do everything that you want to at this point. However, getting a Web-based database application up and running by clicking and dragging is powerful stuff. You might be asking yourself "What's the drawback?" If left untouched, the performance for EOF-based applications can be fairly poor.

This chapter is dedicated to helping you identify and fix EOF-related performance problems. The following topics will be discussed:

- Identifying performance problems

- Debugging the SQL outputted to the database

- Various EOF optimization options, including pre-fetching, batch faulting, and shared objects

Identifying Performance Problems

As a general rule of thumb, you will want to create your application assuming that nothing you do will create a performance problem. Some basic performance improvements can be included from the beginning of development simply because of your previous experiences. However, you don't want to get in the habit of anticipating the performance problems before they occur. You run the risk of wasting your time solving performance problems that don't really exist rather than solving the problem at hand.

So, let's say that your application is finished, and you're testing it. Your users say it's slow. Unfortunately, there are many potential reasons for this slowdown, considering the nature of these types of applications. It's a good idea to determine the nature of the performance problem before you fix it.

One assumption this chapter makes is that the servers are running on appropriate hardware/software combinations with enough RAM (more is better). Also, the assumption is made that the operating systems on the machines for the deployment environment are tuned appropriately.

Web Server

As you will learn in the Chapter 14, "Deploying Your Application," you have the option of deploying your application on the same machine as your Web server or on separate machines. In general, any decent Web server can process more requests than the best application server, so this is probably not a location for your initial performance problems. There are exceptions to this rule, and there are some general ways to increase your performance here, which will be discussed in Chapter 14, "Deploying your Application", as well.

Network

The most commonly overlooked area for performance problems is the network. This includes the network from the client to the Web server, the Web server to the application server, and the application server to the database server. This is a matter of making sure that you have enough bandwidth to handle all the requests being routed to each of the servers. Tuning networks is a complicated task, and the topic is out of the scope of this book. For more information on tuning networks and Web servers, check out *Web Performance Tuning: Speeding Up the Web* by Patrick Killelea and Linda Mui (1998 O'Reilly, ISBN 1565923790).

Application Server

If you have found that your network activity is not at its peak most of the time, and your Web server is mostly idle, the next place to look is your application server. First identify the requests that take the longest. The easiest way to do this is to simply test the application or interview the complaining users. You might find that testing the application yourself takes longer, but will be less stressful, depending on the user.

After you have identified the problem spots, the next step is to examine the SQL that is being generated. This is discussed in the "SQL Debugging" section, later in this chapter. There you will find a majority of your problems, depending on how much time you have spent tuning your application. This chapter is dedicated to solving the database performance problems.

Other areas of the application server could potentially pose performance problems, such as the unnecessary use of sessions, and non-optimization of components. In general, you will want to avoid the use of sessions unless absolutely necessary. Also you should make attempts to use common components (rather than creating new components all the time) when using sessions. Some of these topics, including preparing your application for deployment, will be discussed in Chapter 14.

Database Server

If you are still having problems after you have determined that the SQL being generated by EOF is appropriate and should cause no significant delays, your focus should turn to the database. Make sure that the appropriate tables have indices that will be used in the queries you are generating. This chapter discusses turning on SQL Debugging to display the SQL generated by EOF. Most databases have an option to show the plan for SQL execution. You can then run the SQL directly in a separate application and take a look at the plan that is generated. You will need a skilled database administrator to help with complex database schemas.

You might want to identify any large tables that can be split into live and archive tables. Depending on the amount of data you have, you might need to create read-only and live databases. In a shopping site example, you might want to have product and order databases. You will then have the ability to configure the product database for increased performance.

There are many other options for database tuning; it's quite a large topic. For more information about database tuning, you will have to get a book specific to your database server. For example, *Oracle Performance Tuning* by Mark Gurry and Peter Corrigan (1996 O'Reilly, ISBN 1565922379) is a good book on optimizing Oracle databases.

Locating Performance Problems

To properly tune your application, you must first determine the location of the slowdown. The built-in profiling tools provided with the WebObjects and EOF frameworks can be used to locate potential problem spots in your application. After it is configured properly, objects in the WebObjects and EOF frameworks will log the amount of time spent on various operations. This logging is done in memory and is quite efficient compared to the time spent handling most requests. Two pages are used for profiling: the WOEventSetup and WOEventDisplay.

WOEventSetup

The WOEventSetup page is used to configure the types of events that will be logged, which is the first step to profiling the application. To retrieve the WOEventSetup for a running application, enter the URL:

`http://host/adaptor/application/wa/WOEventSetup`

For example, the following URL is used to retrieve the event logging setup page for the Rental application that is being run via direct-connect:

`http://localhost:4796/scripts/WebObjects.exe/Rental.woa/wa/WOEventSetup`

The port number will be different each time the application is run. This page will appear as shown in Figure 13.1.

Figure 13.1
The WOEventSetup page.

This page sets up the events that will be logged, and defaults to none being logged. All the registered event types are listed. You have the ability to add custom event types if you want to track your own routines: See the EOEvent and EOEventCenter class documentation found in the EOF control layer.

The submit buttons for the form are located at the bottom of the WOEventSetup page as shown in Figure 13.2. You have the option of logging specific types of events or all events. The best way to start is to list all the events.

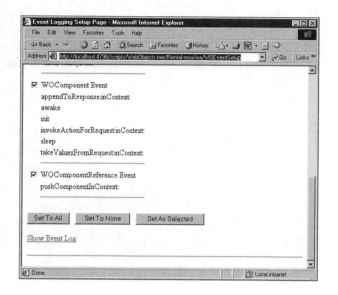

Figure 13.2
You can select the events to log on this page.

After you have selected the events to log, the next step is to use the application. Make sure that you use a number of pages for a number of times to get some accurate data, and then use the WOEventDisplay page (see Figure 13.3). The URL for this page is the following:

```
http://host/adaptor/application/wa/WOEventDisplay
```

For example, the event display page for the Rental application is as follows:

```
http://localhost:4796/scripts/WebObjects.exe/Rental.woa/wa/WOEventDisplay
```

There are a number of different ways to view the events, as shown in the options at the top of the WOEventDisplay page. The default is the Aggregated hierarchical events, which displays events based on the items that logged the times. The views that display events by the page, such as Show Events Grouped by Page, might be more comprehendible. The Event Display page is shown in Figure 13.4.

By default, WebObjects will store up to 200,000 events, which will take about 4MB of RAM. This value is configurable using default settings. For more information on advanced options for event logging, consult the WebObjects documentation supplied in WOInfoCenter. There's an area for "What's new in WebObjects 4.5" in the "Release Notes" section that describes all the settings in detail.

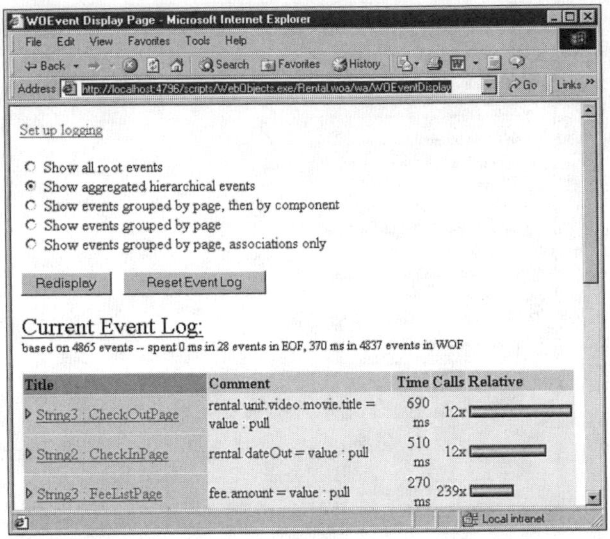

Figure 13.3

The WOEventDisplay *page.*

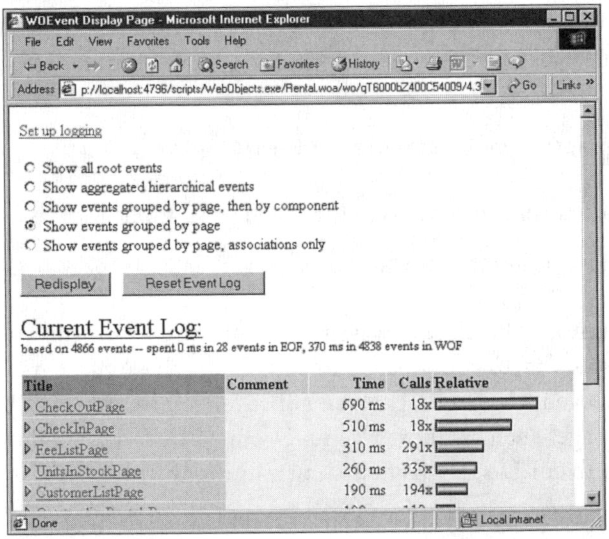

Figure 13.4

The Event Display page.

SQL Debugging

Given the different areas of performance tuning for your application, this chapter focuses on tuning the EOF layer. The first step is to determine the SQL that is being generated. This can be done either in code or by using a defaults setting.

Using the EOAdaptorContext

You can turn on SQL debugging by using a static method in the EOAdaptorContext class called setDebugDefaultEnabled(), similar to this:

```
EOAdaptorContext.setDebugEnabledDefault( true );
```

The SQL generated by EOF will then be echoed to the standard output. When running the application in Project Builder, the standard output is placed in the launch panel, as shown in Figure 13.5.

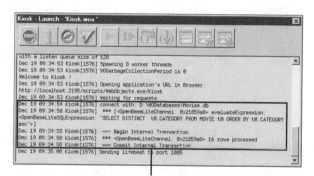

SQL debugging messages

Figure 13.5

When debugging SQL, the SQL is placed in the launch panel. Here is an example of some OpenBaseLite SQL.

Using the Defaults

A lot of times you will not want to hard-code the SQL debugging line in your application. There is another option. When your application starts, the defaults for your application are loaded. All the application defaults are stored in the defaults database. These can be accessed through the defaults command-line command. You can run this command in the Terminal on the OS X Server or by using the command prompt in Windows.

Every application has a domain in the `defaults` database. You can view the available domains by typing the following:

```
defaults domains
```

You should be able to find your applications in this list of domains. To read all the settings for a domain, type the following `defaults` command:

```
defaults read <domain>
```

There will probably not be keys for your any of your applications in this database. The key to set that will turn on SQL debugging for your application is `EOAdaptorDebugEnabled`, and the value to set is `YES`. Here's an example:

```
defaults write <domain> EOAdaptorDebugEnabled YES
```

The `<domain>` is the name of your application, which could be different from the name of the directory in which your application resides. You can determine the application name from the project inspector. Click on the inspector icon in Project Builder and select Project Attributes from the drop-down list (see Figure 13.6).

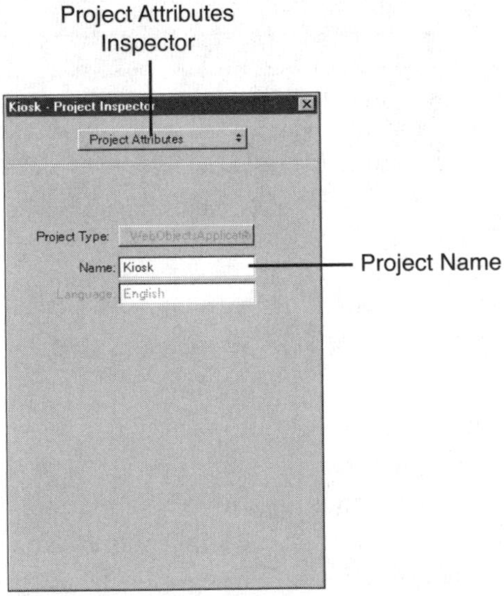

Figure 13.6
The name of the project can be determined in the Project Attributes inspector.

For example, turning on SQL debugging for the application represented by Figure 13.6 could be done with the following defaults command:

```
defaults write Kiosk EOAdaptorDebugEnabled YES
```

Faulting

There are a number of options for optimizing database access within EOF. The options mostly have to do with changing the way records are retrieved and also with how many times they are retrieved. Most of these optimizations have to do with the way that relationships are represented in memory, and the way they are retrieved from the database.

As described in Chapter 2, "Creating a Model," *to-one* relationships are resolved as a simple reference to another object, and a *to-many* relationship is a reference to a NSArray of objects. These references are resolved *lazily*; meaning that they are only populated with data when necessary. Before they are populated with data, they are represented as an EOFault (see Figure 13.7).

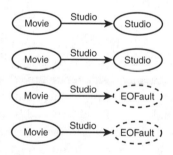

Figure 13.7
Before objects are retrieved for relationships, they are represented as an EOFault.

The EOFault stores the entity and the primary key information. Essentially, enough information to be able to retrieve the object when necessary is stored in the fault. When the fault is tripped, the actual data is retrieved.

Some Methods Dealing with Faults

The EOEditingContext has methods that refault objects. When an object is *refaulted*, it is discarded and replaced with a fault. The next time that object is requested, the data is retrieved from the database. Table 13.1 lists methods in EOEditingContext that refault objects.

Table 13.1

Methods in the `EOEditingContext` *that Refault Objects*

Method	Description
`public void refaultObjects()`	This method saves any pending changes to the database and turns all objects that were not updated or inserted back into faults.
`public void invalidateAllObjects()`	Refaults all objects, discarding any pending changes.
`public void refault( Object sender )`	Refaults only the object passed in as the argument.

A fault can be created using the `EOObjectStore` method called `faultForRawRow()`, which has the following signature:

```
public EOEnterpriseObject faultForRawRow( NSDictionary row,
        String entityName, EOEditingContext editingContext )
```

The dictionary used for the first parameter must at least contain the primary key for the entity.

An Example of Faulting

So, consider the `Movie` entity, which has a to-one relationship with `Studio` called `studio`. One SQL statement is used to retrieve all the `Movie` objects. As the studios are required, a separate SQL statement is generated to retrieve each studio. If 10 movies are selected, there's a potential for 11 SQL statements to be generated. If more than one movie has the same studio, that number would be reduced, but the worst-case scenario is fairly bleak. Note that this performance penalty is levied the first time these rows are returned. When the objects are in memory, the relationship is resolved using the objects in memory.

In this chapter, three methods for improving performance in this area are discussed: batch faulting, prefetching relationships, and batch fetching.

Batch Faulting

Batch faulting works on the premise that if a database trip is required to retrieve records for a relationship, you might as well retrieve a certain number of records. This is similar to a beer run. If you're going to the store to get some beer, you shouldn't return with just one beer, unless you think you are only going to drink one beer. If you think you will need a six-pack, return with a six-pack. If a good game is on and you have a bunch of friends over, come back with a case. Batch faulting works the same way: You specify how many enterprise objects to retrieve when the relationship is used. The difference is, of course, that you do not have to specify EOs in 12-packs.

The batch faulting size is set in the advanced relationship inspector in EOModeler, as shown in Figure 13.8.

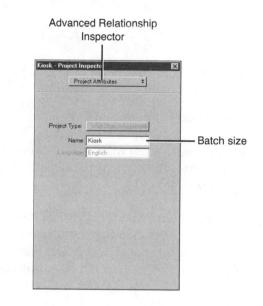

Figure 13.8
The batch fetch size is modified in the advanced relationship inspector.

This number represents the number of faults that are resolved when one is tripped. This number corresponds to the numberOfToManyFaultsToBatchFetch() method in the EORelationship class. You can only set this number for to-many relationships.

Setting the number of to-many faults to batch fetch causes EOF to look for other objects of the same type that have a fault for the same relationship. It will then fault the number of relationships specified. This causes the SQL to have a number of OR statements in the where clause.

For example, consider the to-many relationship from Studio to Movie called movies. Let's say that the batch fetch size for this relationship is 10. When the movies for one studio are requested, EOF will find up to 10 other Studio objects that contain faults for the movies relationship, and construct one SQL statement that will retrieve all the Movie objects for the identified relationships. The SQL generated will be similar to the SQL in Listing 13.1.

Listing 13.1

SQL Debugging Output for Retrieving Batch-Fetched Movies

```
<OpenBaseLiteSQLExpression:
"SELECT  t0.CATEGORY, t0.DATE_RELEASED, t0.MOVIE_ID, t0.POSTER_NAME,
t0.RATED, t0.REVENUE, t0.STUDIO_ID, t0.TITLE, t0.TRAILER_NAME

FROM MOVIE t0

WHERE
(t0.STUDIO_ID = ? OR t0.STUDIO_ID = ? OR t0.STUDIO_ID = ? OR t0.STUDIO_ID = ?
OR t0.STUDIO_ID = ? OR t0.STUDIO_ID = ? OR t0.STUDIO_ID = ? OR t0.STUDIO_ID =
?
OR t0.STUDIO_ID = ? OR t0.STUDIO_ID = ?)"

withBindings:(1:24(studioId), 2:25(studioId), 3:26(studioId), 4:27(studioId),
5:28(studioId), 6:29(studioId), 7:30(studioId), 8:34(studioId),
9:33(studioId), 10:31(studioId))>]
```

This SQL will probably be a little unfamiliar because it is OpenBaseLite SQL. However, you will probably notice that the FROM table is the MOVIE table, and there are 10 OR statements, the same number as the batch size. The implication here is that if the batch size is 100, there might be up to 100 OR statements.

Prefetching Relationships

Another option is to prefetch a relationship when the fetch specification is formed. *Prefetching* means that the objects across a relationship are fetched with the initial fetch specification. For example, assume that we are fetching studios in which the name starts with W. The SQL generated for this fetch specification is given in Listing 13.2.

Listing 13.2

The SQL Debugging Output for Returning All the Studios Whose Name Starts with W

```
<OpenBaseLiteSQLExpression: "SELECT  t0.BUDGET, t0.NAME, t0.STUDIO_ID

FROM STUDIO t0

WHERE t0.NAME like ?

ORDER BY t0.NAME asc"

withBindings:(1:W%(name))>
```

Assume that we will want to display all the movies with these studios. If we set the fetch specification to prefetch the `movies` relationship, the SQL generated contains a similar `WHERE` clause. This SQL is shown in Listing 13.3.

Listing 13.3

The SQL Debugging Output for Prefetching the `movies` *Relationship*

```
<OpenBaseLiteSQLExpression:
"SELECT  t0.CATEGORY, t0.DATE_RELEASED, t0.MOVIE_ID, t0.POSTER_NAME,
t0.RATED, t0.REVENUE, t0.STUDIO_ID, t0.TITLE, t0.TRAILER_NAME

FROM STUDIO t1, MOVIE t0

WHERE t1.NAME like ?
AND t0.STUDIO_ID = t1.STUDIO_ID"

withBindings:(1:W%(name))>
```

Setting Up Prefetching

The relationships to prefetch are determined in the fetch specification as a set of keys to be prefetched. If you are working with a model-based fetch specification, these keys are specified in the Prefetching tab, as shown in Figure 13.5.

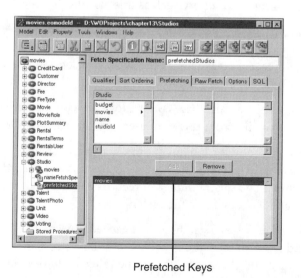

Prefetched Keys

Figure 13.9

The keys to be prefetched are set in EOModeler for a model-based fetch specification.

If you are constructing the model in code, the keys to be prefetched are set in the EOFetchSpecification method:

```
public void setPrefetchingRelationshipKeyPaths( NSArray keyPaths )
```

The performance improvement for this is significant. However, there are still at least two select statements: One for the initial entity, and one for each relationship to prefetch. To combine this into one select statement requires using raw-row SQL, which might not be desirable.

Caching Objects

One of the areas for improvement in EOF is to cache objects from the database and make them available across sessions and components. If commonly used objects can be reused, space will be saved. Objects will not be duplicated across editing contexts, and time will be saved because the objects will not need to be retrieved multiple times. Currently there are two mechanisms for caching objects in EOF. One is using cached objects, and the other is by using shared objects. There are benefits to each type.

Cached Objects

One method of caching objects is to configure an entity to cache objects in memory. This will force all the objects for an entity to be loaded the first time an object is requested. Every time an object is requested for that entity, one of the cached objects is returned. To configure an entity such as this, use the Advanced Entity Inspector as shown in Figure 13.10.

The objects are cached in the EODatabaseContext. The EODatabaseContext shares the same EOObjectStoreCoordinator with the EOEditingContext objects used by your application code (see Figure 13.11).

Because there is a separate database context for each connection dictionary, you can receive the most benefits from this if all users use the same connection information.

Cached objects are useful for lookup entities that rarely change, such as the FeeType entity in the rentals database. The FeeType entity has two records, one for Late and another for Rental. The small number of records and the nonvolatile nature of the data make this an ideal candidate for caching.

Care should be taken when deciding to use cached objects. Read-only entities should be the only entities with cached objects because the objects are retrieved from the database only once and changes might not be reflected in the objects. Also, entities with lots of data should be avoided because all the objects will be loaded into memory on the first request. Also, these objects can only be used for qualifiers that can be resolved in-memory.

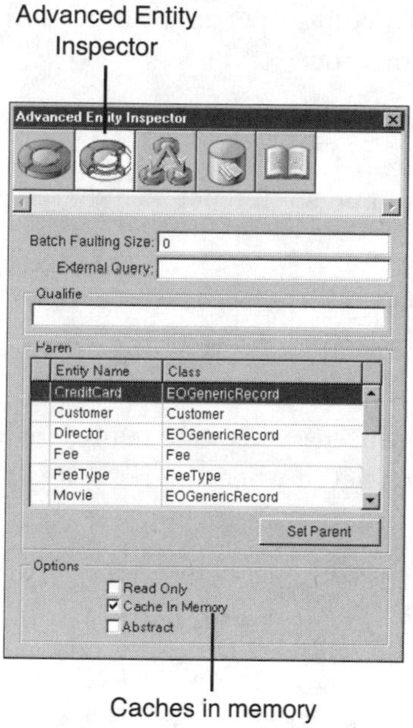

Advanced Entity
Inspector

Caches in memory

Figure 13.10
Setting shared objects in the inspector panel.

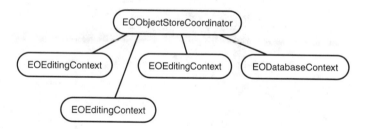

Figure 13.11
The relationship between the editing contexts, object store coordinator, and database context.

Shared Objects

Another mechanism for reusing objects is to share objects. Objects are shared by
being placed in a shared editing context. Because the shared objects are stored in an
editing context, they do not have all of the same restrictions as the cached objects
stored in the database context. Shared objects can be used by users who implement
different database connection dictionaries. Also, shared objects do not have to include
all the records for a particular entity as required by cached objects.

There is one shared editing context per application, and it can be accessed by the following WOApplication method:

```
public EOSharedEditingContext defaultSharedEditingContext()
```

EOEditingContexts also contain a reference to a shared editing context, which can be retrieved using

```
public EOSharedEditingContext sharedEditingContext()
```

Configuring the Entity

One way to get objects in the shared editing context is to configure the entity so that a certain set of objects are retrieved when any request is made for that entity's objects (see Figure 13.12).

Figure 13.12

Objects returned as shared are configured by inspecting the entity and selecting the shared objects inspector.

Three options are in this inspector for using shared objects. These options are for the automatic placement of objects in the editing context when the first objects are requested, similar to cached objects. The difference, however, is that you can specify a fetch specification that identifies shared objects to be placed in the shared editing context.

Share No Objects

This option doesn't disallow placing objects for this entity in the shared editing context; it just does not place any objects in the shared editing context by default.

Share All Objects

This option requires a model-based fetch specification that does not have a qualifier; that is, one that returns all objects. If you do not currently have a model-based fetch specification without a qualifier, clicking on this option will create one for you. When any objects for this entity are requested, that fetch specification is used to place all the objects in the shared editing context. This is similar to caching objects, except cached objects are stored in the database context.

Share Objects Fetched With

This option allows a better level of flexibility, allowing you to place a subset of objects in the shared editing context. Create a fetch specification that defines the set of objects you want to share; then specify this option and select the fetch specification. This is useful in a scenario with a large lookup table in which a small percentage of records are used. To gain the performance advantage of using shared objects without paying a large storage penalty, identify the most commonly used objects in a fetch specification.

Fetching Objects into the Shared Editing Context

If you want to retrieve shared objects during runtime, use the `objectsWithFetchSpecification()` method in the `EOSharedEditingContext` object. This will place all objects retrieved from the fetch specification into the shared editing context.

Modifying Shared Objects

All the objects in the shared editing context are read-only due to the nature of the shared editing context. Because of this, you will have to use a standard `EOEditingContext` to modify objects. When `saveChanges()` is called in the editing context, the changes are propagated to the shared editing context.

For inserts, insert the object as normal in the editing context (not the shared one) and call `saveChanges()`.

For updates and deletes, you will need to temporarily disconnect the shared editing context from the editing context. This can be done by passing `null` in to the `setSharedEditingContext()` method. An example is given in Listing 13.4.

Listing 13.4

When Updating or Deleting Objects in a Shared Editing Context, Disconnect the Shared Editing Context from the Normal One

```
EOEditingContext ec = this.session().defaultEditingContext();
ec.setSharedEditingContext( null );

// perform any updates or deletes on 'ec'

ec.saveChanges();

// now turn on object sharing again

ec.setSharedEditingContext(
    EOSharedEditingContext.defaultSharedEditingContext() );
```

Summary

When considering application performance tuning, there are a lot of factors to examine, and it is important to understand the bottleneck before you begin the tuning process. WebObjects provides tools to assist in profiling that help identify performance hits in the application server.

A few techniques are used to assist in the improvement of performance for EOF objects, including the following:

- Caching objects in the database context
- Prefetching relationships
- Sharing objects in a shared editing context
- Batch-faulting relationships

It is important to understand the performance improvements that each of these topics provide in order to use them effectively.

CHAPTER 14

DEPLOYING YOUR APPLICATION

Eventually, you will need to get your application in front of some users. Sure, you could click the launch button on Project Builder and e-mail them the URL that's generated, but what if your machine crashes? What if you have to do some other work? This is obviously not a good solution. You will need to deploy your application on a suitable deployment machine.

Deployment involves creating a deployable version of the application, and using a tool called the Monitor to deploy the application. This chapter discusses these activities.

Deployment Overview

WebObjects applications can be deployed using multiple instances on multiple hosts. An application instance is a process running on the host machine. Each process has its own memory space and its own instance of WOApplication.

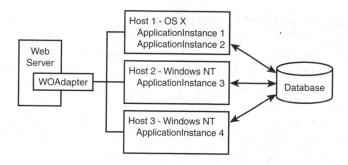

Figure 14.1

A typical deployment scenario.

Because the application instances run in separate memory spaces, you can never assume that some data in memory will be shared across all running instances. For example, it isn't a good idea to store the number of times the application has been accessed in the Application class. That will store the number of times a particular instance has been accessed.

The application instances do not need to run on the same operating system. However, for deployment simplicity, it's probably a good idea to keep the OS the same if using multiple hosts. The main reasons to deploy on multiple hosts are redundancy and scalability. If one host goes down, the requests are routed to the other hosts. Any sessions on the downed host will be lost, however.

wotaskd

The hosts used must be running `wotaskd`. `wotaskd` is a daemon on OS X and Solaris and a service in Windows NT/2000. This daemon manages the communication between the instances and the adaptor, as well as managing the startup and shutdown of the application instances. Using `wotaskd`, you can also set scheduled shutdown times for the application instances if you anticipate having memory problems. (However, if you anticipate having memory problems, you should probably attempt to fix them...)

`wotaskd` uses a configuration file located in the `Local/Library/WebObjects/Configuration` directory to determine how it operates. You have the option of either modifying the configuration file to add instances or using the Monitor. There is no real reason to modify the file directly; Monitor works just fine, and its usage will be discussed in this chapter.

Building an Installable Version

If you are ready to install, you need to build an installable version of the application. An installable version contains everything necessary for the application to be installed, which includes the application executable, resources, and Web server resources.

The Install Directory

The installable version of the application will be placed in the install directory. The install directory is set in the project inspector.

The installation path is set to the following:

```
$(LOCAL_LIBRARY_DIR)/WebObjects/Applications
```

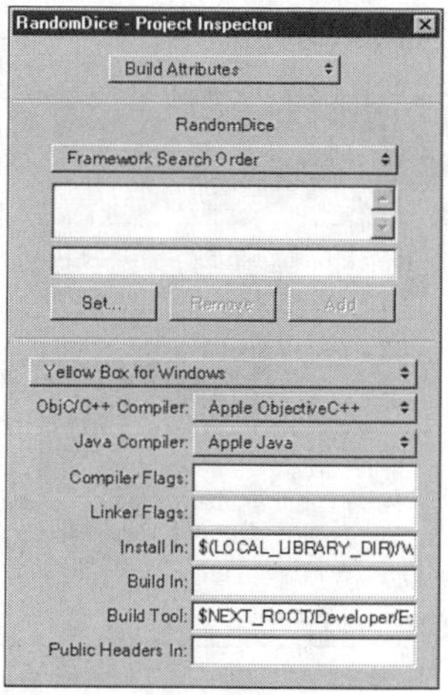

Figure 14.2
The install location will determine where the self-contained application is placed.

On Windows, $(LOCAL_LIBRARY_DIR) resolves to the /Apple/Local/Library; and on OS X, it resolves to /Local/Library. There's really no need to set this any differently because once the application is created, it can be copied to another location.

The Web server resources are also copied to the Web server's documents directory, which was set when you installed WebObjects. The WebServerConfig.plist file can be modified to set the Web server's document directory. It's located in the following location on Windows:

```
\Apple\Library\WebObjects\Configuration
```

And in the following directory on OS X:

```
/System/Library/WebObjects/Configuration
```

If you move the application to another server, you should remember to move the Web server resources as well.

Installing the Application

To install the application, set the target in the Build panel to Install as shown in Figure 14.3, and build the application. The Target can be set by clicking on the Build Options icon in the Build panel and selecting the target from the next panel.

Build options

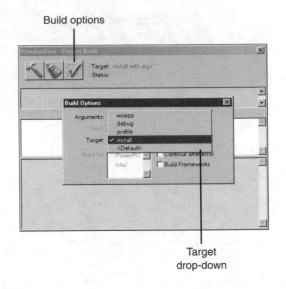

Target
drop-down

Figure 14.3
To install the application, select the Install option in the build panel.

Now by building the application, it will be installed in the location specified in the project inspector. The next step is to start the application using the Monitor application.

> **Note**
> If you are using multiple hosts with the same platform, you can simply copy the installed version of the application to the different hosts. If you are using different platforms, make sure that you build and install versions of the application on each platform.

Go ahead and choose an application to install. If you choose one that uses OpenBaseLite, you will not be able to install multiple instances because OpenBaseLite is a single-user database. The applications created in Chapter 3, "WebObjects Components," do not use the database, and would be good choices.

The Monitor

Monitor is a Web-based application that can be used to install and monitor WebObjects applications (see Figure 14.4). Monitor is actually a front end to the wotaskd service/daemon. On Windows, wotaskd is implemented as a service, and on OS X/Solaris it is implemented as a daemon. This service routes requests from the WebObjects adaptors to the applications.

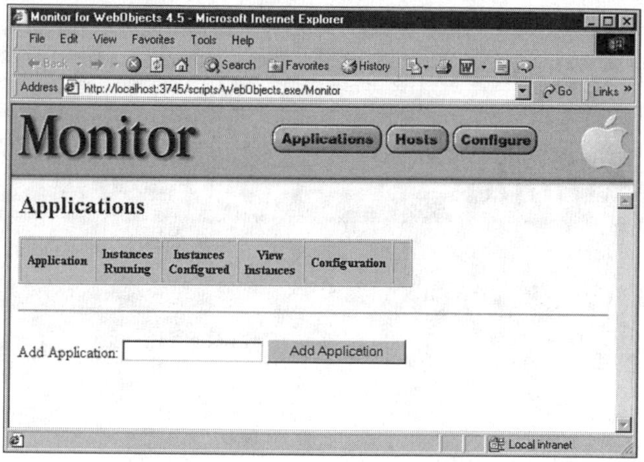

Figure 14.4
The Monitor is used to start, stop, and monitor applications.

Using the Monitor

Monitor is located in the following directory in Windows:

```
\Apple\Library\WebObjects\Applications\Monitor.woa
```

On OS X, it's located in the following directory:

```
/System/Library/WebObjects/Applications/Monitor.woa
```

Monitor has three main locations: Applications, Hosts, and Configure. The primary operations involved in the Monitor are to manage hosts that can have deployed applications, and manage instances of those applications on those hosts.

Adding a Host

To add a host to configure, click on the Hosts button on the main page, type a hostname into the Add host text field, and click on the Add Host button (see Figure 14.5).

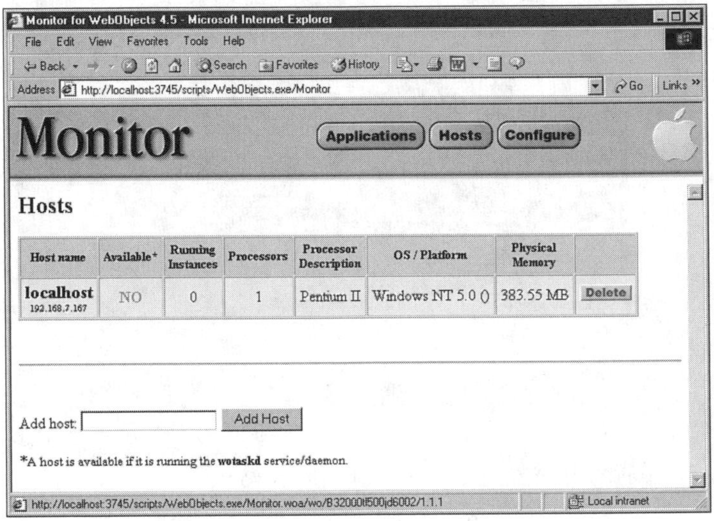

Figure 14.5
It is common for the Available column to display NO for a host that has just been added. When the page is refreshed, the column will change to YES as long as the wotaskd daemon/service is running on that host.

Adding an Application

The Applications page is used to add Applications. This page is retrieved by selecting the Applications button on the main page. To add an application, enter a name for the application on the Applications page and click on the Add Application button (see Figure 14.6). The name that you give the application is a symbolic name and does not need to represent the actual project name, although this name should not contain spaces.

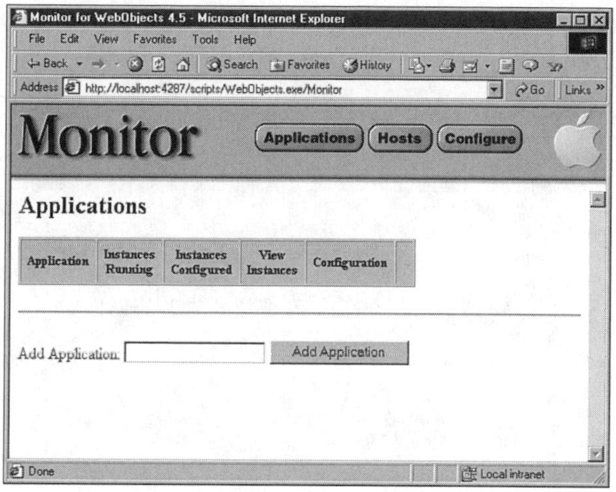

Figure 14.6
The Applications page.

You will then be prompted with the Application detail page, as shown in Figure 14.7. You will enter all the details of the application in this page, such as the location of the application in the file system.

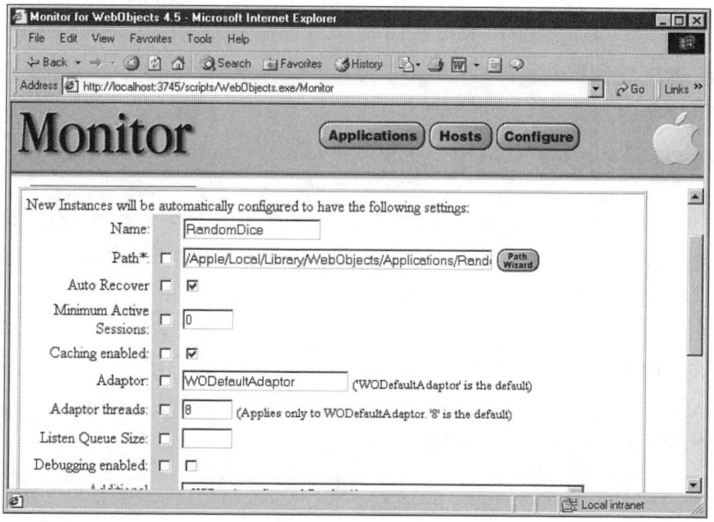

Figure 14.7
The Application Detail page.

To set the filename for the application executable, use the File Wizard button on the Application Detail page as shown in Figure 14.8. This will prompt you for the host, and then present a file chooser type window.

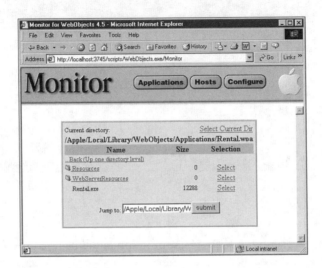

Figure 14.8
The File Wizard that is part of the new instance defaults.

When choosing the application executable, make sure that you choose the executable inside the .woa directory. An example of a file path placed in this text field is as follows:

```
/Apple/Local/Library/WebObjects/Applications/RandomDice.woa/RandomDice.exe
```

The default settings for the other fields are fine for now. When you're finished selecting the path, click on the Update for new instances button. This means that any new instances of this application will use the path you have chosen.

Creating Instances

Creating the application does not actually *start* it; an instance of the application is required for this. Instances can be started and configured by clicking on the Detail View button for an application on the Applications page (see Figure 14.9).

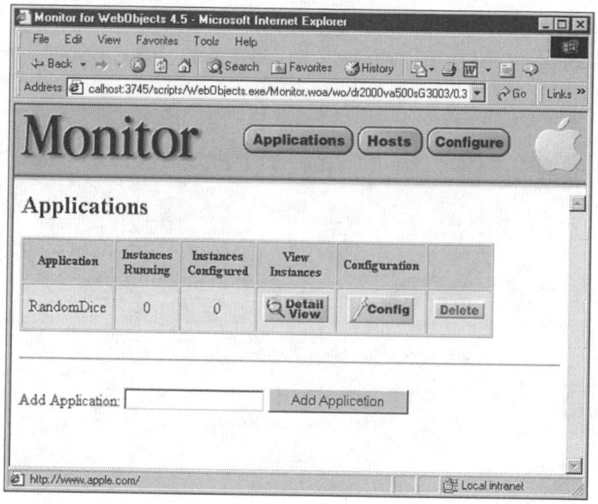

Figure 14.9
After the application has been created, click on the Detail View button to create and configure instances of the application.

When the Detail View button is clicked, the Application Detail page is displayed (see Figure 14.10).

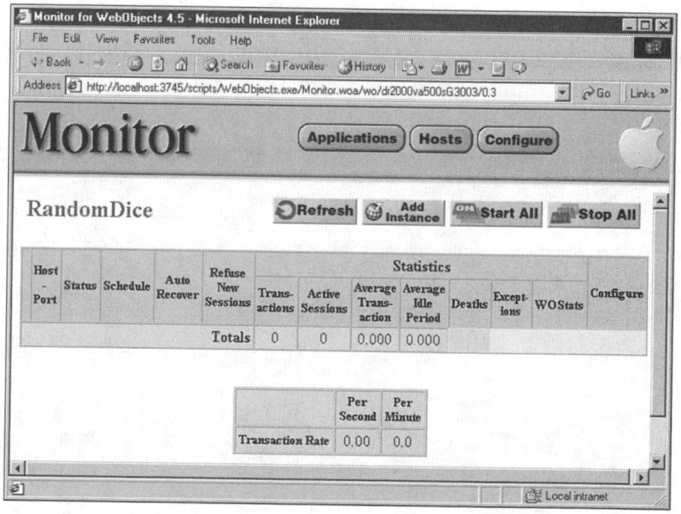

Figure 14.10
The Detail view lists all the instances for the application, and allows you to start and stop the instances along with adding more instances.

To add an instance, click on the Add Instance button on the Application Detail page. You will then have the option to pick the host and the number of instances to add (see Figure 14.11).

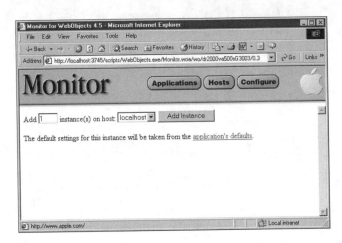

Figure 14.11

Adding an instance of an application.

To start the instance, click on the button that has a "switch" icon in the Status column for the instance. It should be labeled Off because the instance has not been started (see Figure 14.12). Clicking on this will turn it into an animation of the switch turning on. Wait about 30 seconds and click on the Refresh button on the page (not the browser's refresh button). The Status icon should now be changed to On.

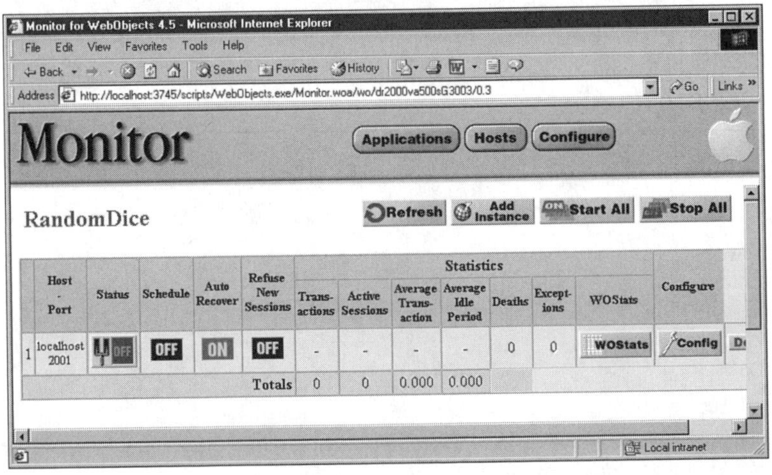

Figure 14.12

The new instance of the application

At this point, you can test the application by selecting the hyperlink or by typing in the URL in the Web Browser.

Deploying on Windows NT/2000

There are a couple of issues to consider when deploying on the Windows platforms.

First, you should limit the number of instances used. Each instance is a separate process running in the operating system, and NT is notoriously inefficient in its handling multiple tasks at the operating system level. WebObjects is multi-threaded, so one or two instances on a NT machine should be fine.

Also, when deploying on Windows, make sure that you have installed the latest WebObjects 4.5 patch, available at `http://til.info.apple.com`. Non-patched versions of WebObjects 4.5 will not properly start instances of an application using Monitor.

And finally, make sure that you turn off Dr. Watson's visual notification on the host used for deployment. Dr. Watson is Windows's way of notifying and logging application crashes, usually because of attempts made by the application to access areas of memory outside the application's memory space. When a crash is detected, Dr. Watson kicks in and presents a dialog asking if a log file should be created for the crash (see Figure 14.13). The application is not terminated until the user selects an option. `wotaskd` will start a new instance when the application is terminated, but if visual notification is turned on, this will not happen until human intervention. To turn off visual notification, run the Dr. Watson setup, `drwtsn32.exe`.

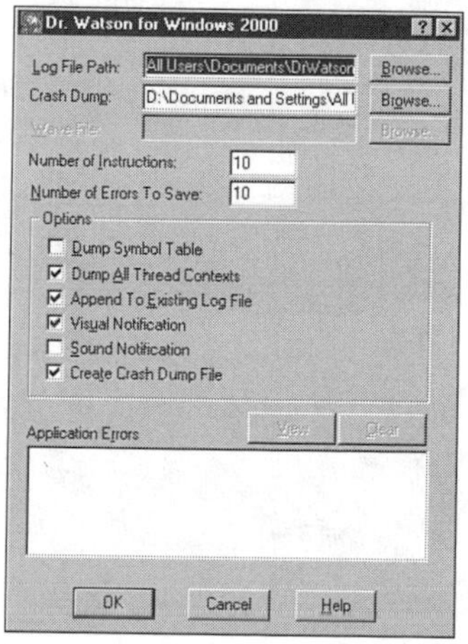

Figure 14.13
The Dr. Watson configuration panel.

Summary

So, to deploy an application, you need to make an installable version and use Monitor to configure and install it. A considerable amount of documentation is available in WOInfoCenter about deploying applications, including deploying on Solaris. There are also answers to commonly found problems at Apple's Web site, `http://til.info.apple.com`.

INDEX

Q